Political Parties in the UK

CONTEMPORARY POLITICAL STUDIES SERIES

Series Editor: John Benyon, *University of Leicester*

Published

Contemporary Political Studies Series
Series Standing Order ISBN 978–0230–54350–8 hardback
Series Standing Order ISBN 978–0230–54351–5 paperback
(outside North America only)

You can receive future titles in this series as they are published by placing a standing
order. Please contact your bookseller or, in case of difficulty, write to us at the address
below with your name and address, the title of the series and the ISBN quoted above.

Customer Services Department, Macmillan Distribution Ltd
Houndmills, Basingstoke, Hampshire RG21 6XS, England

Political Parties in the UK

Alistair Clark

palgrave
macmillan

First published 2012 by
PALGRAVE MACMILLAN

Palgrave Macmillan in the UK is an imprint of Macmillan Publishers Limited, registered in England, company number 785998, of Houndmills, Basingstoke, Hampshire RG21 6XS.

Palgrave Macmillan in the US is a division of St Martin's Press LLC, 175 Fifth Avenue, New York, NY 10010.

Palgrave Macmillan is the global academic imprint of the above companies and has companies and representatives throughout the world.

Palgrave® and Macmillan® are registered trademarks in the United States, the United Kingdom, Europe and other countries

ISBN 978–0–230–24249–4 hardback
ISBN 978–0–230–24250–0 paperback

This book is printed on paper suitable for recycling and made from fully managed and sustained forest sources. Logging, pulping and manufacturing processes are expected to conform to the environmental regulations of the country of origin.

A catalogue record for this book is available from the British Library.

A catalog record for this book is available from the Library of Congress.

10   9   8   7   6   5   4   3   2   1
21 20 19 18 17 16 15 14 13 12

Printed in China

Contents

List of Tables

List of Figures

List of Abbreviations

AES   Alternative Economic Strategy
AM   Assembly Member (National Assembly of Wales)
AMS   Additional Member System
AV   Alternative Vote
AWS   All Women Shortlist
BNP   British National Party
CCO   Conservative Central Office
CLP   Constituency Labour Party
CLPD   Campaign for Labour Party Democracy
CPF   Conservative Policy Forum
CSPL   Committee on Standards in Public Life
DUP   Democratic Unionist Party
EEC   European Economic Community
ENEP   Effective Number of Electoral Parties
ENP   Effective Number of Parties
ENPP   Effective Number of Parliamentary Parties
ERM   Exchange Rate Mechanism
EU   European Union
FEC   Federal Executive Committee (Liberal Democrats)
FPC   Federal Policy Committee (Liberal Democrats)
GFA   Good Friday Agreement
GLA   Greater London Authority
IMF   International Monetary Fund
IRA   Irish Republican Army
JCC   Joint Cabinet Committee
MEP   Member of the European Parliament
MLA   Member of the Legislative Assembly (Northern Ireland)
MMP   Mixed Member Proportional
MSP   Member of the Scottish Parliament
NAW   National Assembly of Wales
NEC   National Executive Committee (Labour)
NHS   National Health Service
NOC   No Overall Control
NPF   National Policy Forum (Labour)

OBR	Office for Budget Responsibility
OMOV	One Member One Vote
PC	Plaid Cymru
PDF	Policy Development Fund
PLP	Parliamentary Labour Party
PPB	Party Political Broadcast
PPEA	Political Parties and Elections Act (2009)
PPERA	Political Parties, Elections and Referendums Act (2000)
PSNI	Police Service of Northern Ireland
SCA	Shadow Communications Agency (Labour)
SDP	Social Democratic Party
SDLP	Social Democratic and Labour Party
SF	Sinn Fein
SNP	Scottish National Party
STV	Single Transferable Vote
UKIP	United Kingdom Independence Party
UUP	Ulster Unionist Party

Acknowledgements

I would like to thank a number of people who have helped with the development and writing of this book. I owe particular gratitude to my editor, Steven Kennedy, for the initial encouragement to write this book, and to Justin Fisher for his encouragement to follow up his predecessor volume, *British Political Parties* (1996). I am also grateful to Justin Fisher for permission to cite some of the data reported in Table 9.1. The help and editorial advice of Helen Caunce and Stephen Wenham has also been invaluable in producing the final book, for which I would also like to record my thanks.

Others also deserve thanks. Lynn Bennie has long supported my study of political parties and has also encouraged me during the writing process. Others have volunteered to read various sections and chapters. These include: Richard Grayson, Karin Bottom, Robin Pettitt, Justin Fisher, Nick Randall and Peter McLoughlin. I am grateful to them all. I'd particularly like to thank Undala Alam for her willingness to read and comment on a sizeable amount of material from earlier drafts, providing insightful comments and ensuring clarity in both my thinking and what I had written. Any errors and omissions are of course my own.

The UK is fortunate in having a lively scholarly community interested in political parties and elections. Much of what is contained in this volume draws on the research from that community, to whom I am collectively grateful. I would also like to extend thanks to my students in the 2010–11 running of PAI3062 Political Parties and Democracy in the UK at Queen's University Belfast. They were, albeit unwittingly, an early audience for much of this material and on numerous occasions their insights helped sharpen my arguments.

Finally, I'd like to thank Arianna Andreangeli for her support and patience. She has had to put up with me arguing about the issues in this book for several years, listened patiently and then dragged me back to earth again. Grazie infinite. Questo libro è per lei.

ALISTAIR CLARK

1

Introduction: The Development of the UK Party System

On the morning of Wednesday 12 May 2010, Conservative Party leader David Cameron stood with Liberal Democrat leader Nick Clegg on the steps of Number 10 Downing Street. After a hard fought and momentous general election campaign, the Conservatives had returned to power for the first time in thirteen years. While the Conservatives' electoral recovery from their 2005 position had been impressive, the party had not done well enough against an unpopular Labour administration to achieve a majority in parliament and form a single party government. Claiming that an unstable minority government might have led to a further economic crisis in Britain, the Conservatives and Liberal Democrats negotiated a coalition agreement after both sides had made a number of concessions. The most notable of these was the referendum on electoral reform, a key Liberal Democrat concern, that was held in May 2011. David Cameron and Nick Clegg therefore stood on the steps of Downing Street, as Prime Minister and Deputy Prime Minster respectively, at the head of the first UK coalition government since the end of the wartime coalition in 1945. Later that afternoon, the two leaders gave a press conference in the garden of Downing Street, commented on widely for the congeniality it was conducted with. This was a stark contrast to the traditionally competitive and oppositional debate of British party politics, epitomized in the public mind by, for instance, weekly jousting at Prime Minister's Questions, and that had been evident just days earlier during the general election campaign.

There had been much talk during the election, primarily originating from the Liberal Democrats, about 'the new politics' and the need to 'do things differently'. According to Clegg, this was necessitated by the declining ability of the two main parties to command the loyalties of voters. The coalition talks, eventual agreement and joint appearances by Cameron and Clegg were the most striking and visible example of the changes that British party politics had been undergoing. However, the

1

British party system had been gradually changing in nature for several decades. These changes were not necessarily immediately obvious to casual onlookers, having been downplayed not only by media coverage but also suppressed by the first-past-the-post electoral system used for elections to Westminster. Nevertheless, as Mair (2009, p. 282) put it before the 2010 elections 'The British party system is ... increasingly vulnerable, and possibly stands on the cusp of a dramatic change.' Later he went on to argue that 'if [the Liberal Democrats] can succeed in entering government as a non-threatening junior coalition partner, then they will succeed in changing the game of British politics at its very core' (Mair, 2009, p. 299). Whether Liberal Democrat participation in coalition fundamentally changes British party politics in the longer term remains to be seen. The fact is that their participation in government marks the first occasion in the post-war period that a party outside the Conservative and Labour parties has formed part of the UK government.

In his seminal volume *British Political Parties*, McKenzie (1963, p. 3) argued that 'party is now the overwhelmingly dominant factor in British politics'. The centrality of parties to political life remains, although whether they are 'overwhelmingly dominant' is at least now open to question. To assess whether or not this remains the case requires an up-to-date understanding of the role played by parties across the UK. Yet, as Heffernan (2009, p. 457) observes, the literature comparing across political parties in the UK is much thinner than that which focuses on just one party at a time. The novel circumstances of the post-2010 election period is therefore an opportune time to be examining developments in UK party politics, both within individual parties and comparatively across parties. There are a number of important questions to answer in order to understand how British party competition arrived at this juncture. What have been the challenges that parties have faced in the UK, and how have parties responded, developed and adapted to meet these challenges? Continually the topic of political dissatisfaction amongst voters, to what extent can we say that political parties are fulfilling their democratic functions in the UK? As one academic asked, 'are British political parties in decline' (Webb, 1995)? Or, as more recent terminology might have it, to what extent do political parties in the UK remain 'fit for purpose'?

This book is dedicated to these questions, each of which is discussed in the chapters to come. To provide context for the discussions to follow, this chapter introduces debates about the party system and party competition in the UK. The first section provides an understanding of party systems and the various criteria by which they might be understood. It introduces the idea of political 'cleavages', and outlines the cleavages around which party systems are said to have developed, and become 'frozen'. It then builds upon this to briefly introduce a number of ways of classifying party systems, and understanding and categorizing the nature of party system change. The second part begins to apply these ideas to the main features of the British party system from 1945 to the early 1970s. Discussion revolves around the dominant cleavages structuring party competition, primarily class, but also stable partisan loyalties, and the post-war British party system is placed firmly in the stable, 'two-party' category. The third section assesses the nature of change in the British party system from the early 1970s onwards. Discussion relates to the increasing importance of different cleavages, for instance the centre–periphery and sectoral cleavages, and the increasingly dealigned British electorate and its impact upon party competition. The consequences of this for the classification of the British party system are then discussed.

Understanding Party Systems

The idea of a party system relates to more than the sum of the number of parties evident in a country. Instead, a party system relates to the patterns of democratic conflict, competition and co-operation between the parties within a country. While some countries – notably authoritarian regimes – can be run by one party, the notion of a one party *system* is at least problematic since there is no meaningful democratic competition between different party options. In short then, the idea of a party system relates to the patterns of interaction between different parties (Sartori, 2005 [1976]).

A historical distinction is often made between parties that formed through co-operation of representatives within parliament, and those parties that initially formed by organizing in society to challenge established interests, before being elected to parliament. The roots of party systems are therefore often traced back to the development of social and political conflicts within societies. The classic statement of this is by Lipset and Rokkan (1967) who identify four major cleavages, or sources of political conflict, in the development of West European party systems. Simplifying their argument considerably, the initial conflicts involved in consolidating the nation-state as a political entity revolved around *church–state* and *centre–periphery* issues. Somewhat later, the second major juncture related to the industrial revolution. Economic interests were central to political interests and the two key cleavages to emerge were the *urban–rural* (sometimes called *land–industry*) cleavage and the *owner–worker* class cleavage. In different countries, different parties formed around these cleavages. However, Lipset and Rokkan's argument was that the widespread extension of the franchise in the early twentieth century essentially 'froze' these political conflicts and the party options that had been dominant at that moment in time. Indeed, writing in 1967, they noted how these party options remained dominant more than forty years after the extension of voting rights in most countries. Party systems, their argument went, were thus more stable than changing.

Early approaches to understanding party systems used numerical criteria to differentiate between different types. Duverger (1964) makes a simple distinction between two-party systems and multi-party systems, i.e. systems with more than two parties in them. Blondel (1968) attempted to include the relative strength of parties, thereby distinguishing between two, two-and-a-half and multi-party systems. What these accounts lacked however was an emphasis on how parties interacted with each other. The seminal classification was provided by Sartori (2005 [1976]). He argues that parties should only be counted as 'relevant' if they have either coalition potential, or can hold the business of government and government formation up through what he calls 'blackmail' potential. Sartori innovates by introducing the concept of ideological distance, or left–right polarization, into his classification. He therefore proposes four different types of party system. *Predominant* party systems are those where one party has governed alone for a considerable period of time, winning at least three if not more elections. *Two-party* systems are marked by minimal ideological distance on the left–right spectrum, centrist competition and alternation in office. *Moderate pluralist* systems also operate in a centrist manner, have a low degree of ideological polarization and involve between three to five parties competing for a position in governing coalitions. Finally, *extreme or polarized pluralism* is multipolar, characterized by a high degree of ideological distance and the presence of anti-system parties at both ends of the ideological spectrum. The centrifugal pressures that such a configuration brings result in radical and bilateral oppositions to the centre-placed governing party or parties.

Five main sources of party system change can be identified. First, *institutional or constitutional changes* can lead to party system change. These can take various forms, but might most often be seen in the adoption of a new electoral system and electoral laws with different thresholds of representation. Second, *changes in social structure* can lead to changes in support for parties. Third, *value change* can impact upon party competition. Thus Inglehart (1990a) highlights a move towards values concerned less with material security and more with quality of life issues. Fourth, the *combination of social and value change* has led to a weakening of political cleavages as electorates become increasingly dealigned. Finally, the *strategy adopted by parties* themselves can also contribute to party system change (Wolinetz, 1979).

Smith (1989) endeavoured to combine both stability and change by defining this in relation to a party system's 'core'. The core consists of the features of that system which appear most resistant to change. This means the party, or parties, that have been in leading positions for a considerable period, and the party alignments, particularly in coalition and government formation that have emerged and endured (Smith, 1989, p. 161). He goes on to propose four potential degrees of change in party systems. These are:

- temporary fluctuations
- restricted change
- general change
- transformation. (Smith, 1989, p. 166)

A three-election time span is suggested to be necessary to distinguish temporary fluctuations from restricted change, while the difference between restricted and general change is not clearly specified. Transformation, while rare, need not mean the wholesale establishment of a new party system. Instead, it may be highlighted by one of the major parties going 'into a steep and irreversible decline' (Smith, 1989: p.167).

Assessing developments in any party system must therefore take into account a range of features before it is possible to classify the nature of the change that has occurred. In other words, classifying the party system, identifying which of these elements has changed, and returning to how this has impacted upon patterns of party competition are crucial areas of investigation for party scholars.

The British Party System, 1945–1970

There has been some debate about the origins of the British party system and parties. Some trace the development of British parties back to the seventeenth century (Ingle, 2008, ch. 1), while others date the development of parties to the mid to late nineteenth century (Fisher, 1996; McKenzie, 1963). Prior to this, two groupings could be found in parliament. The Tories were supportive of the Monarchy and the Church, while the Whigs aimed to restrict Monarchical powers and were religious nonconformists. Both groups were loosely organized in parliament with little or no party discipline as we understand it today. The Reform Acts of 1832 and 1867 ushered in the beginning of the extension of the franchise and saw parties begin to organize outside parliament for the first time in an attempt to gain support from the newly enfranchised electorate. This also saw the two parties become more disciplined in parliament, and the development of now standard elements of party competition such as election manifestos and campaign activity (Fisher, 1996; McKenzie, 1963). The Liberal Party of the late nineteenth–early twentieth century claims descent from the Whigs, while the modern Conservative party traces its history from the Tories of the seventeenth century.

Regularly portrayed as a stable two-party system through much of the twentieth century, there has nevertheless been more change in the British party system than many popular accounts suggest. Bogdanor (2004) highlights a number of permutations of party competition in Britain from the beginning of the twentieth century. The first he dates to between *1906–1914* when a multi-party two bloc system existed with the Conservatives supported by Liberal Unionists on one side, and the Liberal Party supported by the nascent Labour Party and Irish parties on the other. Between *1918–1931*, the rise of the Labour Party meant that, despite other smaller groupings being relevant, there were effectively three main parties in competition, the Conservatives, Liberals and Labour. The extension of the franchise in 1918 contributed considerably to the decline of the Liberals and the rise of Labour. His third period, *1935–70*, equates to what he calls the 'heyday of two-party competition' with Labour having cemented its position to become the main alternative to the Conservatives.

It is the post-war period from 1945 to 1970 which has become the epitome of the British party system in much literature, and from which any change tends to be measured. While this approach has been rightly criticized (Bogdanor, 2004; Dunleavy, 2005), it nevertheless marks an important juncture from which to understand recent developments. The British party system was presented as the foremost example of a two-party system as defined by Sartori (2005 [1976]). The Conservative and Labour parties alternated in office in this period. Labour governed in the immediate post-war period from 1945, narrowly winning the 1950 general election before being defeated, at least in terms of seats, by the Conservatives in 1951. The Conservatives then governed for a thirteen year period until defeated in the 1964 general election by Harold Wilson's Labour Party who went on to increase their majority in 1966 and governed until 1970. This period was also notable for the centrist direction of political competition. In particular, the idea that two-party systems are marked by minimal ideological distance was highlighted by a consensus between the two main parties over the aims of public policy. Labelled 'Butskellism' after two prominent chancellors – R. A. Butler for the Conservatives, and Hugh Gaitskell for Labour – this consensus revolved around the defence of the welfare state that had been set up by Labour after 1945, the pursuit of full employment and Keynesian demand management economic policies. This consensus notwithstanding, some still presented the British party system as an exemplar of strictly competitive political interactions (Dahl, 1966).

This two-party system was supported by twin pillars. The first was stable party loyalties brought about through socialization within the family. The argument was that political attitudes were transmitted through family allegiances. Thus, Butler and Stokes (1969, ch. 3) show that voters' early party preferences were affected by their parents' partisanship. Where both parents were Conservative, 89 per cent of their respondents also initially identified with the Conservatives. Similarly, where both parents were Labour, 92 per cent of respondents' initially identified with Labour. While these preferences weakened with age, this was only by a relatively small amount. Political socialization within the family therefore had a lasting effect, leading to essentially stable political attitudes. Consequently, party identification was at high levels, with around 80 per cent identifying with either the Conservative or Labour parties during the 1960s (Denver, 2007, p. 62).

The second pillar related to the cleavage structure of political conflict. The centre–periphery and land–industry cleavages had been evident in the nineteenth and early twentieth centuries. These were ultimately superseded by the rise of the worker–owner cleavage and the increasing political organization of the working class. For instance, the trade unions played a large part in the formation of the Labour Party. Class therefore became increasingly important, and, underlining Lipset and Rokkan's (1967) suggestion, the extension of the franchise was central in cementing the role of the Labour Party as the main party of opposition to the Conservatives. Indeed, in the post-war period, class was regularly found to be a major explanation for party choice, and the influence of the class cleavage had steadily increased (Butler and Stokes, 1969; Pulzer, 1967). Butler and Stokes (1969) found that in the early 1960s, 72 per cent of the working class identified themselves as Labour supporters, a figure which rose to 77 per cent for the lower working class. By contrast, more than 75 per cent of the middle classes, and

Table 1.1   UK General Election results, 1945–2010

	Con		Lab		Lib (Dems)		Nationalists		Others	
	Vote share %	*Seats*	*Vote share %*	*Seats*	*Vote share %*	*Seats*	*Vote share %*	*Seats*	*Vote share %*	*Seats*
1945	39.8	213	48.3	393	9.1	12	0.2	0	2.5	22
1950	43.5	299	46.1	315	9.1	9	0.1	0	1.2	2
1951	48	321	48.8	295	2.5	6	0.1	0	0.6	3
1955	49.7	345	46.4	277	2.7	6	0.2	0	0.9	2
1959	49.4	365	43.8	258	5.9	6	0.4	0	0.6	1
1964	43.4	304	44.1	317	11.2	9	0.5	0	0.8	0
1966	41.9	253	47.9	363	8.5	12	0.7	0	0.9	2
1970	46.4	330	43	288	7.5	6	1.3	1	1.8	5
1974 Feb	37.8	297	37.1	301	19.3	14	2.6	9	3.2	14
1974 Oct	35.8	277	39.2	319	18.3	13	3.5	14	3.2	12
1979	43.9	339	37	269	13.8	11	2	4	3.3	12
1983	42.4	397	27.6	209	25.4	23	1.5	4	3.1	17
1987	42.3	376	30.8	229	22.6	22	1.7	6	2.6	17
1992	41.9	336	34.4	271	17.8	20	2.3	7	3.5	17
1997	30.7	165	43.2	418	16.8	46	2.5	10	6.8	20
2001	31.7	166	40.7	412	18.3	52	2.5	9	6.8	20
2005	32.4	198	35.2	356	22	62	2.2	9	8.2	21
2010	36.1	307	29	258	23	57	2.2	9	9.6	19

Note: Nationalists refers to the Scottish and Welsh nationalist parties, while the Liberal column refers to the Liberal Party, the Liberal–SDP Alliance and the Liberal Democrats.
Sources: Data from Kavanagh and Cowley, 2010, Appendix 1; Tetteh, 2008.

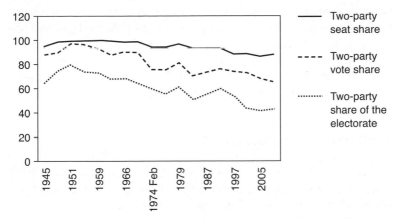

Figure 1.1   Two-party vote, seat and electorate share in the House of Commons 1945–2010 (%)

Source: Data from Kavanagh and Cowley, 2010.

100 per cent of the upper class, identified themselves as Conservative. Other methods of measuring the effects of class on voting similarly found class a dominant factor in explaining party choice in this period (Denver, 2007). Combined with the influence of stable political attitudes and identifications, such class-based voting led to stable patterns of party choice in British general elections.

Changes in government could not have happened however without at least some voters changing their party preference during elections. Nevertheless, elections in this period were low volatility contests, with the most net volatility being evident in the swing back to the Conservatives in 1951 (see Table 1.2 below). The result of these essentially stable voting patterns was therefore a stable two-party system, rooted in the class cleavage. Indeed, as can be seen from Table 1.1, Labour and the Conservatives dominated British party competition, the Conservatives achieving more than 49 per cent vote share in 1955 and 1959, and Labour achieving 47.9 per cent and upwards in 1945, 1951 and 1966. This two-party dominance is underlined by examining the combined voteshare for the Conservatives and Labour (Figure 1.1). Between 1951 and 1959, the two parties accounted for upwards of 93 per cent of the UK vote. While this had weakened slightly during the 1960s, the two-party share nevertheless remained at high levels of around 87–89 per cent. During the same period, the vote share for parties other than the main two was at its lowest in 1951–55 and averaged around nine per cent between 1945 and 1970 with most of that being accounted for by votes for the Liberal Party. In terms of representation, this two-party dominance was reinforced by the first-past-the-post electoral system which militated against smaller parties such as the Liberals gaining extensive representation. As Figure 1.1 demonstrates, from 1950 to 1970, the Conservative and Labour parties held between 98–99 per cent of the seats in the House of Commons.

The British Party System, 1974–2010

Bogdanor's (2004) fourth period of party competition dates from 1974, when voters had the unusual experience of two general elections being conducted in the same year. The February 1974 election was a watershed moment for the British party system. This contest recorded the highest net volatility (14.5) of all post-war UK elections. As Figure 1.1 highlights, the two-party share of the vote fell from 89.4 per cent in 1970 to 74.9 per cent in February 1974. Aside from 1979 when the two-party share of the vote was 80.9 per cent, this proved to be the beginning of a lasting erosion in the combined ability of the two main parties to command the British vote. From 1979 onwards, this has never been higher than the 1992 figure of 76.3 per cent. By the tightly fought election of 2010, the combined two-party share had fallen to 65.1 per cent, with the Conservatives on 36.1 per cent and Labour with its second worst performance in the post-war period on 29 per cent. However, the electoral system still ensured that the Conservatives and Labour dominated the House of Commons, commanding more than 90 per cent of seats up to 1992, and between 86–88 per cent since 1997.

In 1974, the corollary was a rise in the vote for the non-mainstream parties, particularly the Liberals and the Scottish and Welsh nationalist parties, the Scottish National Party (SNP) and Plaid Cymru (PC) (Table 1.1). Thus, Liberal vote share jumped from 7.5 per cent in 1970 to 19.3 per cent in February 1974 and the party increased its number of seats from six to 14. Similarly, Nationalist vote share doubled and the Nationalist parties' representation increased from one MP to nine. In 1983, the Liberal–Social Democratic Party (SDP) Alliance achieved 25.4 per cent of the national vote, and after the Liberals and SDP merged to become the Liberal Democrats in 1988, the third party has shown a steady increase in both its vote share, peaking at 23 per cent in 2010, and its number of seats, winning 62 in 2005. After a decline in their representation in the 1980s, the Nationalist parties elected 10 MPs in 1997 and have since stabilized at a combined 9 MPs in elections from 2001 onwards.

The rise of third and other party votes and the decline of the main-stream party votes highlights a weakening in the position of the two main parties. This is underlined further when election turnout is taken into account. Voters have been decreasingly willing to vote in general elections, with turnout falling to 59.4 per cent in 2001. Despite rising slightly in the two subsequent contests, the 65.1 per cent turnout achieved in 2010 was still the third lowest turnout figure recorded in the post-war period. This means that the two main parties competing for office in Britain are commanding the loyalties of an ever smaller proportion of the declining numbers of people who cast a vote. Indeed, as Figure 1.1 shows, the two-party share of the electorate has declined from 79.9 per cent in 1951, to only 42.4 per cent in 2010. Even accounting for the recent rise of the Liberal Democrats, the three-party share of the British electorate only averaged 55.3 per cent in the three elections from 2001. As Mair (2009) observes, this is hardly a mark of a party system comprised of strong or thriving political parties.

Three large Conservative victories under Margaret Thatcher in 1979, 1983 and 1987, followed up by a much narrower Conservative victory in 1992, led to speculation that the two-party system had been replaced by a *predominant* party system where one party governs alone for a period of three elections or more. Analysts pondered after the Conservatives' fourth win in 1992 whether that had been 'Labour's Last Chance?' and suggested that if the Conservatives won again it would 'no longer be realistic to describe Britain as a two-party democracy' (Heath et al., 1994, p.275). When the Conservatives were replaced by Labour in 1997 a similar pattern appeared to have asserted itself, with Labour winning three successive large majorities in 1997, 2001 and 2005 leaving commentators to assess the 'Conservatives in Crisis' (Garnett and Lynch, 2003). Both the 1979 and 1997 changes of government were marked by large scale vote-switching, 1997 in particular being the second most volatile post-war election after February 1974. In other words, from 1979–2010, the British party system had become marked by the extended predominance of the governing party heralded by a sharp change of direction for voters first in 1979, then in 1997 in what Mair (2009, p.288) suggested might be termed 'alternating predominance'.

Table 1.2 shows that this is not however the whole story. It tracks net electoral volatility, measured through the widely-used Pedersen index (Pedersen, 1990), from 1950–2010. This shows that the most volatile British general elections were February 1974, 1983 and 1997. These are generally followed by low volatility elections as in October 1974, 1987 and 2001. In short, the popularity of governments declines the longer they are in office. From 1974, it appears that once the British electorate have changed direction sharply, they appear to be broadly satisfied with the outcome until circumstances conspire to lead to a desire for change. When this desire for change appeared, between 1974–2005, it did so at higher levels of volatility than in the immediate post-war period.

Table 1.2 also tracks the effective number of parties at both the electoral (ENEP) and the parliamentary (ENPP) level. These measures provide an indication of how fragmented or concentrated party competition is at each level and as such are commonly used as an indicator of the number of relevant parties at electoral and parliamentary levels (Lijphart, 1999. pp. 67–9; Webb, 2000, pp. 36–7). From 1983, there have never been less than three relevant parties in electoral competition, although ENPP remains well below that, with effectively only two and a half relevant parties in parliament in 2005 and 2010. Both measures add further

Table 1.2   Net volatility and effective number of parties: British General Elections 1950–2010

	Net volatility	*ENEP*	*ENPP*
1950	3.65	2.44	2.08
1951	7.2	2.13	2.06
1955	2.35	2.16	2.03
1959	3.3	2.28	1.99
1964	5.95	2.53	2.06
1966	4.15	2.42	2.02
1970	5.95	2.46	2.07
1974 February	14.5	3.13	2.25
1974 October	3.0	3.15	2.25
1979	8.2	2.87	2.15
1983	11.6	3.46	2.09
1987	3.4	3.33	2.17
1992	5.15	3.06	2.27
1997	12.25	3.22	2.13
2001	2.5	3.33	2.17
2005	5.8	3.59	2.46
2010	5.65	3.71	2.57

Sources: Data for net volatility, author's calculations; ENEP and ENPP, Gallagher, 2010. ENEP refers to the effective number of electoral parties, while ENPP refers to the effective number of parliamentary parties.

evidence to the case that the British party system has become increasingly fragmented since the 1970s.

How might these changes be explained? The first potential set of explanations revolves around party performance in office. In the late 1960s–early 1970s, there had been numerous policy and economic crises in British government, culminating in Conservative Prime Minister Edward Heath calling the February 1974 election against the backdrop of considerable industrial unrest ostensibly on the theme of 'Who Governs?' Significantly, both parties had been involved in these various crises, Labour from 1964 and the Conservatives from 1970. Thus, poor performance in office can be highlighted as a reason for the sharp decline in two-party vote share in February 1974. A similar dynamic has continued through to the present day, with Webb (1995, p. 315) noting the seeming inability of political parties, from both sides of the political spectrum, to resolve some of the most pressing public policy problems when in office as an explanation for the decreasing popularity of parties. Whiteley (2009a) similarly observes that British government has continued to decline in effectiveness between 1996–2007.

Secondly, gradual changes in the social structure had begun to impact upon the stability of the class cleavage in a process of political dealignment evident through the late 1960s–early 1970s (Sarlvik and Crewe, 1983). Indeed, a weakening of class-based voting had already been noticed in early election studies (Butler and Stokes, 1969) and while absolute class voting remained at 60 per cent or above in the 1960s, this had fallen to around 49 per cent in the 1980s and around 40 per cent in 2005 (Denver, 2007, p. 69). The decline of the class cleavage is therefore a major explanation for the weakening of party support. In part this reflected the decline of traditional working-class occupations in heavy industry. However, it was also partly due to a process of embourgeoisement, with manual workers becoming more affluent and, as a consequence, their political attitudes changing. Other explanations include increased levels of education and television reporting increasing political knowledge and thereby undermining traditional loyalties and political socialization processes (Denver, 2007).

With a weakening class cleavage, other political conflicts increased in prominence. Dunleavy (1980) highlighted a split between the public and private sectors amongst voters, arguing that those who worked in and depended on the public sector for services and housing were more likely to vote Labour, while those more dependent on the private sector were identified with the Conservative Party. The centre–periphery cleavage also reasserted its importance with the SNP and Plaid Cymru both electing

MPs after notable by-election wins in the late 1960s, and following this up by winning a combined total of 14 seats in October 1974, the SNP in particular winning over 30 per cent of the Scottish vote in that election. Moreover, voting patterns increasingly diverged geographically with Conservative representation in decline in the north of England and Scotland, with these areas overwhelmingly electing Labour MPs (Johnston et al., 1988). This geographical pattern weakened in the 1990s (Curtice and Park, 1999). However, by 2010–11 geographical divisions in party choice had again become sharper. Important though they may be, none of these cleavages has however been able to underpin the structure of state-wide political loyalties and party preferences in the same way as the class cleavage was, serving instead to fragment rather than unify.

The grounds of political debate have also shifted rightwards away from the 'Butskellite' social democratic consensus of the 1950s and 1960s. This was the result of policies followed by Conservative governments of the 1980s. For instance, one of the aims of the Conservatives' privatizations of various state-owned industries and giving council tenants the 'right to buy' their council house was to encourage voters to become small-scale owners and capitalists in the hope that this would undermine collective working class identities and turn such voters towards the Conservatives in the longer term (Norris, 1990). Party policy therefore attempted to engender value change in society. Prior to Labour returning to office in 1997, it had to adapt itself to these realities, abandoning many of its previously held positions, not least Clause IV of its constitution which many understood as committing the party to nationalization of industry. As two keen commentators observe, Labour did little in its 1997–2010 period in office to combat and change these underlying values (Toynbee and Walker, 2010).

Finally, institutional change has also undermined the party system at Westminster. Parties must now operate in complex multi-level environments. The devolution of power to the Scottish parliament and Welsh Assembly in 1999 means that the structures of party competition in the devolved institutions differ from those found at Westminster (Bennie and Clark, 2003; Dunleavy, 2005; Massetti, 2008). This is also the case in elections to the European parliament. Mair (2009) argues that the structure of British party competition is therefore no longer reinforced in these important institutions. Instead, the focus of voters and parties in these jurisdictions is increasingly focused on the new institutions, thereby undermining the claim of the Westminster-based party system to represent the UK as a whole.

Classifying Party System Change in Britain

How might these changes to the British party system be classified? A number of accounts have argued that Britain has a suppressed or latent moderate pluralist party system (Webb, 2000, ch. 1; Webb and Fisher, 1999). As per Sartori's (2005 [1976]) classification, moderate pluralism has between two to five parties competing for a place in a coalition government and is marked by both centrist competition and ideological moderation. The argument was that the first-past-the-post electoral system had restricted the ability of third and smaller parties to win seats in parliament, thereby ensuring that the full consequences of the changes outlined above did not wholly feed through into the question of government formation at Westminster. While party competition at the electoral level may have become more fragmented, in parliament the two-party 'core' of the system, Labour and the Conservatives, were until 2010 at least, able to continue operating as if little had changed.

Liberal Democrat leader Nick Clegg's argument during the 2010 election campaign that the two main parties commanded a decreasing proportion of the electorate nevertheless had considerable evidence behind it. The dramatic outcome of the 2010 election, a Conservative–Liberal Democrat coalition, would appear to suggest that change in the British party system is no longer suppressed and has become a moderate pluralist party system. In the 2010 parliament, this is undoubtedly true. Nevertheless, some caution is advised before jumping to longer term conclusions. As noted earlier, Smith (1989) suggests a three-election time span to distinguish between temporary fluctuations and what he calls restricted change. Polling early in the 2010 parliament suggested that the Liberal Democrats would be severely punished by voters for joining a Conservative Party embarking upon controversial cuts to public services. This came to pass in 2011 with large Liberal Democrat losses in that year's devolved and local elections. Under these circumstances, one possible eventual outcome is the resumption of two-party competition for office at Westminster between Labour and the Conservatives. However, if coalition governments continue to be the norm, over the next two elections and beyond it would also not be unreasonable to talk of restricted and eventually even general change in the British party system insofar as competition for office is concerned.

Nevertheless, it is possible to make the case that the British party system has already undergone a process of general change since February 1974, particularly at the level of electoral competition. There are three key reasons for this. First, as noted earlier, the processes of class and partisan dealignment that have resulted from social structural and value change appear to be in steady decline. The importance of the owner–worker cleavage and the values associated with that therefore no longer support the British party system in the way they did. Evans and Norris (1999) term this process one of secular dealignment, suggesting that even the apparently sharp shift from Conservative to Labour in 1997 can be explained through this gradual process. Some have argued that this has led to long-term attitudinal scepticism about parties and politicians (for instance: Webb, 2009). Although 73 per cent trusted politicians not at all or not very much in 2010, it is harder however to make the case that this has changed; voters have always been sceptical about political parties (Hansard Society, 2010). They most likely always will be.

Second, the new devolved institutions have fragmented party competition across Britain, and this has been compounded by the geographical spread of the vote, with the Conservatives predominant again in the south of England, and Labour further north with competition from nationalist alternatives in Scotland and Wales. Third, elections to these new institutions and the European parliament utilize assorted forms of proportional representation. This means that the dominance of the two main parties is no longer underpinned by an unproportional and unrepresentative electoral system. This opens up opportunities for other parties to build their representation in a way that they have seldom been able to at Westminster. The consequence is that 'the two-party system that the parties both create and depend upon is being isolated ever more effectively within the confines of Westminster, with little purchase beyond the core institutions' (Mair, 2009, p. 299). Moreover, party membership and activism is also in decline which means that British political parties appear ever more rooted in the institutions of state, not in the communities they claim to represent (Katz and Mair, 1995; Whiteley, 2009a).

Despite much talk from party politicians of the need to 'reconnect' with the public, none of these developments is likely to be reversed, hence it is both possible and appropriate to classify the British party system as having undergone general change from 1974 onwards. Whether the more recent experience of a hung parliament and coalition government ultimately becomes a part of this picture of general change in the British party system depends on whether or not the Liberal Democrats can survive the electoral consequences of their first participation in British government in such a way that again makes them potential coalition partners for either Labour or the Conservatives.

The Structure of the Book

The following chapters investigate developments in British party politics in more depth. Chapter 2 investigates the democratic functions of political parties, outlining how these are, or are not, fulfilled by parties as organizations, in the electorate and in office. Chapters 3, 4 and 5 examine each of the main three British parties – the Conservatives, Labour and the Liberal Democrats – in depth. Each of these chapters has a common structure to enable comparison. Party ideology and policy begins the discussion and the extent of ideological and policy change in each party is assessed. Discussion then proceeds to questions of party leadership performance and selection, before going on to examine the representativeness and candidate selection processes of each of the three parties. The final part of these chapters goes on to discuss and assess each party's performance in office.

Subsequent chapters proceed on a thematic basis. Chapter 6 analyses the rise, and fall, of small parties such as the Green Party, UK Independence Party (UKIP) and the British National Party (BNP). These parties are introduced individually before moving on to discuss the reasons for their rise and broader systemic impact. Chapter 7 moves on to examine the question of Britain's 'multi-level' party systems. A number of parties active only in Scotland, Wales and Northern Ireland are introduced and their territorial party systems outlined and classified, before extending the analysis to party systems in local government and in competition for the European Parliament. Chapter 8 addresses the important question of parties' relationship with the media, outlining a model of political communication, examining patterns of press partisanship, professionalization of communication activity and the use of the internet. Chapter 9 addresses the crucial issue of party organization and funding, highlighting where power lies in the main parties as well as examining the often parlous state of party finances. Most people associate political parties with campaigning for election. Chapter 10 therefore examines the structure of the British electorate in 2010, before analysing developments in party campaign techniques at both national and local constituency level. The final chapter reviews each of these themes and returns to the question of the challenges faced by political parties in the UK today, arguing that parties and the party system face a range of challenges, some of which are specific to the UK's parties, but many of which are also common to political parties elsewhere.

2

The Role of Political Parties in the UK

According to Schattschneider (1942) 'modern democracy is unthinkable save in terms of political parties'. Yet although political parties are a recognizable feature of democratic politics, they are also often the source of much disillusion among electors. In recent years parties have been said to be in decline in a number of ways, whether in terms of their membership, or in their ability to motivate electors to turn out to vote for them. Against this backdrop, this chapter assesses the current literature on British parties to ask two key questions: what is the role of political parties in the modern UK; and to what extent are parties successfully fulfilling their democratic functions? The first part of the chapter begins by setting out various definitions of political parties and highlighting their functions in democracies. The second part of the chapter addresses itself to the question: to what extent are the UK's parties successfully fulfilling these roles? British parties are argued to be fulfilling these functions to varying degrees. While they continue to simplify the electoral choices available to voters, they are decreasingly able to command the loyalty of voters. Nevertheless, through their position in organizing both government and opposition in the House of Commons, parties play a crucial, if not always necessarily central, role in providing political accountability in the UK. Arguably political parties have become decreasingly rooted in the communities they aspire to represent, thereby leaving governing and electioneering at the heart of what parties currently do in the UK today.

Defining Political Parties

What is a political party? Definitions of parties can be found from eighteenth-century philosophers such as David Hume and Edmund Burke (van Biezen and Saward, 2008, p. 23), through to the more recent

18

work of specialists such as Sartori (2005 [1976]). Consequently, there are many competing definitions of what parties are and what they do. Rather than try to resolve this longstanding debate with one definition, it is useful to have a conception of the various different understandings of parties that scholars have set out and the different elements that they each emphasize. Sartori's (2005 [1976], p. 57) minimal definition suggests that 'a party is any political group that presents at elections, and is capable of placing through elections, candidates for public office'. Panebianco (1988, p. 6) similarly points to electoral competition as an activity that distinguishes parties from the goals of other political organizations such as pressure groups. While compellingly simple, there are two difficulties with these definitions. Neither considers what parties do if they are successful in being elected to office, and in recent years single-issue pressure groups have increasingly sought influence by contesting elections thereby blurring the distinction between them and parties. Ware (1996, p. 5) attempts to resolve these difficulties by proposing that:

A political party is an institution that (a) seeks influence in a state, often by attempting to occupy positions in government, and (b) usually consists of more than a single interest in society and so to some degree attempts to 'aggregate interests'.

However, this renders the electoral aspect an implicit element of his definition, something that many observers would consider crucial. An understanding and combination of each of these three approaches to defining parties is therefore a necessary initial condition for understanding what parties are and what they do.

Parties come in different organizational shapes and sizes (Gunther and Diamond, 2003). Some have taken a more comprehensive view of what parties are by adding organizational aspects to the definition. LaPalombara and Weiner (1966, p. 6) define a party as: having continuity in organization beyond its present leaders; evident organization at the local level with structured relationships between local and national levels; the determination at both local and national level to win and exercise power; and the aim of seeking popular support at elections. This is quite a restrictive definition. It would exclude parties oriented around loosely organized groups of 'notables', the classic cadre parties of Duverger's (1964) account, or parties which have a central organization but little representation at the local level. LaPalombara and Weiner's definition is nevertheless a useful ideal type from which to assess organizational aspects of political parties.

Observers tend to assume that parties are important. But are they? Despite having been central to the conduct of politics, Bogdanor (2004, p. 717) notes that political parties were not legally and constitutionally recognized in Britain until the end of the twentieth century. While parties contest elections and form governments they often seem unable to either control or make a difference to events. Parties face a range of constraints (Hay, 2007; Rose, 1984). On the one hand, politicians claim to be constrained by global economic conditions and market reactions. Labour governments throughout the 1960s and 1970s were forced to implement severe public spending cuts because of international pressure on the pound, while the post-2010 Conservative–Liberal Democrat coalition's cuts in public services and spending were justified by the fear that markets would punish the UK for running an increased deficit in the aftermath of the 2008–2010 economic crisis. Prior to this, according to former Prime Minister Gordon Brown, the UK was unable to regulate its financial sector heavily because of the prevailing international market culture of low regulation.

On the other hand, politicians increasingly seem to give away what power they do have. On election in 1997, Labour gave independence to the Bank of England for monetary policy. Similarly, an early act of the Conservative–Liberal Democrat coalition in 2010 was to set up the Office for Budget Responsibility (OBR) to provide independent economic forecasts. A range of other independent or semi-independent bodies have been set up in a wide range of policy areas – the famous quangos of much political debate. This depoliticizes many areas of public policy and leads to, at best, unclear lines of accountability, and, at worst, a crisis of policy responsibility. Rather than the model of direct and responsible party *government*, this means that there is a more diffuse network of *governance* relationships at local, national and international levels (Rhodes, 1996; Torfing, 2007).

The role of political parties when these broader conditions are taken into account is unclear. Rose (1984, ch. 8) suggests that 'much of a party's record in office will be stamped upon it by forces outside its control. British parties are not the primary forces shaping the destiny of British society.' He argues that while parties do make a difference, they often do so in a far smaller way than might be thought. Hay (2007, chs 3 and 4) by contrast argues that politicians have much more room for policy manoeuvre than is often claimed. If so, the role of parties would seem to be enhanced.

The Functions of Political Parties

Such contrasting arguments make it necessary to clearly understand what the functions of political parties are. Sartori (2005, p. 21) sees the functional approach as 'particularly rewarding. While all parties perform system-related functions, the interesting thing is that they do not all perform the same functions.' Daalder (1991, pp. 285–6) observes that scholars may be reaching the wrong conclusions about the health of parties because they concentrate on some functions to the exclusion of others. He argues for well-specified empirical analyses of how parties are carrying out their functions. As Lowi (1963, p. 571) conceptualizes the debate, party functions should not be just presented as an inventory, but be conceived of as 'standards for the proper functioning of party ... they should be guides for enquiry'. Such an approach can be used at all levels of party organization, from the national to the local (Clark, 2004; Lowi, 1963), and can be used to distinguish the performance of parties generally, and between individual parties in particular.

What are the functions of political parties? There are almost as many lists of party functions as there are party scholars. Broadly, literature on party organization identifies two main approaches to this question. First, parties play an integrative function in society, integrating citizens into the complex world of democracy by educating them, helping them identify with one or other particular party, and ensuring that citizens participate politically either through party membership and activism or, at minimum, going out to vote. Such a view is typically associated with broadly left-wing models of party organization which aimed to mobilize and integrate the working class, such as Duverger's (1964) 'mass party', or Neumann's (1956; also Kirchheimer, 1966) 'party of democratic integration'.

Others have seen parties as playing an essentially electoral role in democratic life, in what Schumpeter (1965 [1942], p. 282–3) calls the 'competitive struggle for political power'. Competing for office, selecting candidates to stand for election and honing the party's message in this conception is the limit of party functions. Thus, Duverger's (1964) cadre parties are organized around local 'notables' who can bring either money to the party, or know how to organize election campaigns for the candidates, while Wright's (1971) 'rational-efficient' parties have similar organization and aims.

As broad approaches to party functions, the idea of integration and electoral competition focus on the input side of the party politics equation. Parties campaign for election on both a programme for office derived from their ideological background, and their record either as a government or opposition. If elected, parties claim to have received a mandate to govern. So that these post-election aspects can also form part of the assessment of party functions, what is also needed is some sense of what parties should do after they have been elected to public office. Table 2.1 therefore sets out a comprehensive list of party functions as summarized by Dalton and Wattenberg (2000a). They posit a threefold understanding: parties in the electorate, as organizations and in government. The remainder of this chapter assesses whether and to what degree political parties continue to fulfil these functions in the UK.

Table 2.1   The functions of political parties in advanced democracies

Parties in the electorate	Parties as organizations	Parties in government
Simplifying choices for voters	Recruiting political leadership	Creating majorities in government
Educating citizens	Seeking governmental office	Organizing the government
Generating symbols of political identification and loyalty	Training political elites	Implementing policy objectives
Mobilizing people to participate	Articulating political interests	Organizing dissent and opposition
	Aggregating political interests	Ensuring responsibility for government actions
		Controlling government administration
		Fostering stability in government

Source: Adapted from Dalton and Wattenberg (2000a).

Parties in the Electorate

The electoral function is the least demanding view of what parties should do in advanced democracies (Webb, 2009). If parties successfully structure and simplify electoral choice, we should expect them to, at minimum, offer candidates for election for public office. In the UK, evidence suggests that there has been an expansion of party competition in this regard. In 1900 more than a third of parliamentary constituencies were uncontested, while 107 candidates were returned unopposed in 1918. Even into the 1920s and 1930s it was not uncommon for around 10 per cent of MPs to be returned unopposed. From 1955, with the exception of the Speaker of the House of Commons, every constituency has been contested (Rallings and Thrasher, 2000). Between 1918 and 1935, the average number of candidates was around 1400. From 1945 onwards there has been a considerable increase in contestation, rising from 1659 in 1945 to 4133 in 2010 (Tetteh, 2008, p. 12; Cracknell et al., 2010, p. 6). It is now highly uncommon for any of the three major parties not to offer a candidate in every British constituency.

The rise in numbers of candidates has come from three sources. First, numbers of Liberal Party candidates contesting elections grew from a low of 104 in 1951 to 639 in 1997–2001. Second, between 1966 and 1970 the number of candidates from the Scottish and Welsh nationalists more than doubled, thereby enabling them to contest all constituencies in their countries. Finally, the number of 'other' candidates has increased substantially from 95 in 1966 to 1470 in 2005 (Tetteh, 2008, p. 12). This comprises some ephemeral small organizations and local candidates. It also comprises a number of smaller parties which are becoming significant actors in their own right, such as the UK Independence Party (UKIP), and which are discussed in Chapter 6 below. Whether this simplifies or confuses choice for voters is debatable. Rather than parties having a declining role in structuring electoral choice, it can be argued that parties actually offer more choice in Britain than they ever have.

Political parties are meant to play a central role in educating citizens about politics. Competing for election means that parties must, at minimum, set out what they stand for and what their policies are during election campaigns. They must then communicate this to voters, thereby attempting to persuade them of the merits of their party's arguments. This has an educational role since it feeds into what one country's constitution suggests is the main purpose of political parties, 'forming the political will of the people' (German Basic Law Article 21). Viewing this from an integrative perspective suggests a more active role for parties, with party organizations providing information direct to voters, being active in local communities and enabling political debate to take place.

The extent to which parties in the UK have been able to educate voters directly is debatable. It is unlikely that any 'golden age' of direct party activity existed in the way that some suggest (Scarrow, 1996, pp. 194–5). While parties must indeed set out their position and attempt to persuade voters of their case, the size of the electorate in advanced democracies means that this is essentially done via the media. Analysts are divided about whether this has an impact on political behaviour. Lloyd (2004) argues that the media have a detrimental effect on political life, portraying parties and politicians in negative terms and routinely distrusting and questioning their messages. Norris et al. (1999) suggest that while parties do try to control how their message is portrayed, there is a divergence between the media and the parties. The media concentrate on reporting party strategy, while the parties themselves do attempt to discuss substantive issues and policies. While parties may attempt to educate the public, their views may not be getting through. However, Norris et al. (1999, ch. 7) do find that greater exposure to political media over the long term does make a positive difference to greater levels of civic engagement. If so, the media might be argued to share the political education role with parties.

The relationship between parties and various media has become more complex in recent decades, with the fragmentation of the television market, and the rise of the internet. While the internet allows parties to supply information direct to voters, it also provides considerable space for critical debate and commentary on parties and politics. Webb (1995, pp. 316–17) therefore points to the reduced capacity of parties to get their message across and that the sources of most political information are apt to be critical of parties. The relationship between parties and the media is returned to in Chapter 8.

To what extent do parties generate symbols of identification and political loyalty? Given widespread scepticism about politics, it might be expected that parties have been decreasingly successful in fulfilling this function. Figure 2.1 shows that levels of party identification have been on a downwards trend from the 1960s onwards. Although high levels of voters still indicate having party identification, this has declined from 94 per cent in 1992 to 81 per cent in 2005. Fewer people report identifying with either the Labour or Conservative parties, and this has also declined from 81 per cent in 1964 to 63 per cent in 2005. The decline in identification is most apparent when those who 'very strongly' identify with a party are considered, having fallen from 43 per cent in 1964 to only 10 per cent

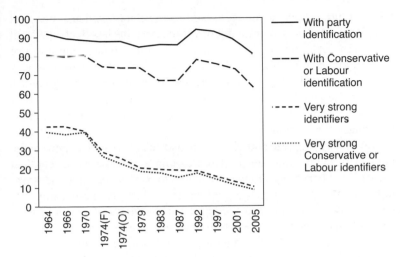

Figure 2.1   Party identification (% of the electorate), 1964–2005

Sources: Data from Denver (1994, p. 54; 2007, pp. 62, 72).

in 2005. Such a decline is closely mirrored by those who strongly identify with either Labour or the Conservative Party, falling from 40 per cent in 1964 to just nine per cent in 2005. Parties have therefore been decreasingly able to act as symbols of political identification and loyalty, becoming instead more like 'necessary evils' to voters (Dalton and Weldon, 2005). The decline in party identification has important political consequences. It means that voting patterns have become more volatile and that people with weak party loyalties are less likely to turn out to vote. This weakens the base of support for the leading parties in the UK. It also calls into question both the legitimacy of any party elected on a minority of the vote, and ultimately of the party system itself if voters stop going to the polls in large numbers (Dalton and Weldon, 2005; Holmberg, 2003).

Concerns about turnout were brought to the forefront when it fell sharply from 71.4 per cent in 1997 to 59.4 per cent in 2001. While turnout recovered slightly to 65.1 per cent in the 2010 general election, this is still substantially below the post-war record of 84 per cent in 1950 and even the 77.7 per cent recorded in 1992. In recent elections turnout has struggled to get much above 40 per cent in some constituencies, while in others it is well above 70 per cent. Reasons for declining participation are complex and revolve around social (age, class, education), political (competitiveness of the constituency) and practical factors (the ease of getting to the polls) (Clarke et al., 2004, ch. 8; Denver, 2007, ch. 2). Low levels of turnout among younger voters have been of particular concern, since if they do not learn the habit of voting early, the less likely they will be to turn out in future, thereby undermining the future legitimacy of party political competition in the UK. Low levels of turnout have also plagued the devolved institutions, created in an attempt to bring politics closer to the people in Scotland and Wales. Parties across the UK then have been decreasingly able to mobilize voters to participate in elections to a range of institutions.

Mobilizing people to participate can also be understood in terms of the number of people that are prepared to join and be active in political parties. Members bring a range of benefits to parties, including subscriptions and donations, acting as volunteer workers, communicating the party's message locally and feeding back the views of voters to their party's higher echelons. At election time, their activity can make a positive difference to the result in their local area (Scarrow, 1996; Whiteley et al., 1994; Seyd and Whiteley, 1992). Party membership is therefore a key indicator of the democratic health of political parties. Party membership figures should always be treated with caution. Parties have incentives to overstate their membership and may not keep accurate records, while other sources also have problems with reliability. Nevertheless, in the absence of more reliable methods of estimating membership size, researchers have to make use of what figures are available (Mair and van Biezen, 2001). As Figure 2.2 illustrates, the estimates that are available for the mainstream British parties show an unmistakable pattern of

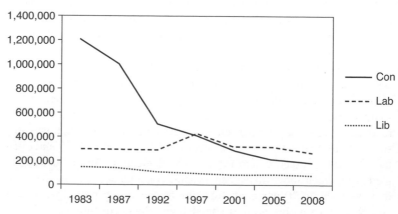

Figure 2.2   Party membership in Britain, 1983–2008

Source: Data from Marshall, 2009, pp. 8–9.

decline. This is most evident with the Conservative Party, declining from an estimated 1.2 million members in 1983 to around quarter of a million in 2008. Labour enjoyed a membership boom after Tony Blair was elected leader in 1994, but this was short-lived. The Labour membership declined from around 405,000 in 1997 to 156,000 in 2009, although this increased slightly during the party's 2010 leadership election to succeed Gordon Brown; around 177,000 members were issued with ballot papers in that contest. The Liberal Democrats have similarly lost a sizeable proportion of their membership, declining from around 100,000 in the early 1990s to around 59,000 in 2008–09. Britain is not alone: this phenomenon of membership decline is replicated across many advanced democracies (Mair and van Biezen, 2001). In sum, parties are decreasingly able to fulfil their democratic function of mobilizing people to participate not only in politics more generally, but also in their own organizations.

Parties as Organizations

The second group of party functions revolves around the idea of parties as organizations. Dalton and Wattenberg (2000a) highlight seeking governmental office as a party function. This relates to the broader discussion about parties contesting elections and providing choice for voters. It is ultimately dependent upon parties being able to recruit candidates to stand for election, as discussed above. Consequently, this section concentrates on the four remaining aspects: recruitment and training of political leadership, and articulating and aggregating political interests.

While parties may have trouble in recruiting members, they play a central role in recruiting political leadership. It is difficult to think of a major political figure without a party affiliation. Political parties therefore act as 'gatekeepers' with their candidate selection processes determining who stands for and is elected to public office. Norris and Lovenduski (1995) suggest that this might be understood in terms of 'demand and supply'. Supply reflects the willingness of people to come forward and offer themselves as a potential candidate, while demand relates to the idea that selectors choose candidates on the basis of certain characteristics that they are looking for. Candidate selection is often seen as the 'secret garden' of politics (Gallagher and Marsh, 1988), since, as an internal party process, it tends to take place behind closed doors. However, it is crucial because conflicts over which candidate to select can often be struggles over the direction a party should take. The result of such disputes can determine the composition and direction of parliamentary parties. This is particularly important in Britain where there have traditionally been many safe seats due to the first-past-the-post electoral system. Selecting a candidate for the dominant party in a safe constituency means selecting the future MP. The conduct of candidate selection processes can also reveal just how democratic a party is in its own internal affairs. Candidate selection can therefore reflect conflicts over political power within parties, which also impact upon the broader conduct of politics.

Parties have a number of issues to face in this regard. Candidate recruitment and selection used to be, along with electioneering, the key role of parties' local organizations. In the UK, recent attempts to extend the role of party headquarters into the candidate selection process have proved controversial, particularly in the Conservative and Labour parties. For instance, Labour's efforts to impose an all women shortlist (AWS) in one Welsh constituency in 2005 led to the party's original candidate standing as an independent in protest and being successfully elected to parliament. Similarly, since David Cameron became leader, local Conservative associations have resisted efforts from party HQ to interfere in their selection processes. Parties have also experimented with new methods of candidate selection. In what are known as 'open primaries', some Conservative associations have opened up their selection process to include not just paid-up party members but also voters, thereby weakening the grip of local activists. A key question underpinning much of the debate on candidate selection relates to the extent to which it leads to candidates who are representative of the electorate as a whole, or whether parties' 'gatekeeping' leads to the exclusion of certain groups such as women and ethnic minorities (Norris and Lovenduski, 1995). These debates are returned to below. Parties nevertheless remain at the centre of recruiting political leadership in the UK.

A closely related issue is the role that parties play in training political elites. Parties can act as a kind of 'political training ground' in a number of ways. Party organizations socialize members into the party's procedures and larger value system. They allow political novices to test their aptitude and motivations for political activity and gain first-hand experience of political processes. Prior party service is crucial if a member wishes to become a candidate. This can take numerous forms. Typically, these include being active in the local party organization, being an office holder in the local constituency party, or acting as an election agent for candidates. Virtually all successful candidates will have had a history of contesting a number of 'hopeless' constituencies before eventually being elected to parliament. Norris and Lovenduski (1995) underline this idea of previous party service being important and offer what they call a 'ladder of recruitment' with constituency or party posts being the step before an ambitious member becomes, or is allowed to become, a candidate at an election. Other paths available to a small number of ambitious members include being recruited to the party's central organization, acting as a researcher or special advisor for instance. Both David Cameron and George Osborne, and four of the five contenders for the 2010 Labour leadership demonstrate such a career path. While local activity remains central, this type of experience within parties is increasingly important. While only 3 per cent of MPs in 1979 had previous experience as a politician or political organizer, acting for instance as a party or ministerial advisor before they were elected to the House of Commons, this had risen to around 14 per cent in the 2005 and 2010 parliaments (Gay, 2009, p. 11; Kavanagh and Cowley, 2010, p. 327).

The argument about parties articulating interests is rooted in the idea, highlighted in Chapter 1, that parties evolved from the conflicts evident in society at the time of the extension of the franchise (Lipset and Rokkan, 1967). In other words, parties exist to articulate the interests of a specific section of the electorate. Thus, the Labour Party, having emerged from a mixture of the trade union movement and socialist societies, represented and articulated the interests of the working classes. By contrast, the Conservative Party has been associated with the interests of business and the middle classes and perceived to be speaking up for them. There are a number of difficulties with such a conception of parties articulating interests in advanced democracies. First, the electorate has become increasingly affluent at the same time as collective group identities have been challenged by economic and social change and an increasing individualization of societies. This weakens the importance of parties, and, as noted earlier, leads to declining party identification and mobilization.

Second, and as a consequence, Kirchheimer (1966) highlights the rise of what he calls the 'catch-all party'. Key features are that such parties drastically reduce their reliance on ideological stances, party leaders stop identifying with particular social groups in favour of society as a whole, and the parties place distance between themselves and the traditional social class and group that the party's original support was built upon. Such dynamics have had an impact on the ability of both Labour and the Conservative Party to articulate interests in the UK, with both seeking to distance themselves from their respective core groups and attempting to persuade uncommitted voters (Smith, 2009). In 1997, for instance,

Labour was keen to downplay its links with the trade unions for fear of alienating voters, a difficulty that the party still faces today.

Moreover, parties are not the only organizations that articulate political interests in the UK. Many interest or pressure groups also do so, taking their various demands to policy-makers either directly or through campaigns designed to highlight particular issues, often more effectively than parties do. These can be high profile such as environmental protests designed to draw attention to issues relating to environmental degradation. Other interest groups prefer to work within the political system, bringing their expertise to government and parties in order to highlight their issues. Although articulation remains important for parties, they essentially share this political function with such actors. Moreover, if the 'catch-all' argument is correct, this means that parties in the UK have been decreasingly willing to articulate the interests of their core supporters. As Webb (1995, p. 316) summarizes, this means that parties 'do not fulfil the function of articulating and representing interests as efficiently as was once the case'.

Aggregating interests is a closely related function. There are numerous difficulties with this and, like interest articulation, parties are not necessarily the only bodies which perform such a role (King, 1969). What is meant here is simply converting demands into general policy positions (cf. Almond and Powell, 1966, p. 98). When assessing these questions, it is worth briefly considering how parties compete. There are two influential approaches to this. Downs (1957) develops a rational choice model of party behaviour, summarized in Figure 2.3. He posits a two-party system,

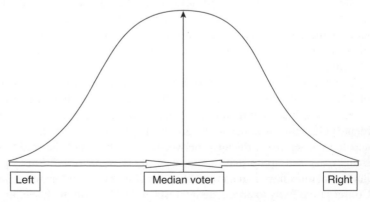

Figure 2.3   The 'Downsian' model of party competition
Source: Adapted from Downs, 1957.

where political conflicts revolve around the division between left and right of the political spectrum. Voters are evenly distributed along this spectrum, with few voters at the extreme ends, but rising on both sides so that most voters are found in the centre. If parties are to maximize their vote, it is therefore sensible for parties to concentrate their efforts on such 'median voters', thereby meaning that parties' policy programmes are moderate and centrist.

More recent models of party competition have attempted to incorporate the rise of new issues into political debate. The argument is that in advanced democracies, citizens' needs for physical and material security have largely been met. Consequently, their political thoughts and demands have moved away from 'materialist' politics of order, economic growth and stability, towards 'post-materialist' issues. While 'materialist' issues might be thought of as essentially quantitative in nature, 'post-materialism' is more qualitative, revolving around quality of life issues. Typical post-materialist causes have included environmentalism, the women's movement and campaigns against nuclear weapons and power (Inglehart 1990a; 1990b; Kitschelt, 1994). How this feeds into party competition is conceptualized around two axes. The first is a horizontal axis which represents the left–right economic dimension. The vertical axis by contrast represents post-material versus materialist issues, with post-material views at the top of the spectrum and materialist views at the bottom. In most democracies, the main area of party competition spreads diagonally across these two axes, revolving mainly around left-leaning post-materialist issues and right-leaning materialist issues (Kitschelt, 1994; 1997) (see Figure 2.4).

There are difficulties in aggregating interests under either model of party competition. To aggregate interests parties must prioritize between competing sets of interests. The Downsian model (Figure 2.3), often applied in post-war Britain where there have been predominantly two main parties in competition, means that as parties move close to the centre to address the interests of voters there, it becomes difficult for them to include the interests of voters at the more extreme left and right ends of the spectrum. Indeed, Wolinetz (1979) highlighted how instead of catch-all parties being able to aggregate all interests, a fragmentation of party systems resulted as space opened up for the articulation of other issues. Similarly, in the post-material model (Figure 2.4), large areas of issue space are also left empty. Thus, a post-material right-wing voter or left-wing voter concerned about material issues may find little of interest in the policy programmes that mainstream parties put together. While these are generalizations, such difficulties have been utilized to explain, for instance, the rise of small and radical parties of both the far-right and

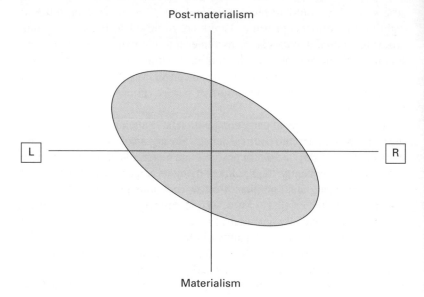

Figure 2.4   Model of party competition including the material–post-material axis

Sources: Adapted from Inglehart, 1990a, 1990b; Kitschelt, 1994, 1997.

environmental parties such as the Greens (Ignazi, 1992). In the British case, this can be equated to the rise of small parties such as the British National Party (BNP), the Greens and the Respect Party (Clark et al., 2008). This also highlights the interlinked nature of interest articulation and aggregation for parties. When mainstream parties choose to prioritize some interests over others in their programmes, they necessarily leave others out. This means that space is opened for other parties to articulate interests revolving around the vacant issue space, albeit often on a much narrower platform. While parties share both the articulation and aggregation functions with other actors, these are still key roles that parties fulfil. How parties choose to do so can directly impact on how parties compete and interact more generally.

Parties in Government

The third group of functions revolve around what parties do after elections, particularly if they are successful and form the government. Dalton and Wattenberg (2000a) identify seven such functions. Many of these overlap and can therefore be combined into a more manageable list. Thus: parties create majorities and foster stability in government; organize the government and control government administration; implement party policy objectives and ensure responsibility for government actions; and organize dissent and opposition.

Political parties are clearly the central actors in creating majorities in order to form governments in the UK. Table 2.2 summarizes the composition of UK governments from 1945 and their majorities. In the UK, the Westminster model of government has, in the post-war period at least, traditionally relied upon a single party being able to form the government, often with a large majority of seats. For instance, under Tony Blair's leadership the Labour Party governed with majorities of 179 in 1997, 167 in 2001 and 66 in 2005, while Margaret Thatcher achieved majorities of 43 in 1979, 144 in 1983 and 101 in 1987. The UK has therefore appeared to

Table 2.2   General Elections 1945–2010: governments and majorities

Year	Government	Majority	Post-Election Prime Minister
1945	Labour	147	Clement Attlee
1950	Labour	6	Clement Attlee
1951	Conservative	16	Sir Winston Churchill
1955	Conservative	59	Sir Anthony Eden
1959	Conservative	99	Harold MacMillan
1964	Labour	5	Harold Wilson
1966	Labour	97	Harold Wilson
1970	Conservative	31	Edward Heath
1974 (Feb)	Labour	None	Harold Wilson
1974 (Oct)	Labour	4	Harold Wilson
1979	Conservative	44	Margaret Thatcher
1983	Conservative	144	Margaret Thatcher
1987	Conservative	101	Margaret Thatcher
1992	Conservative	21	John Major
1997	Labour	178	Tony Blair
2001	Labour	166	Tony Blair
2005	Labour	65	Tony Blair
2010	Conservative–Liberal Democrat	76	David Cameron

Source: Adapted from Tetteh (2008).

be the epitome of strong party government. That the UK has tended to have single party majorities is at least in part due to the nature of the first-past-the-post electoral system used for Westminster. Indeed, those opposing electoral reform often argue that the need for strong party government is one good reason to maintain the first-past-the-post system. Even in closer elections, parties have still been able, on the whole, to form single party governments; Labour governed alone with small majorities in 1950, 1964 and between 1974 and 1976.

This is not necessarily the same as saying that parties will be able to foster stability in government. It is important to make a distinction between different sources of instability. These can come from inside the governing party, or externally from opposition parties. Instability can also come from a party that has been supporting the main governing party, whether through a formal coalition or on a more informal case-by-case basis, removing that support, thereby leaving the main governing party vulnerable. Examples of each can be found in British politics. Even majority governments can give the impression of instability. A good example is the Conservative Party after the 1992 general election, despite the 21 seat majority achieved by John Major. The party's majority was eroded over time for a variety of reasons, including withdrawing the whip from Eurosceptic internal critics. This left the party reliant on the Ulster Unionist Party (UUP) for support and contributed to perceptions of a government lurching from crisis to crisis.

When no party has an overall majority over the other party groups, this is commonly referred to as a 'hung' parliament. If a party is the largest group in parliament under such circumstances, they may have the option of forming a minority government. The perception of minority governments in mainstream British commentary has tended to be that they are inherently unstable. This is not necessarily so. After the 2007 Scottish parliament elections, the Scottish National Party (SNP) formed a minority government which proved to be relatively stable, and enacted some party policies with support from other parties. This does not mean that the SNP could implement all its policies. For example, the other parties in the Scottish parliament combined to block the SNP's plans for a 2010 referendum on Scottish independence. Minority governments can however be vulnerable when other parties withdraw support. The decline in Labour's majority in the 1974–79 parliament saw it become reliant on the Liberals in what was known as the Lib–Lab pact. The withdrawal of Liberal support in 1978 led to the Labour Party becoming more reliant on less formal support from other parties and eventually defeated in a vote of no confidence in 1979.

The main way of dealing with such difficulties outside the UK has been to try to form a coalition to provide both a majority and stable government. Broadly, coalitions can be built when the parties involved have enough seats to achieve a viable majority, and when the parties involved also have ideological and policy approaches which overlap (Laver and Schofield, 1990). The formation of the Conservative–Liberal Democrat coalition in 2010 appeared to shock media commentators. However, coalitions are not unknown in British politics, having been in evidence both in devolved and local government in the UK. One of the justifications given for the Conservative–Liberal Democrat coalition was the need for stable government to steer the country through the economic crisis. While both parties had major differences, there was enough common ground between them – on reducing the size of the state for instance – for the two parties to agree a formal coalition. Despite criticisms from within both parties, the coalition initially proved to be a stable government. Forming majorities and providing stable government has therefore been central to the role of UK parties.

Dalton and Wattenberg's (2000a) organizing the government function is more accurately described as organizing the activities of government in the national legislature. There are two aspects. The first is organizing the party's legislative programme and ensuring that this is passed by parliament. At Westminster, these are organized by party appointees in the form of the Leader of the House of Commons, and in the party 'Whips' who attempt to maintain party discipline in votes in parliament. A common myth is that party whips are able to enforce discipline to the extent that MPs become little more than sheep voting for the party line. In recent years this has been challenged. Cowley (2005; Cowley and Stuart, 2008a) has demonstrated how, despite the party's 'control freak' reputation, Labour Party MPs increasingly voted against their party. Once an MP had rebelled, evidence suggested that this was just the beginning of a longer term habit of voting against their party.

The second aspect is the appointment of party personnel to head important committees and positions within the legislature. Prior to 2010, parties were able to appoint members to standing and select committees in relation to their strength in the chamber, with the government holding the power of appointment of the committee chair. This changed in the aftermath of the parliamentary expenses scandal as demands for parliamentary reform became urgent. From 2010, committee chairs and members are elected by all MPs, thereby weakening the power of patronage of party leaders. These issues notwithstanding, parties are still central to formulating a governing programme, legislating and getting that legislation through parliament.

Parties are also still central to controlling government administration. In the UK, selected MPs are appointed as minsters to run the various departments of state. This also applies in each of the devolved administrations thereby extending the role of parties in controlling government to different levels. Where single party governments are formed, this involves the party leader appointing his 'cabinet' from senior members of their parliamentary party, attempting to achieve a balance of expertise and opinion from within the party. This is more difficult when the government is a coalition because more than one party is involved and the need for compromise inevitably sees some potential ministers lose out to MPs from another party, as was the case when Conservative spokespeople had to give way to senior Liberal Democrats in the aftermath of the 2010 election. Under Gordon Brown, recruitment of ministers to the Labour government briefly included business and military figures who were given peerages and co-opted to the so-called 'governments of all the talents'. While this appeared to broaden out the traditional party-based route into government, it is important to note that these figures were appointed by the Labour Party and served in a Labour government. Parties therefore remain central in providing leadership for government administration.

It is more difficult to argue that parties are the key actors in implementing policy objectives. Parties may appoint minsters to run departments and direct the broad sweep of policy. However, implementation requires not just direction from above, but a number of people working together in public administration to actually deliver the outcomes desired. These include civil servants, administrators, departmental and occasionally interdisciplinary committees, arms-length agencies and those who have to actually carry out work to deliver the policy. In education the latter may include primary and secondary school teachers, while in health it includes nurses and doctors. Policies can often be delayed or amended because of the sheer complexity of the organization required to implement them. This can be frustrating for governments. Tony Blair regularly complained that his efforts to reform public services and deliver policy were hindered by public sector workers that he perceived to be opposing his reform process. The private sector also has a role to play. The Conservative–Liberal Democrat government may have wanted to concentrate on growth, but found this exceedingly difficult because the banks were unwilling to lend despite numerous ministerial statements and efforts encouraging them to do so. Parties are therefore reliant on many other actors to implement policy for them. At best their role is one of setting aims and trying to direct policy outcomes through constant persuasion and cajoling of the actors involved, not always successfully. This has implications for parties. As Webb (1995, p. 315) observes, 'persistent failures by governments to resolve national policy problems are bound to undermine the popular status of parties – especially when these failures are associated with both sides of the partisan spectrum'.

Any model of party government necessarily reverts back to the electoral process as a means for holding parties responsible for their achievements, or failures, in office. The idea of 'responsible political parties' has been influential in political science debates about how parties should behave (APSA, 1950). In short, parties present programmes to which they are committed and have been sufficiently cohesive to carry out. The argument is that voters can then choose between them, rewarding or punishing parties for their performance while running the government. Commonly referred to as 'valence' politics, performance voting has become an important explanation for voting behaviour in UK general elections. This informed early British voting studies (Butler and Stokes, 1969). It has recently gained in importance as an explanation of British voting behaviour against the backdrop of declining turnout and identification. As Clarke et al. (2009, p. 305) argue in regard to the 2005 election:

> To the extent that the parties and party leaders can convey a sense of their collective competence to deliver goods and services to the electorate, citizens will respond by increasing their support.

This provides an incentive for parties in office to strive to provide good government, since their future in office can depend upon it. The important functional point is that it is parties and their leaders which are central to this process. Parties and elections therefore provide a crucial link in the chain of political responsibility and accountability.

Britain has often been utilized as an example of where dissent and opposition to the government consists of strictly competitive behaviour in elections and parliament by the party that does not, at that time, form the government. Dahl (1966) suggested that the purpose of party-based opposition in Britain is ultimately to seek to win an election, form a government and take a new policy direction. Such behaviour would seem readily apparent; party leaders spar weekly in Prime Minister's Questions, while opposition spokespersons routinely criticize government proposals and even occasionally offer their own solutions. Such opposition is a crucial element in holding governments responsible (APSA, 1950).

A number of observations are necessary. First, while opposition parties routinely challenge the government, even in the competitive two-party system Dahl highlights, parties choose to compete on some issues and not on others. In opposition between 2004 and 2005, for example, the Conservatives chose to highlight immigration policy since it had an opinion poll lead over Labour on the issue, but chose to downplay European issues since these could play badly for the party. Second, parties do not necessarily only compete and oppose. They can also collaborate, co-operate and collude, thereby neutralizing certain policy areas as issues (Katz and Mair, 1995). This is most obvious when parties form a coalition. It can also be the case when parties decide an issue is not worth competing over. Prior to being elected in 1997, Labour agreed to stick to Conservative spending limits in office for two years, while the Conservative Party made a similar pledge in opposition before the 2008 economic crisis. This took public spending – perhaps *the* crucial political issue – off the agenda and meant that the official opposition was not actually fulfilling one of the major roles of political parties. This also has implications for party competition, articulating political interests and ensuring responsibility and accountability in government. Thirdly, such agreement, explicit or otherwise, can be exploited by other smaller parties; Liberal Democrats were able to exploit anti-Iraq war sentiment in 2005 for instance when the two main parties had voted for war. Finally, to see parties as playing the key role in dissent and opposition necessitates a narrow focus on political institutions. However, dissent and opposition can also be found in broader society. Many civil society organizations have opposed the Conservative–Liberal Democrat coalition's public spending cuts, while mass opposition to the poll tax in the late 1980s was a key moment in explaining why the Conservative Party removed Margaret Thatcher from office. Parties may therefore have an important role in dissent and opposition, but only on some issues, not all the time and not on their own.

Conclusion

There has been considerable debate about how important parties are in modern democracies, given that they face numerous constraints upon their actions. Being clear about what parties are and what they do in the UK is therefore a necessary starting point in any assessment of party-based democracy. Definitions of parties highlight several aspects of what parties do. They stand for election for public office, they aggregate interests and they govern. While some argue that integrating voters into political life through participative activity is crucial, others however highlight the importance of competing for election as being all that parties need do. Consequently, three main groups of party functions have been identified against which these ideas can be explored, revolving around parties in the electorate, as organizations and in government. The chapter suggested that while some of these functions are fairly obviously in decline, there are some functions that parties share with other political actors and some that parties remain absolutely central to in the UK today.

If parties link society and the institutions of government, then it is the societal end of what parties do in the UK that seems in most difficulty. As membership organizations, temporary fluctuations notwithstanding, parties are fairly obviously in decline and have been so for some time. Similarly, the proportions of strong party identifiers in the UK have declined sharply to a point where only around 10 per cent claim to have strong party loyalties. This impacts upon turnout; UK turnouts are considerably lower than a generation ago, and those for institutions such as the devolved assemblies and European Parliament are considerably lower again. Parties also appear to have a reduced ability to get their message out to the public through the media. These developments would seem to put integrative approaches to the study of parties in some difficulty. Some other important functions parties share with other actors, and how parties perform them can directly impact upon both party competition and the role of these other actors. Thus, parties share articulation and aggregation functions with interest groups, and must ultimately rely upon other actors to implement their policies for them. Failure to do any of these things convincingly can lead to protest, opposition and smaller party options filling the gap left by more mainstream parties.

Parties remain central to a group of functions that revolve around the electoral process, government and ensuring political accountability in the UK. Parties offer greater numbers of candidates than ever in the UK and continue to play the central, if occasionally controversial, role in recruiting and training political elites. They have also been the key actors in forming majorities and providing stability in government, and organizing the government in both parliament and public administration. By standing for election on a policy platform, and being willing to be judged on that platform, parties are held responsible for their performance in public office and consequently remain central actors in the provision of political responsibility and accountability in the UK today. The broader difficulty for parties lies in the interaction of their strengths and weaknesses. Their declining ability to integrate citizens into political life impacts negatively upon perceptions about their legitimacy to govern. This is a difficulty in

all democracies, but is increasingly important in the UK where governments have recently been elected on ever smaller shares of the electorate.
Analysts are pessimistic about parties' ability to resolve this situation
(Webb, 2009). Indeed, Holmberg (2003, p. 298) goes so far as to argue
that 'if [parties'] place in the minds of the electorate weakens, we may,
indeed, see the eventual downturn in support for democratic regimes'.
The chapters to follow examine in more detail some of the questions
raised in this chapter, before returning to these broader questions in the
conclusion.

3

The Conservative Party

The Conservative Party has been the most successful political party in the UK over the past century. Post-war, it had two long spells in office from 1951–64, and 1979–97. In opposition between 1997 and 2010, the Conservative Party struggled to compete with the Labour Party, particularly under Tony Blair. It had four different leaders during this period – William Hague, Iain Duncan Smith, Michael Howard and David Cameron. This lack of success had consequences for policy and party positioning, with the Conservatives alternating between periods of seemingly 'one nation' paternalistic Conservatism, followed by periods where the party has emphasized more 'Thatcherite' and nationalist polices. Acting as the lead partner in a coalition government with the Liberal Democrats, the Conservatives returned to power in May 2010. This chapter therefore assesses developments in the Conservative Party. Discussion progresses in four sections. The first sets out the key elements of Conservative ideology and policy and assesses how this may have changed in recent decades. The second part discusses the question of party leadership. In addition to evaluating perceptions of the party's recent leaders from Edward Heath onwards, it also analyses the party's procedures for selecting a party leader. Under David Cameron, the issue of the party's representativeness has been a high-profile topic. The third part therefore outlines the party's candidate selection processes and, through an assessment of the representativeness of the party's MPs, asks whether or not initiatives to make the party more representative have been successful. The final section reflects upon the Conservative Party's performance in office, particularly during the Heath and Thatcher–Major years. To what extent did they achieve their aims, and does the legacy of these governments continue to haunt the Conservative Party?

Ideology and Policy

Before beginning discussion of specific parties and their ideologies, it is worth considering two questions. What does it mean to say that a party

41

has an ideology? What uses do parties put their ideologies to? There is considerable controversy amongst political theorists about the nature of ideologies. A number of brief points are nevertheless useful for guiding discussion in the following chapters. First, ideologies are generally assumed to offer a coherent and recognizable structure of principles, values and ideas which guide political action. Second, these ideologies can be assessed by examining their views relating to the individual, society and the state. Third, parties use their ideological positioning as a way of guiding voters in their electoral choice. Fourth, such ideological positioning is often expressed and given practical form through the policy pledges that parties make both between and during election campaigns.

One difficulty in understanding conservatism is that its general pragmatism and scepticism over proposals for change mean that it is often viewed not as an ideology, but instead as a disposition or frame of mind (Seawright, 2010, ch. 2; Vincent, 1994). This makes it to some almost an 'anti-ideology'. Conservatives tend to view the term 'ideology' itself in disparaging terms. Analysts have dealt with this difficulty by setting out a number of core elements of conservatism (Barnes, 1994; Garnett, 2003a, pp. 110–14; Ingle, 2008, pp. 22–7; Seawright, 2010, ch. 2; Webb, 2000, pp. 88–92). The first three are closely interrelated. First, conservatives recognize the value of *tradition* in both politics and social life. Second, conservatives have an *organic view of society* through which they have a desire for orderly change. Third, they also demonstrate a *scepticism* about the limits of the power of reason and human ability to reform society. Fourth, conservatives defend the *rule of law* and highlight the importance of property rights. Fifth, a *strong but limited state* is a key element of conservative philosophy, as is, sixth, the desire to have a *prosperous economy*. Seventh, a further element is a respect for *hierarchy, leadership and authority* within politics and society. Finally, conservatives have a close attachment to the nation and the *national interest*.

Two main variants of conservatism have traditionally been identified in the UK. The first is commonly known as *'one nation' conservatism*. This is generally traced back to Benjamin Disraeli, who wrote of the division between two nations, shorthand for two different classes, in Britain and the need to improve the condition of the working classes to bring them together (Disraeli, 1927; Seawright, 2010, pp. 4–8). 'One nation' conservatism was therefore a paternalistic idea which aimed to create social unity by using the state to provide aid to the worst off in society. This was intended to be a safety net which would provide the basis for individual autonomy. The state's role was not unlimited; such conservatives equally encouraged individual and community provision (Gamble,

1980). 'One nation' conservatism is commonly perceived to be on the left of the Conservative Party, so much so that some authors have also referred to it as 'progressive conservatism' (Smith and Ludlam, 1996). It was most commonly associated in the post-war period with the leaderships of Anthony Eden, Harold MacMillan and Edward Heath.

The second variant is now commonly known by the name of its most famous advocate, former Conservative leader, Margaret Thatcher. While *Thatcherism* contains many contradictory narratives, it is nevertheless possible to highlight some key features (Bevir and Rhodes, 1998; Gamble, 1994). Thatcherism had three key elements to it: the free market; the minimal state; and individual liberty and responsibility. In short, the argument was that as free markets created prosperity, they also led to a greater degree of human freedom. This could however only be achieved through minimal state intervention in the economy. This is a very different conception of social justice to that set out by 'one nation' conservatives, having individual responsibility rather than the enabling state at its heart. These ideas manifested themselves in tax-cutting, privatization and deregulation programmes and in a monetarist approach to economics. Additional elements to Thatcherism included arguments for strong law and order and defence, and a re-emphasis on the importance of British nationalism coupled with anti-European sentiment.

The main terms of ideological debate in the post-war Conservative Party tend to fall between 'one nation' and Thatcherite perspectives. Recently some have also highlighted what they call *liberal conservatism* (Beech, 2009; Dorey, 2007, pp. 140–7; Snowdon, 2010, pp. 225–6). The free-market, small-state rhetoric of Thatcherism certainly drew upon economic liberal arguments. However, the idea of liberal conservatism has been used in a different way. Instead, it refers to a social liberalism which places an emphasis on the tolerance of difference, for instance towards the politics of race, immigration and a variety of social and family relationships. This could be extended further to include concern for post-material issues such as the environment. Liberal conservatism has therefore been used as a sign of moderation, placing its advocates on the left wing of the party (Denham and O'Hara, 2007, p. 187; Heppell and Hill, 2009). Underpinning this remains a vision of liberty for the individual from the state, albeit in a version which is more socially acceptable to modern circumstances than the harder-edged economic liberalism of Thatcherites (Beech, 2009, p. 27).

These differing perspectives suggest a degree of ideological change over time in the Conservative Party. Discussions about such change are generally measured from the paternalistic 'one nation' post-war period

(Evans, 2009; Gamble, 1996). During this period, the concern to use the state to help both promote economic growth and at the same time to provide welfare programmes paid for by high rates of taxation, while also recognizing the trade unions as significant economic actors, can be seen as attempts to maintain social unity in classic conservative terms – a scepticism about the ability of grand plans to bring about reform and the consequent desire to manage change in an orderly and organic fashion without challenging the institutions that conservatives sought to defend. These included political institutions, but also social and economic institutions such as private property (Gamble, 1996: pp. 22–3). This period can broadly be summed up in the words of the 1965 policy document *Putting Britain Right Ahead*, which, although it contained some free-market ideas, also included the argument that 'the state should serve the people not dominate them' (cited in Garnett, 2005, p. 201). British membership of the European Economic Community (EEC) under Conservative Prime Minister Heath can also be seen as standing in the tradition of 'one nation' imperialism running through the party (Gamble, 1996, p. 22).

Under Thatcher, the Conservatives moved from an acceptance of the post-war consensus towards a neo-liberal approach to economics. This was accompanied by both an increasing rhetorical hostility to the EEC and European project, and a greater use of British nationalist sentiment to stake out the party's position. Gamble (1996, p. 21) points to Thatcherism as being a 'decisive rupture' for the party. He notes that:

> [h]er call to roll back the state was a repudiation not just of the consensus of post-war politics but of the main line of direction of Conservative politics in the twentieth century. In defining the Conservatives as the party of national independence, economic liberty and moral order the Thatcherites were attempting to ... abandon many of the causes and commitments which had come to define the Conservative Party. (Gamble, 1996: p.23)

That Thatcherism was different to what had gone before was evident in internal party conflict at the time. 'One nation' conservatives saw Thatcher as a liberal and an 'alien import into the Conservative tradition' (Evans, 2009, p. 103), while Thatcher (1993, pp. 13–14) herself dismissed such Conservatives as little more than socialists.

Thatcherism also drew on many traits already evident in conservative ideology. The concern with strong leadership, private property and the role of markets in creating prosperity all had echoes in previous conservative thought (Bevir and Rhodes, 1998). Despite the undoubtedly 'one nation' nature of Heath's conservatism, he prefigured some Thatcherite free-market ideas in the party's 1970 election manifesto, leading one key Conservative thinker to label these policies as being more Thatcherite than those contained in her first two manifestos (Willetts, 1992, p. 42). Indeed, it is well recognized that Thatcherism was initially cautious, only growing gradually in its radicalism during her premiership. As Evans (2009) and Seawright (2010, p. 25) both note, Thatcher exploited earlier 'one nation' conservative themes in relation to patriotism and creating a property-owning democracy as a means of introducing many of the themes which would later be seen as Thatcherite.

These two ideological strands run deep within the party, although there has been a shift over time as to which is dominant. Whiteley et al. (1994, p. 140) point to party members' views in the early 1990s being divided between those who favour free markets and have anti-trade union, anti-immigrant and chauvinist views, and another group who had 'centrist' tendencies concerned with protecting consumers from market excesses, providing welfare to the unemployed and also regulating privatized industries. A more recent membership survey suggested that the dominant members' attitudes between late 2009 to early 2010 revolved around less public spending, pro-tax cuts, deregulation, anti-immigration and Eurosceptic issues (ConservativeHome, 2010a). Webb and Childs (2011) however detect a three-way split in membership attitudes between liberal conservatives, Thatcherites and traditionalists. They suggest that these differing attitudes mean that there remains scope for intra-party conflict between the three groups, particularly over cutting public expenditure.

Heppell and Hill (2009, p. 398) broadly confirm the picture of ideological division amongst party members in their analysis of the orientation of Conservative MPs in 1992. Since 1997, Conservative MPs have become increasingly Eurosceptic, conservative in social policy and free market in economics. In other words, the party's MPs have also become increasingly Thatcherite since Labour's victory in the 1997 general election. Cowley (2009) nevertheless highlights divisions in Conservative parliamentary ranks – Thatcherites against modernizers, and social liberals versus social conservatives, for instance, with some MPs proving rebellious. Expert analysis of party manifestos tends to place the Conservative Party in economically right-wing and socially conservative territory (Benoit and Laver, 2006).

How might the modern Conservative Party's ideological position be characterized? Outlining clear values was an early aim for the Cameron leadership. In the document *Built to Last* (Conservative Party, 2006), these values were those of the liberal conservatism noted above: emphasizing quality of life, social injustice, the environment, public services and empowering communities. Similar emphases were put on responsibility, inclusiveness and tolerance, social policy and understanding and dealing with the causes and problems of poverty (Beech, 2009, pp. 26–7; Dorey, 2007, p. 146). Cameron appeared to distance the party considerably from Thatcherism while also making apologies for past mistakes (Dorey, 2007, pp. 144–5), thereby leading some to wonder if Cameron was 'consigning the party's past to history' (Evans, 2008). Some cast Cameron clearly in the 'one nation' camp (Wilson, 2006), while senior party figures referred to themselves as 'compassionate conservatives' or as being the 'progressive' party in British politics (Cameron, 2009a; Osborne 2009a, 2009b). This meant building up what has been variously called 'associative society' or the 'big society' to encourage groups to take responsibility for resolving problems and providing social services in their communities (Blond, 2010; Cameron, 2009b, 2011; Norman, 2010). In short, the state would encourage social entrepreneurs and community activists to provide solutions to social problems. Such an idea has a long history in conservative political thought.

Not all have been convinced by this ideological repositioning. *Built to Last* (2006) was not well received either on the right of the party or amongst party supporters, with many viewing it as a disappointment (Bale, 2010, pp. 309–11; Snowdon, 2010, pp. 230–1). Beech (2009, p. 24) and Evans (2008, 2010) both argue that despite the early focus on social issues Cameron is fundamentally Thatcherite, being in favour of less state intervention and of Eurosceptic persuasion. The economic crisis of 2007–2010 forced the party's position on economic issues into sharp focus and eventually highlighted a more Thatcherite emphasis than the party's earlier repositioning suggested. With the public deficit increasing largely because of the need to rescue the banks, the party argued for cutting this sharply within the term of a single parliament. This would be achieved through extensive public spending cuts and public service reform starting in 2010, including reducing the civil service Whitehall budget by a third, public sector pay and pensions freezes. It also included the aim of improving the UK's rankings for tax competitiveness and business regulation through corporation tax cutting and deregulation measures (Conservative Party, 2010; Osborne, 2009b, 2010a, b, c). Even one of the thinkers credited with influencing the party's renewed emphasis on society pointed to Shadow Chancellor George Osborne, responsible for the party's economic policy, as being a 'convinced Thatcherite' and appeared unsure how far this meant Osborne supported the party's emphasis on empowering society (Blond, 2010, p. 33). Many have seen the 'Big Society' as simply a mask for spending cuts, noting the damage such cuts were making to precisely the type of community organization the Conservatives claimed to want to encourage. These cuts invariably fell heavily on poorer areas more reliant on public spending. Even when defending the 'Big Society' idea, Cameron (2011) has been clear that cutting public spending is the party's priority. Calls for a referendum on the EU's Lisbon Treaty, the party's subsequent argument for a referendum on transferring any further powers to the EU (Cameron, 2009a), and leaving the mainstream conservative grouping in the European Parliament in favour of a group opposed to the EU all suggested that the Thatcherite anti-EU nationalist agenda remained a significant force within the party even if other strands of conservatism are sometimes evident.

Leadership

Party leaders are significant political figures. To the electorate, they are often the only recognizable face of the party. Their political statements are closely examined by analysts for a sign of the direction the party is taking. Offering strong and decisive leadership is commonly perceived to be a key factor in ensuring that leaders become an electoral asset to their parties. Leadership is therefore important, not least to a party like the Conservatives which professes to privilege hierarchy and authority.

Table 3.1 lists the post-war leaders of the Conservative Party. The party first began to break with the post-war consensus under the leadership of Edward Heath. Heath is generally perceived as having been ineffective. Of the four elections he contested as leader, he only succeeded in winning office in 1970, despite also winning marginally more votes but fewer seats than Labour in the February 1974 contest. Most accounts of Heath's period of leading the party in opposition between 1965–70 are highly critical. Burch (1980) highlights how Heath was poor at communicating the party's message and preferred not to vigorously oppose the Labour government's programme. Burch (1980, p. 171) also observes that Heath 'seldom seemed to inspire the party faithful', while Garnett (2005, pp. 198–9) refers to him being 'aloof and insensitive', lacking social skills and upsetting his own MPs. He was most concerned with developing policy, some seeing his policy review in opposition as being the highpoint of his leadership (Burch, 1980; Garnett, 2005, p. 205). Policy priorities included an attempt to modernize the British economy,

Table 3.1   Leaders of the Conservative Party, 1940–2010

	Term of office
Winston Churchill	October 1940–April 1955
Anthony Eden	April 1955–January 1957
Harold MacMillan	January 1957–October 1963
Alec Douglas-Home	November 1963–August 1965
Edward Heath	August 1965–February 1975
Margaret Thatcher	February 1975–November 1990
John Major	November 1990–June 1997
William Hague	June 1997–September 2001
Iain Duncan Smith	September 2001–November 2003
Michael Howard	November 2003–December 2005
David Cameron	December 2005–

Sources: Data from Seldon and Ball, 1994; Cooke, n.d.

the so-called 'Selsdon Man' project, and attempts to reform the machinery of government by proposing, for instance, Scottish devolution and membership of the EEC. Heath's economic policies were opposed by the trade unions when implemented after the 1970 victory. After strikes in the coal industry led to extensive power cuts and a three-day week, Heath performed an embarrassing U-turn, adopting more corporatist and consensual economic and industrial policies. Unrest led Heath to call a general election in February 1974, challenging the unions by asking the electorate to decide 'who governs?' These matters notwithstanding, Heath's lasting achievement was to bring the UK into the EEC in 1973, albeit not without opposition within the parliamentary party (Ludlam, 1996, pp. 103–6).

Margaret Thatcher is often associated with being a strong leader. Under her leadership, the Conservatives achieved three large victories in the 1979, 1983 and 1987 general elections with a majority of more than 100 in 1987, leading to 'a perception almost of invulnerability' (Norton, 1993, p. 29). Thatcher is commonly held to have had a lasting effect on politics, with at least one author referring to her as a revolutionary leader (Jenkins, 2007), and others suggesting that her 'statecraft' had returned the Conservative Party to its natural place as a party of government (Bulpitt, 1986). Her style and demeanour certainly contributed to the perception of strong leadership. She came across as being combative, decisive and uncompromising and these features were cemented by various successes, such as her three election victories, defeating striking miners, European Heads of Government, and the Argentinean invasion of the Falkland Islands. As Norton (1993, p. 33) notes, she 'conveyed a sense of purpose, of knowing what she wanted to achieve and how to achieve it'.

A number of qualifications are however necessary. First, at least in her early days as leader, Thatcher was more cautious than this 'strong leadership' narrative might suggest. The relative caution of her first two policy platforms has already been noted (Willetts, 1992, p. 42). In opposition and in her early governments, experience was more important in senior colleagues than ideological purity and loyalty to her policy aims. This began to change halfway into her first term in office when she began to replace so-called 'wets', traditional or 'one nation' conservatives not necessarily convinced by Thatcher's ideas, with those who were more ideologically in tune with her, the so-called 'dries' in the terminology of the time. Second, her election victories had as much to do with the difficulties being experienced by the Labour Party at the time and the rise of the Liberal/Social Democratic Party (SDP) Alliance which had split the vote for the left. Third, studies show that public opinion remained unconvinced by the merits of Thatcherism (Crewe, 1993, pp. 18–23; Norton, 1993, p. 33). As Bale (2010, p. 23) comments:

Thatcher didn't win elections because she converted a majority of citizens to her cause (she didn't) or because she was personally popular (she wasn't). She won them because her governments delivered just enough tangible benefits to just enough voters at just the right times.

Ultimately, Thatcher was a divisive leader. King (2002) suggests that she chose to operate as a social and psychological outsider both in the party and in government. Bale (2010, p. 23) similarly highlights her 'iconoclastic instinct'. She often ignored cabinet procedures and the need to manage relationships within the party among backbenchers and minsters. This was the downside of 'strong leadership'; by being increasingly convinced of the merits of her arguments, and by surrounding herself with similarly minded advisors, she alienated many within the party. Senior ministers such as Michael Heseltine, Nigel Lawson and Geoffrey Howe all resigned due to personality and policy clashes with Thatcher, with the latter two over economic and European policy being particularly damaging. Thatcher's 1989–90 decision to introduce the poll tax – a form of local government financing which individuals and not households were liable to pay – despite considerable public opposition, led to a leadership challenge by Michael Heseltine in November 1990.

This was mishandled by Thatcher's campaign team, and she failed to win the first round outright. Before a second round could be organized, Thatcher resigned, advised by many cabinet ministers to do so in the interests of the party. As the leadership election results demonstrated, her legacy was to leave the party divided between those who supported her, and tended to see her as being betrayed by the cabinet, and those who were either less Eurosceptic or 'wet' in terms of economic policy (Norton, 1993).

John Major is regularly seen as having been a weak leader. Although he had risen to become Chancellor of the Exchequer, Major was nevertheless inexperienced by comparison with the other leadership contenders, Michael Heseltine and Douglas Hurd. Major was a pragmatic politician and his 'ideological agnosticism' enabled him to become leader by not alienating the competing factions in the parliamentary party during the leadership election (Heppell, 2007a). A key factor in his success was that those ideologically opposed to European integration – the Eurosceptic right of the party – supported him in the leadership election (Cowley and Garry, 1998). His accession to the leadership was initially rewarded by a rise in the opinion polls. Major was more consensual, and paid more attention to conventions of cabinet government. Against expectations, Major led the Conservatives to a fourth general election victory in 1992, achieving a small Commons majority of 21 seats.

From 1992, Major was beset by seemingly never-ending difficulties. On 16 September 1992, so-called 'Black Wednesday', a run on the pound forced Major's government to withdraw from the European Exchange Rate Mechanism (ERM), raise interest rates to 15 per cent and, ultimately, lose the Conservative party's reputation for economic competence. Other difficulties included the much ridiculed 'Citizen's Charter' and 'Back to Basics' initiatives. It was the nexus between European policy and party division that proved the running sore of Major's leadership. In short, Major was initially relatively constructive towards Europe. This did not please the Eurosceptics who had supported him for the leadership, and who rebelled throughout the 1992–97 parliament, constantly undermining Major in the process and reminding voters of the divisions within the party.

Jones and Hudson (1996) argue that the sense of ineffectiveness about his leadership damaged him in the eyes of voters. Heppell (2007b) however argues that the party's leadership election rules, which permitted an annual challenge to the leadership, meant that Major was never secure in his position as leader. Potential challenges were regularly rumoured, with Major even standing down in 1995 before regaining the leadership, in an attempt to silence his critics. Ultimately, Major had been the 'default' leader of the party since on both occasions he had contested the leadership, he had been the least unacceptable option. Many of Major's actions in party management, such as withdrawing the whip from nine Eurosceptics, only exacerbated his difficulties. Heppell (2007b, p. 487) suggests that 'the leadership of Major did not provide competent governance, nor did it offer electoral appeal'. It is nevertheless worth remembering the small parliamentary majority that Major had, the divided party that he inherited, and his relative inexperience in high office. He may not have been effective, but such circumstances would have made it difficult for anyone.

The three leaders to follow Major – William Hague, Iain Duncan Smith and Michael Howard – met with little success. Under both Hague and Duncan Smith, the party initially sought to move to the centre, in classic Downsian style (Downs, 1957), in an attempt to regain lost voters. According to Bale (2010, p. 132), Hague was never really convinced by this attempt at repositioning. Duncan Smith's concern with the under-privileged did appear to be sincere, despite his origins on the party's traditionalist right. Voters were convinced by neither, nor their attempts to portray themselves as 'compassionate Conservatives', and the party flat-lined in the polls under both. Consequently, Hague retreated to what many perceived to be a 'core vote' strategy, highlighting issues where the party was seen as having a lead in public opinion, such as Euroscepticism and immigration, as subsequently did Duncan Smith and his successor, Michael Howard (Bale, 2010). Both Hague and Duncan Smith also had to contend with considerable levels of division within the parliamentary party, which undermined their leaderships and neither handled well (Bale, 2010; Garnett, 2003b; Hayton and Heppell, 2010). Hague resigned after a net gain of only one extra seat for the party in 2001, Duncan Smith was essentially deposed by the parliamentary party after long-running concern at his poor performance as leader, while Howard also resigned after his essentially negative campaign was defeated by an unpopular Labour government in the 2005 election.

Collectively, these three leaders are seen as being ineffective leaders who failed to bring electoral renewal to the party. This is not to say that their tenure did not leave its mark. Hague, for instance, made a sizeable contribution to the modern Conservative Party by initiating the range of organizational changes to the party structure and procedures outlined below and in Chapter 9 (Parkinson, 2003). Duncan Smith initiated a concern with social justice and the underprivileged that the party subsequently developed to some effect in opposition. On the other hand, his time as leader also discredited a particular brand of traditionalist right-wing politics within the party (Bale, 2010, p. 193; Hayton and Heppell, 2010). The party appeared more disciplined under Michael Howard but the focus on issues like immigration in 2005 risked reminding voters of it being 'the nasty party' in the words of one former party Chairperson. As Bale (2010, p. 253) observes, Howard 'tested to destruction the idea that [the party] could win power on a platform of populist promises and taking up where Thatcher left off'. The same could largely have been said about Hague in 2001.

By contrast, David Cameron was an effective leader of the Conservative Party in opposition. He was media savvy, impressive in debates in the Commons and gave the appearance of decisiveness when necessary. His early period as leader was noted for moderating the party's image, emphasizing public services, social justice and the environment, while downplaying issues such as the economy and Europe (Bale, 2008; Snowdon, 2010, Ch. 6). Commonly presented as a way of 'decontaminating' the party brand, it also highlighted a move towards the centre, and into the post-material and social liberal areas of competition that have also become important in positioning parties. Consequently, Cameron delivered a sustained opinion poll lead over Labour for most of his leadership in opposition. Bale (2010, p. 389) argues that he was 'one of the most skilful leaders of the opposition Britain has ever seen'. Voters appeared to agree; 49 per cent of respondents to a pre-election YouGov/*Sunday Times* poll (fieldwork 18–19 March 2010) thought that David Cameron was doing well as Conservative Party leader, as opposed to 39 per cent who thought he was doing badly. In the 2010 general election, Cameron led the Conservatives into government for the first time in 13 years, albeit in coalition with the Liberal Democrats.

Some have nevertheless highlighted criticisms of Cameron's leadership. As Table 3.2 shows, despite a convincing win in the final membership ballot, he was only MPs' second choice in the first round. In a number of occasions Cameron's judgement has been questioned, such as in the controversy over grammar schools in 2007 (Elliott and Hanning, 2009; Snowdon, 2010), or appointing the controversial former *News of the World* editor Andy Coulson as both party and then government Head of Communications. The party's initial response to the financial crisis of 2007–2010 also appeared less than assured (Dorey, 2009). Others indicate that Cameron had done just enough, but no more, to modernize the party and its appeal to voters, noting the party stressing more traditional Conservative issues from mid-2007 and backing away from the consequences of some of its earlier repositioning in relation to environmental

Table 3.2   2005 Conservative Party leadership results

Candidates	First ballot (MPs)	Second ballot (MPs)	Third ballot (Members)
David Cameron	56	90	134,446
David Davis	62	57	64,398
Liam Fox	42	51	
Kenneth Clarke	38		

Source: Data from Denham and O'Hara, 2008, p. 206.

politics, green taxes and public services. Indeed, many suggest that the Thatcherite nature of the parliamentary party acted as a brake on any further modernization (Bale, 2008; Buckler and Dolowitz, 2009, pp. 26–7; Denham and O'Hara, 2007; Dorey, 2007; Evans, 2008, 2010).

There have also been a number of controversial decisions; leaving the mainstream right party group in the European Parliament after the 2009 European elections may have appeased Eurosceptics within the party, but risked perceptions of being allied to parties perceived to be extremist. Northern parts of Britain have appeared largely oblivious to the party's revival under Cameron, nor did revival in the polls lead to an increase in the size of grassroots party organizations (Pattie and Johnston, 2009; Randall, 2009). Finally, some have criticized Cameron's leadership in the 2010 election, arguing that the Conservatives should have performed better (Ashcroft, 2010; ConservativeHome, 2010). Criticisms include the vague nature of the 'Big Society' theme, providing the Liberal Democrats with publicity by allowing them to appear in the televised leaders' debates, and not campaigning hard enough on traditional themes such as Europe, immigration and taxes. Others are critical of the coalition with the Liberal Democrats, suggesting that Cameron has given up too much to the junior coalition partner.

Conservative leaders have often appeared to be selected because they had made the least enemies within the party and had therefore become 'compromise' candidates (Bale, 2010; Garnett, 2003b; Hayton and Heppell, 2010; Heppell, 2007a; 2007b). Once elected the key criteria for holding on to the leadership has been electoral success. The procedures for electing a Conservative leader have changed considerably since the mid-1960s. These are outlined in detail by Denham and O'Hara (2008) and Quinn (2005). A number of key developments can be identified. First, prior to 1965, new Conservative leaders 'emerged' through an opaque process amongst senior party members, the so-called 'magic circle'. Second, concerns about the legitimacy of a leader emerging through such an undemocratic process led to the introduction of selection by the parliamentary party from 1965. Provision was made for three ballots of MPs, with the worst-performing candidates eliminated in each round. Victory on the first ballot required a majority plus a 15 per cent lead over the nearest rival, and it was open to new candidates to enter the race in the second round. This method was used six times between 1965 and 1997, with a third ballot only necessary in 1997 when William Hague was elected leader. Third, Edward Heath's reluctance to stand down after electoral defeat meant that the rules were changed in 1975 to permit an annual leadership challenge if a candidate came forward. Such a challenge required only two anonymous proposers, although this was changed to 10 per cent of the parliamentary party after 1991.

Fourth, the most drastic changes to the party's leadership selection rules came as part of William Hague's organizational reforms of 1998. A challenge to an incumbent leader was made slightly harder, with 15 per cent of MPs required to propose a vote of no confidence. Once candidates had come forward, MPs would vote, in a number of elimination ballots, to decide the final two candidates that would go forward to a one-member-one-vote (OMOV) postal ballot of the party membership. This process has been used twice, to elect Iain Duncan Smith and David Cameron. Presented as a 'democratization' of the party, it has nevertheless had some interesting consequences. Holding such a ballot extends the leadership contest over a longer period of time than previous procedures, and risks the party being seen as divided by voters. Moreover, members may prefer a candidate who turns out to be an ineffective leader, as in the case of Iain Duncan Smith. After Duncan Smith's poor performance, it appeared that MPs had lost faith in these rules; Michael Howard was unopposed in what seemed like a return to the pre-1965 'magic circle' (Denham and O'Hara, 2008, p. 7). Members have nevertheless defended these powers, resisting an attempt under Michael Howard to return the whole leadership selection process to MPs. This notwithstanding, MPs also retain considerable power under this system; they ultimately decide who the candidates that go through to the final ballot of the members are. The election of David Cameron appears to have restored some legitimacy to the Hague rules. What is clear is that Conservative Party leaders hold their position on what Quinn (2005, p. 804) calls a 'leasehold' basis. In other words, they are subject to a challenge if they are not seen to be performing successfully.

Candidate Selection and Representativeness

The make-up of any parliamentary party can create difficulties for party leaders, party positioning and the policies parties follow. A fundamental element contributing to the composition of parliamentary parties is the question of how their candidates are selected in the first place. In most parties, candidate selection has historically been one of the main rights reserved to local associations. However, this has been a controversial element in party politics in recent years, with party headquarters often getting involved in an attempt to have more favoured, and what are perceived to be more electable, candidates selected. Candidate selection has therefore become a key location in which power struggles within parties, between the centre and the local associations, are played out.

A key difficulty for the Conservative Party is that it has often been seen as unrepresentative of the population as a whole. Conservative MPs coming from the privileged upper or upper-middle classes, white males, and educated at elite institutions such as Oxford before going on to political careers may be a caricature, but such caricatures often form an important part of public perceptions. This difficulty was arguably made more acute by the election of David Cameron to the leadership. Despite his highly articulate attempts to communicate with the public, Cameron and many of his inner-circle typified this elite perception. In his leadership acceptance speech, David Cameron (2005a) identified representativeness as a problem for the party, referring to the 'scandalous under-representation of women in the Conservative Party', and in a subsequent speech to the under-representation of ethnic minorities in the parliamentary party (Cameron, 2005b).

Efforts to address the party's unrepresentativeness have had consequences for candidate selection procedures. Traditionally, these procedures were the preserve of the local constituency association. In short, approved candidates could apply for a vacant seat. From these applicants the local party could shortlist three or four for a final selection meeting, where candidates would make a presentation to the members present who would then vote for a candidate. These procedures have been changed since Cameron became leader, although this has been controversial with the party grassroots who perceive one of their main powers as being usurped by the central party. A week after becoming leader, Cameron (2005b) announced a freeze on candidate selections, until a system had been devised which guaranteed increased diversity, and the creation of a priority list, subsequently dubbed the A-list, with at least 50 per cent women and a significant number of people with disabilities and ethnic minorities. All target seats and Conservative-held seats were expected to select from this list. There was to be a review of progress after three months and the party would introduce a head-hunting programme to try to identify potential women and ethnic minority candidates. Finally, all target seats and Conservative-held seats were also expected to involve the local community in their selection process, whether through holding an open primary selection, which are open to all registered voters in the constituency not just party members, or somehow involving local opinion leaders.

Childs et al. (2009, pp. 205–6) highlight two further sets of changes. From August 2006–January 2008, constituency associations with less than 300 members were expected to hold primary selections, while candidate shortlists in other constituencies were to be balanced between women and men and the final decision made by the constituency executive committee. From January 2008 onwards, associations were allowed to choose from the full list of approved candidates, although at each stage of selection women had to comprise at least half of candidates considered. In the run up to the 2010 election, the high numbers of MPs standing down because of the parliamentary expenses scandal led to further changes with the number of candidates associations could create a shortlist from, reduced to six, selected by a joint group from the central party and the local association. If seats remained without a candidate after the beginning of 2010, by-election rules would be used. This meant that local associations would be given a shortlist of three to choose from by the central party, although candidate selection rules were to revert back to normal post-election (ConservativeHome, 2010b).

How might these changes be assessed? In advance of the 2010 election, McIlveen (2009) suggested that the A-list rules had been successful in allowing more women to be selected, particularly in Conservative-held seats with vacancies, although an earlier assessment was more qualified, calling it only a 'limited success' (Dorey, 2007, pp. 154–5). The Conservatives have certainly innovated in adopting primaries to select candidates. First used by Reading East Conservative association in 2003, in 2009 Totnes Conservative association became the first to run a primary by an all-postal ballot, meaning that voters did not even have to be able to attend a meeting to participate.

There was significant disquiet among the party's members and grassroots activists about these changes to candidate selection in an attempt to widen the party's diversity. One survey of 1,900 party members in late 2009

Table 3.3   Occupation of Conservative Party MPs elected in 2010

	Number	%
Professions	107	35
Business	125	40
Miscellaneous	72	24
Manual workers	2	1
Total	306	100

Source: Data from Kavanagh and Cowley, 2010, p. 327.

found that 79 per cent thought local associations better placed to select their constituency candidates than party headquarters (ConservativeHome, 2010c). Another survey found that party members tended to disapprove of having compulsory minimum numbers of women at shortlisting stage, felt that attempts to increase the proportion of women candidates had increased tensions within the party, and that the leadership had too much influence in candidate selection (Childs et al., 2009, p. 211). Holding primaries also caused tensions, with some members seeing these as taking away rights that local members had, and instead giving them to non-members who may have little or no interest in the party. Some members nevertheless appeared to strongly approve of primaries (Childs et al., 2009, p. 211).

Post-2010, what is the profile of the parliamentary party and does it still conform to an elitist image? Table 3.3 shows the background of Conservative MPs in 2010. The party had around the same proportion of MPs from professional backgrounds as Labour (both 35 per cent). Conservative MPs overwhelmingly came from legal backgrounds, with few coming from public service professions such as health and education. The Conservatives often claim to be the party of business. Indeed, at 40 per cent the party had a higher proportion of MPs from a business background than its competitors, with the Liberal Democrats closest at 20 per cent. The party had the lowest proportion of those classified 'miscellaneous', with 18 being from a journalistic or publishing background, and another 31 already having been active as politicians or political organizers. In terms of education, at 54 per cent the Conservatives had the highest proportion of MPs that had attended fee-paying school of all three main parties, although this has declined from 73 per cent in 1979. Similarly, at 34 per cent the party had the highest proportion of MPs who had attended either Oxford or Cambridge universities, albeit down somewhat from 49 per cent in 1979 (Gay, 2009, p. 12; Kavanagh and Cowley, 2010, p. 326).

In the 2010 parliament, the Conservative Party had the youngest age-profile of its MPs, the average age of Conservative parliamentarians being 48, with 24 per cent being under 40, up from 17 per cent in 2005, and 75 per cent being over 40, down from 83 per cent in 2005 (Gay, 2009, p. 9; Kavanagh and Cowley, 2010, p. 322). Despite having had the only woman Prime Minister in British political history, the Conservatives trail considerably behind Labour in having women elected to parliament. The proportion of women MPs in the Conservative parliamentary party has only gradually increased from 1979 onwards. Women's representation remained at a very low level, reaching only 17, or nine per cent of the parliamentary party, in 2005. This picture changed considerably in 2010, the party electing 49 women MPs, equating to 16 per cent of the parliamentary party (Figure 3.1). Similar under-representation has also applied to ethnic minorities; in 2005, the party had only two MPs from an ethnic minority background. As with women, efforts to increase the party's diversity seem to have had some effect, with 11 Conservative MPs now coming from an ethnic minority background (Gay, 2009; Kavanagh and Cowley, 2010). Despite traditional backgrounds still dominating, the Conservative parliamentary party nevertheless looks younger and more diverse than it did prior to 2010.

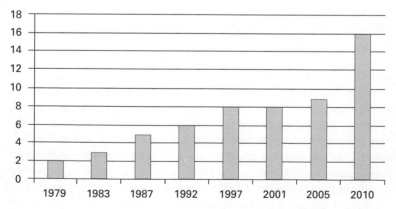

Figure 3.1   Proportion of women Conservative MPs, 1979–2010 (%)

Sources: Data from Gay, 2009, p. 10; Kavanagh and Cowley, 2010, p. 319.

In Office

How has the Conservative Party performed in office? One simple way of assessing this is to examine the performance of Conservative Prime Ministers. Theakston and Gill's (2006) ranking of twentieth-century British Prime Ministers makes mixed reading for Conservatives. Margaret Thatcher is consistently highly rated, generally appearing in the top four or five behind such iconic figures as Churchill, Attlee and Lloyd George. By contrast, both Heath and Major's performances as PM are consistently lowly rated across the various measures, with Conservative respondents actually being harsher to them than Labour and Liberal Democrat respondents.

Heath's time in office between 1970–74 is commonly remembered for industrial unrest, power cuts and his calling an election on the theme of 'Who Governs?'. In short, Heath's attempt to introduce free-market reforms in the early part of his term of office was unsuccessful, and led to increased levels of unemployment and inflation. As part of these reforms, public sector pay was limited, and the Conservative government tried to restrict the powers of the trade unions. The result was disputes with key groups of workers such as mineworkers and those involved in power supply. Industrial unrest led to the calling of a three-day week and to extensive power cuts across the country. Ultimately, the Heath government was forced into reversing its free-market reforms, and introducing an incomes policy in an effort to stabilize the situation. As Taylor (1994, p. 527) rightly notes, the first 1974 election was not necessarily about 'Who Governs?'. Instead, the key issue that will have influenced many voters was simply the party's poor performance in office. The inevitable consequence was to lose support and this allowed Labour to win more seats in February 1974. Nevertheless, Heath's tenure in office did bring lasting reform to the institutions of state, introducing Departments of Trade and Industry and Environment, overseeing reform of local government and leading the UK into the EEC (Smith, 1996, p. 144).

At one point, there was extensive debate about the legacy of Thatcher's period in office, (Hay, 2006). Her legacy remains controversial. One popular account suggests that she presided over two 'revolutions': the first represented an 'assault' on the state sector through privatization, lower taxes and reforms to government, the economy and labour markets; the second involved the centralization of power in Whitehall to regulate this shift towards greater marketization (Jenkins, 2007; see also Gamble, 1994). In these terms, Thatcherism can be said to have achieved some of its aims, not least since subsequent governments, including the Labour Party, have had to adapt to these changes.

There were nevertheless consequences to these policies. Thatcher took Britain further into Europe, by signing the 1986 Single European Act, than her later rhetoric might lead observers to think. Her subsequent Eurosceptic speech in Bruges in 1988 has set the tone for Conservative Party debate, and division, on Europe ever since. Her economic policies led to a rise in unemployment, considerable social unrest in British cities and laid waste to considerable tracts of industrial production in the UK, with the 1984–85 miners' strike remaining perhaps the most totemic. One recent account of inequality in the UK highlights the contribution made by Thatcherite polices to creating and sustaining such inequality (Dorling, 2010). Her time in office was not marked necessarily by a reduction in the size of the state. In other words, it was less than wholly successful even in its own terms. Instead, the state had to pick up the tab for the social consequences of many of these policies, in terms of benefits and social welfare, but also in terms of the increased levels of centralization and control that resulted. Finally, Thatcher's leadership style caused difficulties for the party, particularly in the later part of her premiership when personality and policy conflicts led to the resignation of the Chancellor, Nigel Lawson, and Foreign Secretary, Geoffrey Howe, shortly after each other in 1989–90, with the latter's resignation speech proving particularly damning.

Conservative governments under John Major also experienced difficulties. The economic consequences of leaving the ERM on 'Black Wednesday' saw the public lose confidence in the party's ability to run the economy (Wickham-Jones, 1997), confidence that the party was unable to restore until 2010 (see Chapter 10). Major embarked upon further privatizations, going further than Thatcher by privatizing the rail network, closing the remains of the coal industry and authorizing an unsuccessful attempt to privatize post offices. The Conservative government was forced to raise taxes in 1993 to deal with public borrowing and this also had a negative impact on public trust in the Conservatives' ability to run the economy (Wickham-Jones, 1997). Despite Major's success in negotiating an opt-out from the 1992 Treaty on European Union's Social Chapter and maintaining vetoes on a number of other areas seen as impinging on national sovereignty, European matters were most controversial, with ratification of the Maastricht Treaty leading to considerable intra-party conflict between Major and the party's Eurosceptic backbenchers throughout the parliament, persisting even into the 1997 election campaign (Geddes, 1997). When added to accusations of 'sleaze' against Conservative backbenchers, in addition to mishandling events such as the outbreak of so-called Mad Cow disease, the performance of the Conservatives in office under Major ultimately left the party unelectable between 1997 and 2010, having shed its reputation for governing competently.

The post-2010 Conservative-led coalition government has been controversial. Its ambitious programme of public spending cuts divided opinion, with some claiming they were necessary while others argued that they represent an ideological attack on public services. Critics, including commentators and business figures not known as Labour sympathizers, suggested that there was no necessity to cut public expenditure so quickly (Elliott, 2011a, b; Kaletsky, 2011). There have been overlaps between the coalition parties – on cutting bureaucracy for instance. However, the Conservatives also made some concessions, most obviously by holding a referendum on electoral reform. There were clear conflicts between them, Conservatives sounding more pro-big business and antagonistic towards European institutions and multiculturalism than their Liberal Democrat coalition partners. Conservative ministers however seemed disorganized and rushed, with the consequences of numerous policies not appearing to have been thought through properly and many of these policies having harmful social consequences for poorer areas of Britain. While there was disquiet among right-wing backbenchers who felt the party was not addressing some issues, notably Europe, the coalition agreement nevertheless meant that Cameron could rely on Liberal Democrat votes in parliament and was not held hostage by his more radical MPs.

Conclusion

For much of the twentieth century, the Conservative Party was seen as the natural party of government in the UK, with a reputation of doing whatever it needed to do to retain power. Under the leadership of David Cameron, the 2010 general election returned the party to that position. While the party performed well, it was still not enough to achieve a majority. Consequently, the Conservatives formed a coalition government with the Liberal Democrats their junior partners. The mystery according to Bale (2010) is why the party took so long to change to make it electable again. One simple reason was the dominance of the Labour Party under Tony Blair, and its poor performance under Gordon Brown. However, any explanation must take into account developments within the Conservative Party as well. The first explanation is ideological. Thatcherism represented a break with earlier 'one nation' themes. While this was accepted by the party and over time became the dominant perspective within both the parliamentary and grassroots party, this approach was never widely accepted by the electorate. Primarily because of the constraints of internal party opinion, the Conservative Party continued to 'bang on' about these themes – tax cuts, cutting the state, Euroscepticism – in the 2001 and 2005 general elections, to little effect. Second, after the 1997 defeat, the party went through three leaders who were simply not perceived by voters, as well as some within the party, as prime ministerial material. This was compounded by the tradition in Conservative leadership contests for candidates to be elected for who they were not, instead of for their potential appeal to voters. This was also a consequence of the rightward turn within the parliamentary and grass-roots party. Third, in office, certainly under Heath, Major and Thatcher, the party had experienced divisions, while the potential negative consequences of Conservative governments lingered in the public consciousness, with the loss of the public trust on the party's economic competence hitting the party hard after 'Black Wednesday' in 1992.

Having returned to power against the backdrop of economic crisis and claiming an urgent need to reduce the public debt, the difficulty faced by David Cameron and the Conservative Party has been retaining public perceptions of economic competence and trust while taking measures that will be at best unpopular, and certainly controversial and painful to many of the weakest in society. In opposition Cameron proved to be a skilful politician. Whether these tough measures in government will render the party unelectable once again, remains to be seen. They will certainly call on all the skill and 'statecraft' the Conservative Party can muster.

4

The Labour Party

Under Tony Blair, the Labour Party became a formidable electoral machine, winning large majorities in three successive general elections from 1997. While the leadership of Gordon Brown was much less sure-footed, until its defeat in the 2010 election Labour had been in power for thirteen years, a record for the party. Until 1997 however, Labour had to struggle to become successful against the dominant Conservative Party, with the tension between electability and adhering to the party's principles being fought out internally on a number of occasions. Struggles over the totemic Clause IV of the party's constitution, committing Labour to public ownership, under Hugh Gaitskell and Tony Blair are examples of this, while the 1974 and 1983 manifestos were considerably left-wing documents, by comparison with the party's 1987 and 1997 programmes. Discussion of developments in the Labour Party revolves around four sections. The first sets out key elements of Labour Party ideology and policy. The second part assesses the party's recent leadership, from the Wilson/Callaghan period onwards, while also outlining the party's procedures for selecting a party leader. The issue of Labour's representativeness and role of its candidate selection procedures has been a high-profile topic. The third part therefore outlines the party's candidate selection processes and, through an assessment of the representativeness of the party's MPs, asks whether or not initiatives to make the party more representative, such as women-only shortlists, have been successful. The final section reflects upon Labour's performance in office. To what extent has Labour achieved its aims, and can it claim to have shaken off its reputation for ineffective government?

Ideology and Policy

Formed out of co-operation between the trade union movement and various socialist societies, the Labour Party traces its history back to late nineteenth-century attempts to represent the newly enfranchised working class. Ideologically, the Labour Party's constitution, amended in 1995, now explicitly states that it is a democratic socialist party. Broadly, the main aim of socialism is to create a more equal society. However, socialism does not necessarily have a unified set of ideas, nor can the Labour Party trace its ideology to a number of key texts (Crosland, 1956 [2006], p. 52; Panitch, 1971, p. 189). Experts differ about the extent to which Labour has been an ideological party, with one influential thinker indicating that the Labour Party has 'always preserved a marked anti-doctrinal and anti-theoretical bias' (Crosland, 2006 [1956], p. 52), while others have suggested that Labour is 'the most ideologically inclined of all British political parties' (Randall, 2003, p. 8).

There are two ways of approaching the ideology of the Labour Party. The first is to identify the various strands of socialist thought that have informed the Labour Party's approach. Unlike continental varieties of socialism, revolutionary and Marxist approaches have had much less of an impact in the UK. Most of the socialist influences on the Labour Party have been more moderate. There are a number of categorizations of these influences (Crosland, 2006 [1956], p. 52; Fisher, 1996, p. 80; Ingle, 2008, pp. 41–3; Webb, 2000, pp. 93–4). Three sets of influences can be identified. The first relates to the *Christian and ethical roots* of the party's socialism. In short, the consequence of competitive capitalism is to leave many disadvantaged and in poverty. Highlighting the essential dignity of man, such socialists argue that this is morally wrong. Instead, the main aim of political life should be to reduce equalities as much as possible, whether through co-operative or redistributive means (Foote, 1997, Ch. 2; Tawney, 1964). Second, *scientific socialism* took an essentially top-down approach and sought to use government planning of policies to deliver socialist outcomes such as equality. Scientific socialists rely heavily on the role of the state to create a fairer and more equal society. Such an approach was evident in the work of the technocratic Fabian society, one of the socialist societies which contributed to founding the Labour Party and, through the leading Fabian Sidney Webb, to writing the party's 1918 constitution (Foote, 1997, ch. 2). Finally, the party's roots in the trade union movement mean that *organized labour* has been highly influential. Such 'labourist' approaches argued that workers receive little of the value that their efforts create. Workers had therefore to organize to challenge exploitative capitalists, and aimed to redistribute the wealth that resulted to rectify this injustice. The main aim was therefore the protection and advancement of working-class living standards (Foote, 1997, ch. 1).

The second approach to Labour's ideology is to highlight the key principles that have motivated the party. *Equality* has concerned some of the key thinkers of the Labour movement (Drucker, 1979, p. 9; Tawney, 1964). As Crosland (2006 [1956], p. 87) argues, the 'belief in social equality ... has been the strongest ethical inspiration of virtually every socialist doctrine'. Equality can be conceived of in two main ways: equality of outcome, for instance through equalizing incomes; and equality of opportunity, through creating chances for individuals to overcome barriers that may stop them fulfilling their potential, whether these are socioeconomic or educational. Second, and related, has been the principle of *redistribution*. This has two main strands, through progressive taxation which sought to equalize incomes, or through the provision of universal public services such as welfare benefits, the National Health Service and comprehensive education. The third principle that has been influential has been the *common ownership of industry*. This was most clearly set out in the pre-1995 Clause IV of the party's constitution. The aim was:

> To secure for the workers by hand or by brain the full fruits of their industry and the most equitable distribution thereof that may be possible, upon the basis of the common ownership of the means of production, distribution and exchange, and the best obtainable system of popular administration and control of each industry or service.

The final principle was to seek to achieve these aims not by revolutionary means, but through the process of *parliamentary democracy*. This has meant that the party's principles have been gradualist in nature, seeking to reform the capitalist system from the inside, rather than through revolutionary change.

One former senior Labour figure, Herbert Morrison, famously quipped that 'socialism is what a Labour government does'. In other words, the practical expression of these principles depends on the policies that the party forwards and, when in office, implements. The first opportunity a majority Labour government had to do so was between 1945–51 under Clement Attlee. Attlee's governments drew upon experience of state planning in the wartime coalition and this allowed them to implement a large expansion of the public sector. The ideal of common ownership was achieved through nationalization of the Bank of England, the steel industry and vital services such as coal, electricity and gas. At the same time, the 1945–51 Labour governments dealt with the aspiration to improve welfare by founding the National Health Service, introducing a National Insurance scheme and introducing the welfare state by implementing the 1942 Beveridge report to deal with the conditions of the worst off in society. These Labour governments also achieved full employment and embarked upon a sizeable building programme to provide a decent standard of housing for the working class.

In the aftermath of election defeat in 1951, there was considerable debate about the ideological and policy aims and objectives of the party. This culminated in an attempt by then party leader Hugh Gaitskell at the party's 1959 conference to abolish the Clause IV commitment to public ownership of the means of production, commonly interpreted as necessitating the nationalization of industry. Clause IV was seen as potentially electorally damaging to the party. Although a totemic commitment, Clause IV was in reality ambiguous and compatible with numerous different forms of industrial and economic organization. From a policy viewpoint, nationalization did not necessarily equate to improving the lot of the working class and instead owed more to the scientific planning-based socialist influences within the party (Panitch, 1971, pp. 190–1). A seminal 'revisionist' text was Crosland's (2006 [1956]) *The Future of Socialism*. This argued that many of the party's ideological and policy aims had been met between 1945–51 and that what was required in light of these changed circumstances was a reassessment of how to achieve a further improvement in the circumstances of the least well off. Crosland argued strongly for the pursuit of equality as the party's main objective, although there is ambiguity about what type of equality it was he preferred. Equality and a more just society were to be achieved not by nationalization of industry as Clause IV advocates suggested. This was to be achieved by promoting economic growth through the market and then deploying a progressive, redistributionist strategy of taxation in order to increase social welfare and create a more equal distribution of wealth and opportunity. Gaitskell's attempt to change Clause IV was nevertheless defeated by conference in 1959.

Ideological and policy disputes continued through the 1970s and 1980s. The February 1974 manifesto contained radical commitments to extending workers' control of industry, further nationalization and extending both social and economic equality, although these were watered down for the second election that year. Through the mid to late 1970s, the party developed an *Alternative Economic Strategy* (AES) which eventually fed into the electorally disastrous 1983 manifesto (Shaw, 1994, pp. 12–13). The AES sought to shift power towards workers and citizens, achieve full employment and reduce inequalities through reflation of the economy, redistribution of wealth and power, price and import controls, and a considerable extension of public ownership and planning (Callaghan, 2000).

In the aftermath of the 1983 and 1987 defeats, Labour embarked on an extensive policy review. The resulting 1989 policy document, *Meet the Challenge, Make the Change*, distanced the party from many of its historic commitments to public ownership, heavily progressive taxation, and full employment. It contained an emphasis on personal freedom and gave primacy instead to market mechanisms while indicating that the key role for the state was not extensive intervention and planning in economic matters, but instead welfare programmes to ameliorate the worst effects of the market. Although assessments of the policy review differ (Ludlam, 2001, p. 27), this appeared to be a considerable shift in policy since the party no longer even viewed the pursuit of equality and full employment as viable aims, and also sought to downplay the party's commitment if re-elected to the trade unions (Shaw, 1994, ch. 4).

Distancing the party from Clause IV was finalized formally in 1995 when, under Tony Blair, Labour amended it to do away with the commitment to public ownership, replacing it instead with a relatively anodyne statement which emphasizes individuals realizing their potential, the balance between rights and responsibilities and the need for 'power, wealth and opportunity to be in the hands of the many and not the few'. Such sentiments also fed into the 'Third Way' thinking surrounding New Labour. This highlighted a range of 'dilemmas' which, it was claimed, rendered the opposing philosophies of the New Right and statist social democracy increasingly irrelevant. These included globalization; increasing individualism; the irrelevance of left and right; the decline of traditional democratic institutions; and environmental degradation (Blair, 1998; Giddens, 1998).

Drawing partly upon Christian socialist thinking (Bevir, 2000), and also on aspects of liberalism (Beer, 2001) and social democracy (Fielding, 2003), the 'Third Way' was presented as a way of pursuing traditional centre-left values of democracy, liberty, social justice and community obligation in changed circumstances. It prioritized the concern with social justice while maintaining distance from full employment and collectivist solutions. The concern with equality was recast as the need to promote inclusion, while redistribution was no longer about wealth but 'the redistribution of possibilities'. Instead of the welfare state, the need was for a 'social investment state' which promoted individual capacity (Giddens, 1998). In addition to help from an 'enabling state', partnership would also be sought from the private sector to achieve these goals since, according to Blair (1998, p. 4), 'what matters is what works'. The 'Third Way' also sought to bring environmental matters into this debate, relating them to debates about justice and inclusion.

Whiteley (1983, ch. 2) suggests that ideological attitudes amongst the Labour elite were distributed relatively equally between left and right in the late 1970s–early 1980s. This spread of attitudes continued to exist into the 1990s, although by then the prospects of achieving office meant that dissent was aired less often than previously, giving the impression that the parliamentary party was 'almost faction free' (Seyd and Whiteley, 2002a, p. 50). In office, however, MPs increasingly rebelled against the party whip. Although motivations varied, rebellions were often on issues that some MPs felt ideologically unacceptable to the party, such as cutting welfare benefits, and introducing foundation hospitals and university tuition fees (Cowley and Stuart, 2008a).

In the early 1990s, members saw the key issue in politics as the class struggle and were overwhelmingly concerned with four 'socialist touchstone' issues (Seyd and Whiteley, 1992, pp. 40–9). These included being strongly in favour of further nationalization; the return of privatized industries to the public sector; high levels of public spending, albeit not in defence; and supporting the legitimacy of trade unions. In some of these areas, members' attitudes were contrary to the policies being espoused by the leadership. By the end of the decade, the rise in membership associated with Blair's leadership saw the ideological profile of members change. Members' attitudes moved rightwards between 1992–1997 (Webb and Farrell, 1999). New members who had joined during the 1990s were more accepting of privatization and defence spending, saw issues to a lesser extent through class war lenses and were also somewhat more authoritarian than more long-serving colleagues, showing an acceptance of some of the 'Third Way'. Nevertheless, a large proportion remained in favour of nationalization, sceptical of the market, pro-trade union and also in favour of maintaining high levels of spending on public services (Seyd and Whiteley, 2002a, ch. 3).

To what extent has there been ideological and policy change in the Labour Party? One thing all these changes have in common – from Crosland's revisionism, through the AES, the 1989 policy review and the 'Third Way' – is that they attempted to situate the party's principles and policies in a changing political and socio-economic environment. When these attempts have succeeded, they have done so because of an ability to demonstrate their 'newness' alongside their continuity with previously important ideological themes (Buckler and Dolowitz, 2009; Fielding, 2003). Nevertheless, Labour has consequently been shown to have moved gradually to the right from 1974 onwards, and sharply so under New Labour in order to locate itself firmly in the centre of British political space (Budge, 1999; Hindmoor, 2004; Webb, 2000, p. 123). There have been major shifts away from deeply held commitments that had been seen as central. Shaw (1994, p. 88) observes somewhat critically of the 1989 policy review that 'for the first time in its history, Labour ceased to regard any modification of property relationships as a significant object of political endeavour'. Others similarly pointed to New Labour essentially accommodating itself to the existing 'Thatcherite' economic arrangements rather than challenging them (Finlayson, 2003; Hay, 1999; Heffernan, 2001). Moreover, the 'Third Way' received so much criticism, on various grounds, that one of its architects defended it with a book-length response (Giddens, 2000).

During the later part of Labour's 1997–2010 term of office, changing circumstances forced the party back onto territory it had abandoned in the 1980s. It was forced to nationalize one of the previously private rail franchises, and, more importantly, during the 2007–2010 banking crisis, had to effectively nationalize a number of banks to prevent them, and the financial system, from collapsing. From the mid-1980s on, such a move would have been anathema. Post-recession, the 2010 campaign theme was fairness. In addition to promoting economic recovery, it focused on protecting living standards and front-line services, strengthening communities and society and halving the deficit during the parliament (Labour Party, 2010). In opposition after the 2010 election defeat, Labour began a somewhat tentative rethinking of its principles and policies, which began with the leadership contest initiated when Gordon Brown resigned as leader.

Leadership

The Labour Party has had an uneasy relationship with the idea of leadership. According to Drucker (1979, pp.1, 12), once the party elects a leader, it is very reluctant to unseat them if they do not resign, partly because of the importance of the idea of solidarity and loyalty to the labour movement. Moreover, the party's collectivist and democratic ethos and its internal structure have meant that the very notion of leadership has at times been viewed with suspicion (Morgan, 2004, p. 38; Shaw, 1996, pp. 64–5). Consequently, the party has often thought nothing of engaging in debate, internal conflicts between the left and right and criticisms of the leadership which have made the party at times difficult to lead.

Various accounts of the party's leaders exist (Jefferys, 1999; Morgan, 1992). To understand the recent development of the party, discussion

Table 4.1   Labour Party leaders, 1935–present

	Term of office
Clement Attlee	October 1935–November 1955
Hugh Gaitskell	December 1955–January 1963
Harold Wilson	February 1963–April 1976
James Callaghan	April 1976–November 1980
Michael Foot	November 1980–October 1983
Neil Kinnock	October 1983–July 1992
John Smith	July 1992–May 1994
Tony Blair	July 1994–June 2007
Gordon Brown	June 2007–May 2010
Ed Miliband	September 2010–

begins with Harold Wilson, elected leader in 1963 after Gaitskell's sudden death. In some respects Wilson can be thought of as a successful leader, winning four out of the five general elections he led the party in. Nonetheless, Wilson's reputation is generally low. At worst he is portrayed as paranoid, opportunistic, interested in political tactics over strategy. At best he is seen as an enigmatic figure (Bale, 1999; Davies, 1992; Morgan, 1992). His leadership can be divided into four periods. Between 1963 and 1966, the initial focus was on winning in 1964 and then winning a workable majority in 1966. Wilson is generally credited with having been at his best in this period, having caught the public mood with a message of change, for instance equating technological developments with socialism in a famous 1963 speech. In office between 1964–66, he was able to blame any setbacks on a combination of having a small majority, the previous Conservative government and economic constraints on the pound. From 1966–70, judgements are less favourable. This second period was marked by a lack of consistent policy implementation, assorted economic and industrial crises and a tendency to think of colleagues as plotting against him which led to regular cabinet reshuffles. The main aim seemed to be simply 'keeping the ship of state afloat' (Shaw, 1996, p. 104). Between 1970–74, difficulties continued, with Wilson not proving a particularly active or effective leader of the opposition (Morgan, 1992, p. 257). In office again from 1974 until his resignation in 1976, his leadership appeared calmer, even if he himself had lost much of his original vigour.

Although Bale (1999) credits Wilson with being able to negotiate a way between the party's left and right factions, a key difficulty stemmed from Wilson's leadership style. This was highly personalized, with Wilson advised by a small coterie of close friends – the so-called 'kitchen cabinet' – rather than a collegiate leadership that may have managed the party better. He cultivated the symbolic image of a provincial 'man of the people', and, in a foretaste of what was to come under Tony Blair, Wilson was highly concerned with media management and style. As Morgan (1992, pp. 260–1) suggests, Wilson's failure was one of both substance and style where 'public relations superseded public planning, tactics swamped strategy, and cosmetics dominated economics'.

Wilson's successor James Callaghan is widely associated with weak government, economic crisis and trade union unrest in the 1978–79 'Winter of Discontent'. However, one observer notes that Callaghan was 'consistently underestimated for much of his career' (Morgan, 1992, p. 275). Callaghan was one of the few people to have held all three great offices of state – having served as chancellor, home and foreign secretary – before becoming Prime Minister and party leader in 1976. A former trade union official, he had strong roots in the Labour movement and had built up good relations with the unions, constituency labour parties and the PLP. This helped him as leader in what were difficult political and economic circumstances, leading a minority government during an economic crisis. His was a more collegiate style of leadership and party management. Consequently, he was largely able to maintain good relations with the left and right of the party. For instance, he was able to negotiate an IMF loan, with stringent conditions, to rescue the British economy with no subsequent cabinet resignations. The circumstances Callaghan faced meant that in many ways strategic leadership was unlikely, and the party remained stubbornly divided. Yet judgements on his leadership are essentially favourable, a 'safe pair of hands' who 'inspired trust and confidence' (Morgan, 2004, p. 45; Morgan, 1992, 1999). Only from late 1978, having failed to call an early election, did Callaghan's leadership falter under pressure from a declining majority, trade union militancy and some untypical policy misjudgements.

Michael Foot is remembered as a great parliamentarian, yet his leadership also saw Labour's nadir in recent decades. An author and left-wing radical, Foot had served in government during the 1970s, remaining loyal throughout. His candidacy for the leadership in 1980 was an attempt to prevent the divisive left-wing figure of Tony Benn from doing so and damaging the party further electorally. Three main points can be made about Foot's leadership. First, he spent much of his time involved in trying to resolve intra-party disputes over organization and policy between various wings of the party, whether the Trotskyite Militant faction, the grassroots Campaign for Labour Party Democracy (CLPD), or the trade unions (Shaw, 1999). Second, divided parties seldom win elections and his toler- ance of dissent within the party did nothing to prevent it from appearing divided. Finally, he eschewed the need to cultivate image and did not conform to the dictates of modern broadcasting, preferring instead to write and make speeches. Confronted with Conservative Party resurgence after the Falklands conflict, his leadership style combined with a particularly left-wing manifesto to ensure that the party suffered a large defeat in 1983. Although Foot's leadership is seen as an 'unfortunate interregnum' (Shaw, 1999, p. 166), others have been sympathetic to him as an individual, seeing him as 'an innocent abroad' and 'a beleaguered prophet born a century out of his time' (Morgan, 1992, p. 277). His reign did nevertheless begin to change attitudes about the role of leadership in the Labour Party (Morgan, 1992, pp. 286–7; Shaw, 1999, p. 167).

If leaders were solely judged on winning elections, then Neil Kinnock would be regarded as a failure, losing heavily in 1987 and snatching defeat from the jaws of what was expected to be a narrow victory in 1992. After the policy review of 1989 abandoned some deeply held policies, a regular criticism was that it was unclear what Kinnock stood for (Davies, 1992, pp. 276–80). A fiery Welsh orator, he was often criticized for being long on rhetoric, and short on policy detail. Nonetheless, Kinnock was a pragmatic politician who believed that before a policy programme could be enacted, the party had first to win power. Placed on the moderate left, Kinnock had played a role in ensuring the more right wing Denis Healey won the 1980 Deputy Leadership contest over the left wing Tony Benn (Morgan, 1992; Westlake, 1999). Kinnock faced major challenges when he became leader in 1983. First, the party needed unprecedented reform both organizationally and in policy if it was to become electable again. Second, he had to purge the radical left of the party, while at the same time keeping the party's right wing in line. Third, he faced a major chal- lenge for the centre-left of British politics from a breakaway from Labour, the Social Democratic Party (SDP). This had allied itself with the Liberals, in what became known as the Alliance, winning a vote share of over 25 per cent in 1983. Fourth, he faced a dominant Conservative Party when the centre-left was divided. Fifth, he required trade union support for many of the reforms to the party he wanted to undertake, although these would necessitate reducing the intra-party rights of the very unions whose support he required (Westlake, 1999, pp. 172–3). Finally, he had the misfortune to be leader during the 1984–85 Miners' Strike, the conduct of which placed Kinnock and the party in a difficult position despite their sympathy for striking miners.

Any of these would have been a major challenge on its own. Kinnock's leadership is now perceived to have been a necessary step effecting change which, although it may not have won the party office, would at least lead to the party doing so in 1997. Westlake (1999, p. 189) suggests that Kinnock's legacy can be measured in three ways: structure; policy; and mentality. Taking the first two points together, Shaw (1994, p. 221) observes that Kinnock's key innovations were to ensure that power was effectively centralized in Kinnock's inner leadership group, to the detriment of party bodies such as the National Executive Committee (NEC) and constituency parties, and to ensure that policy was driven by strategic electoral aims with vote maximizing being the party's new core function. In terms of the mentality of the party, Westlake (1999, p. 189) contends that had Kinnock given up the leadership prior to 1992, the modernization process would have stalled. He goes on: 'he was undeniably successful in his aim of reforming and modernizing the Labour Party ... of all the Labour leaders who were never Prime Minister ... Kinnock achieved the most by far'.

John Smith led the party briefly from 1992 until his death in 1994. Shadow Chancellor from 1987, and with a reputation for caution and integrity, Smith won the leadership easily with support from all sections of the party. Under Smith, the pace of change slowed considerably. McSmith (1999, p. 193) indicates that aspects of the future reforms enacted by Tony Blair, such as rewriting Clause IV, would not have happened under Smith. Tensions certainly existed between Smith and modernizers, such as Blair and Brown, who thought the party needed to reform further. A common perception is that under Smith 'one more heave' would have seen the party returned to office. Smith was good at managing the parliamentary party, being tolerant towards different views until a consensus was reached. This mitigated the effects of parliamentary rebellions, while the parliamentary tactics adopted under his leadership did much to exploit the Conservative Party's divisions over issues related to Europe (Stuart, 2006).

Tony Blair became leader in 1994 after agreeing a deal that Gordon Brown, also seen as a potential leader, would not contest the leadership. Throughout his leadership, this Blair–Brown split, as much about personality as policy, was one of the key dividing lines in the party and an important element in understanding the development of the party from 1994 (Naughtie, 2002; Rawnsley, 2001, 2010). Blair was perceived to be good at presentation but would abandon many of the party's most cherished positions by pulling it rightwards to the centre of political space. Indeed, more than half of the membership felt Blair was right-wing, by comparison with only a third viewing Kinnock in such a way (Seyd and Whiteley, 2002a, p. 144). Blair was heavily criticized for 'control freakery', particularly in relation to media and party management. This was to a large extent a function of Blair's heavily personalized leadership style, but also a consequence of the desire to present a united party to the electorate. As a consequence of both this leadership style and a number of controversial policy positions, Labour suffered an increasing number of parliamentary rebellions under Blair. These included, in the vote on the 2003 Iraq war, the largest rebellion within any party in the previous century and a half (Cowley, 2005).

Blair is one of the most significant leaders Labour has had. Electorally, he achieved three consecutive general election victories, winning sizeable majorities in each. He broadened Labour's electoral coalition to appeal to aspirational middle-class voters and to the previously resistant South East (Curtice, 2007). Blair easily saw off four Conservative leaders while the party's occupation of the centre of British politics and presentation of itself as 'New' Labour proved difficult for the Conservatives to compete with. He took the party further than Kinnock, being successful in rewriting Clause IV, and further reforming party structures by downgrading conference and introducing the new policy forum system of policy making described in Chapter 9. While members may have been critical, they nevertheless appreciated his leadership qualities; 90 per cent thought he was a strong leader (Seyd and Whiteley, 2002a, p. 144). Electoral success in 1997 and 2001 bolstered his autonomy as leader. Contrary to accusations of him following an essentially right-wing conservative agenda, others have suggested his ethical and Christian socialist orientation meant he was more closely rooted in the thought of some of the party's founders than many who prioritized public ownership (Rentoul, 1999). Many of the decisions he made were highly controversial with, in the latter part of his leadership, such controversies being utilized by so-called 'Brownites' to challenge Blair's leadership (Rawnsley, 2010). Blair was nevertheless a dominant figure. In the way he increased the leadership's autonomy, emphasized vote and office seeking, and sought to professionalize and personalize campaigning, Heffernan (2007, p. 163) suggests that he was more than just an important leader for Labour but also 'significantly reworked the template of modern political party leadership' more generally.

Blair's successor had great difficulty adapting, in both political and personal terms, to such a 'high-intensity model of leadership performance' (Foley, 2009). Gordon Brown had a long history in the party and had served as Chancellor for ten years. He had a reputation for party management, political strategy and a concern for social justice. His heir-apparent role meant that he was elected unopposed to the leadership. Despite a short-term boost in the polls, acceding to the leadership presented him with a number of problems: the difficulty of distancing himself from both his record as Chancellor and Blair's record as leader; the need to create a distinct 'vision' for his leadership; and the ability to impose his interpretation of events upon crises. Combined with the financial sector crisis from 2007, these challenges proved too much. He was unable to construct a clear leadership identity that was decisive and gave direction (Foley, 2009; Kettell and Kerr, 2008). Party management also failed, with many 'Blairites' critical of his leadership and a number of disaffected cabinet ministers resigning. Brown led the party to defeat in 2010, albeit not by the margin that some had predicted.

Ed Miliband won the subsequent leadership election to become leader in September 2010 (Table 4.2). Former climate change secretary under Brown, his early leadership was concerned with efforts to articulate effective opposition in the new context of Conservative–Liberal coalition government. While the coalition remained initially popular, the scale of the public sector cuts it implemented meant that Labour had an opportunity to re-establish itself as a credible alternative. This was not wholly successful, Miliband's main difficulty being distancing the party and himself from the legacy of the Blair–Brown years.

Electing the leader has been controversial within the Labour Party, with a number of changes made to leadership election rules. The major change came in 1981 when an electoral college consisting of three elements – the PLP, CLPs and trade unions and affiliated organizations – was introduced as a consequence of an attempt to democratize the party. Prior to 1981, leaders had been elected by the party's MPs. Since these tended to be further to the right than constituency activists and the trade

Table 4.2   Labour Party leadership election results, 2010 (percentages)

Candidates	First ballot	Second ballot	Third ballot	Fourth ballot
Ed Miliband	34.33	37.47	41.26	50.65
David Miliband	37.78	38.89	42.72	49.35
Ed Balls	11.79	13.30	16.02	
Andy Burnham	8.68	10.41		
Diane Abbott	7.42			

Source: Data from www.labour.org/results, 26 September 2010.

unions, the left saw the electoral college as a way of ensuring it elected a left-wing leader. Quinn (2005) sets out the rules in detail. There are three stages. The first is the nomination process. Potential candidates originally needed to be nominated by five per cent of the PLP to stand for leader. In the aftermath of a failed attempt by Benn to challenge Kinnock in 1988, this was raised to 20 per cent to discourage frivolous and damaging challenges. When a vacancy exists – for instance after a leadership resignation such as Gordon Brown's in 2010 – this threshold is lower, at 12.5 per cent of the PLP, although the NEC have on occasions (in 1992 and 2010) allowed MPs to switch nominations to ensure more candidates enter the contest. The second stage is when candidates set out their case to MPs, CLPs and affiliated organizations through hustings around the country. Finally, the results of the Electoral College are announced at a party conference. Between 1981 and 1993, the weighting between the three elements was PLP and CLPs 30 per cent each, with 40 per cent given to the unions. CLP and union votes were cast as a block vote. From 1993, the proportion allocated to each element of the Electoral College has been a third each. Moreover, both CLPs and unions have been obliged to ballot their members in a one-member-one-vote (OMOV) process. These votes are then cast in proportion for each of the candidates.

A number of consequences, some unintended, have resulted. First, broadening the process to individual members has ensured both that the leadership has greater autonomy vis-à-vis the relatively atomized membership, and that the leadership has, in principle, greater democratic legitimacy. Indeed, one of the difficulties of Gordon Brown's leadership was that the lack of a contest in 2007 undermined his legitimacy in the eyes of many. Second, despite the left's aim of the electoral college leading to more leadership accountability and electing left-wing leaders, the contrary was thought to have happened, not least because the extension of OMOV led to a weakening of left-wing and union activists' power (Heppell, 2010; Quinn, 2004). However, the 2010 leadership election results, shown in Table 4.2, challenge such an assessment. Ed Miliband trailed his brother, former foreign secretary David Miliband, throughout, only winning in the final ballot because of the influence of the union vote. This was the first time that different elements of the Electoral College had differed, decisively in this instance, leading some to question its continued utility, and others to question Miliband's legitimacy as leader. Finally, despite extensive plotting against the leader under Blair and Brown, in practice the risks of challenging an incumbent Labour leader are considerable. They are seldom challenged formally, and their tenure is relatively secure (Quinn, 2004, 2005).

Candidate Selection and Representativeness

One of the most symbolic images of Labour's 1997 victory was of Tony Blair with the party's 101 women MPs. This did much to cement the idea that 'New' Labour had actually changed from being a male-dominated party populated by MPs with working-class and trade-union backgrounds. This section therefore assesses Labour's candidate selection processes, before outlining the current composition of the parliamentary party.

Candidate selection has been a key factional battleground between left and right. The party traditionally had a localized selection system, whereby constituency party committees were responsible for both short-listing and selecting parliamentary candidates. The NEC however could veto candidates after they had been selected by CLPs. Concerned that the party's MPs were predominantly right-wing, during the 1970s the CLPD pressed for mandatory reselection of all MPs. After ongoing conference debates during the 1970s, mandatory reselection was introduced in 1980 with the left and CLPD arguing that this would make MPs more accountable. Although seldom used to unseat an MP, in reality local selectorates took both electoral and ideological considerations into account when selecting (Bochel and Denver, 1983; Norris and Lovenduski, 1995). The perception amongst modernizers was that mandatory reselection gave too much power to radical local activists. The selection process was further reformed in 1989 when an electoral college with two elements, local party members and local affiliated organizations, was introduced in order to remove some of the perceived power of activists in CLP general committees. The power of local trade unions to influence candidate selection was also limited by weighting their contribution to local electoral colleges at a maximum of 40 per cent. A major change came at the 1993 conference which introduced one-member-one-vote (OMOV) ballots for candidate selection, seen as necessary because the large number of ordinary members were perceived to be less radical than local activists and the trade unions. The vote was carried only after a decisive speech from John Prescott and John Smith's threat to resign if the motion was not passed. Devolution led to further controversies about candidate selection in London, Scotland and Wales, not least in relation to the centralization of the process (Bradbury et al., 2000; Russell, 2005, ch. 4; Shaw, 2001). The main change since, introduced prior to 2001, has been the practice of central approval of candidates by party HQ before they are selected by constituencies. This has been criticized for giving considerable power to the leadership. Nevertheless, after being the source of considerable conflict within the party, Labour's candidate selection processes have settled down with OMOV at the core of the process (Russell, 2005, ch. 4).

The movement to select women candidates was caught up in factional disputes over candidate selection during the 1970s and 1980s. A number of steps have been decisive in achieving women's representation (Russell, 2005, ch. 5). First, the principle of having one woman on a candidate shortlist was approved in 1986 and implemented in 1988, although this was not effective in itself in having more women elected. Second, quotas were also introduced to ensure that women were represented on the party's internal bodies such as the NEC and constituency committees (Norris and Lovenduski, 1995, ch. 4; Russell, 2005, ch. 5). Third, despite efforts to encourage voluntary adoption of all women shortlists (AWS) in the 1980s, conference voted in 1993, in the same vote that passed OMOV, to force a proportion of constituencies to run AWSs at the 1997 general election. Fourth, although AWSs were subject to a legal challenge which ruled against the party, in office Labour passed the Sex Discrimination (Election Candidates) Act 2002 which legitimized their use in future elections for any party which wishes to use such a procedure (Childs, 2003). They have been successful for Labour, for example, leading to the 101 women elected in 1997, while 23 of 30 women selected by AWS were elected in 2005. While there have been perceptions of a backlash against AWS amongst both voters and CLPs, Cutts et al. (2008) show this has not been the case. Consequently, the success of AWSs, along with increasing women's representation at various levels through the party, has 'necessitated a major shift in power from men to women' (Russell, 2005, p. 124).

How representative and distinctive are Labour's parliamentarians? In terms of age, Labour had the oldest cohort of parliamentarians elected in 2010, with an average age of 52 between the party's 258 MPs. Labour nevertheless had the youngest member of the 2010 parliament, Pamela Nash MP elected at the age of 25 for a Scottish central belt constituency.

Labour MPs have origins that are distinct from the other two main parties in four ways. The occupational background of Labour's 2010 cohort is set out in Table 4.3. First, as in the 2005 parliament, only a small percentage of Labour MPs were drawn from business backgrounds. Second, Labour relied to a greater extent on MPs with backgrounds in miscellaneous white-collar occupations particularly among political organizers and union officials. Third, Labour MPs drawn from the working class made up a larger part of the PLP than found in the other two main parties, although this still only accounts for 9 per cent of Labour

Table 4.3   Occupation of Labour MPs elected in 2010

	Number	%
Professions	89	35
Business	20	8
Miscellaneous	127	49
Manual workers	22	9
Total	258	100

Source: Data from Kavanagh and Cowley, 2010, p. 327.

MPs. Finally, of Labour MPs drawn from the professions, a greater proportion of these came from public sector professions such as the civil service and local government or had been school teachers and university lecturers.

Labour MPs were much less likely to have gone to either public school, or attended Oxford or Cambridge, than their Conservative counterparts. The proportion that went to public school in 2010 was 13 per cent, down from 18 per cent in 1979. University educated Labour MPs rose from 59 to 72 per cent between 1979 and 2010, although this is still lower than the 80 per cent of Liberal Democrat and Conservative MPs that had done so in 2010. The proportion of Oxbridge educated Labour MPs fell between 1979 and 2010 from 21 to 17 per cent (Gay, 2009, p. 12; Kavanagh and Cowley, 2010, pp. 326–7).

Labour have been the most successful of the three main parties in having MPs from minority ethnic backgrounds elected to parliament. In 1987 the party elected four non-white MPs. This has risen steadily in every general election since, rising to 13 in 2005 and 16 in 2010 (Gay, 2009, p. 12; Cracknell et al., 2010, p. 42). Consequently, the party has also had senior minority ethnic politicians serve at high levels, with figures such as Paul Boateng, David Lammy and Shahid Malik serving at ministerial level in Labour governments, while in 2010 Diane Abbott became the first minority ethnic candidate to contest the party's leadership.

Labour has also been at the forefront of having women elected to parliament. The numbers of women Labour MPs have risen from 1979 onwards, from 11 in 1979 to the high of 101 in 1997 to 81 in 2010. While the raw numbers have fallen back from the 101 in 1997 noted above, particularly because of electoral defeat in 2010, the party has nevertheless consistently had the highest proportion of women MPs of all the major parties since 1979. Moreover, as Figure 4.1 highlights, the proportion of women in the PLP has risen steadily from 1979, representing 24

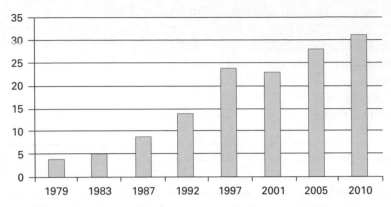

Figure 4.1   Proportion of women Labour Party MPs, 1979–2010 (%)
Sources: Data from Gay, 2009, p. 10; Cracknell et al., 2010, p. 42.

per cent of the PLP in 1997 and 31 per cent in 2010. One of the key reasons has been the move within the party to select more female candidates. In 2010, 191 women contested seats for Labour, 30 per cent of the party's total number of candidates and a greater proportion of women candidates than either of the other two main parties (Kavanagh and Cowley, 2010, p. 319). While the party has never had a female leader, two women have been deputy leader, Margaret Beckett who served as deputy under John Smith and Harriet Harman who was elected deputy leader in 2007.

In Office

Labour formed minority governments in the 1920s, and contributed to the wartime coalition government between 1940–45, before, in 1945, forming the party's first majority government. There have since been four periods of Labour government: 1945–51; 1964–70; 1974–79; and 1997–2010. A popular yet damaging image of Labour in office has been of a party constantly reacting to financial crises as markets put pressure on the UK economy and currency. This was because of market perceptions of high public expenditure and borrowing by profligate Labour governments spending more than the country could afford. Such an image was uppermost in 'New' Labour minds as the party sought office under Tony Blair, and establishing a reputation for economic competence became a key element of the party's appeal under his leadership. How then have Labour performed in office?

The achievements of the 1945–51 Labour governments represent one of, if not the, high points of Labour's history. Indeed, one survey ranked Attlee first out of all Britain's twentieth-century Prime Ministers (Theakston and Gill, 2006, pp. 198–9). As noted above, the 1945–51 Attlee governments introduced the National Health Service and welfare state, achieved full employment, embarked on a large post-war rebuilding programme in addition to nationalizing sizeable swathes of industry. As one popular assessment argues, these outcomes were 'a decisive advance over most pre-war working class experiences' which achieved 'more good for more people than any other British government of the 20th century' (Howell, 2006, p. 136 and p. 140). Nonetheless, the Labour government faced numerous difficulties. These included how to get war-damaged British industry back on its feet as well as sizeable financial crises over sterling convertibility in 1947 and devaluation in 1949. International affairs remained problematic, with a deteriorating cold war situation. Particularly in economics, leadership seemed not always sure-footed, with Attlee often playing a subordinate role to more junior ministers (Morgan, 1992; Pearce, 1999). The main reforms – NHS, nationalization, welfare – were carried out during the party's first two years in office. The financial crises of 1947 and 1949 put considerable pressure on public spending, and consequently these key Labour policies. Instead of cutting programmes, Labour managed demand and consumption through wartime controls, austerity packages and rationing, believing these measures more equitable. When cuts were implemented, they were much smaller than economic advisors and experts had advocated, largely because the government resisted such advice in favour of pressing ahead with their programmes. Consequently Shaw (1996, p. 35) indicates that the 1945–51 Labour governments were highly purposeful, notable for their determination to achieve the goals of full employment and extended social welfare, and their ability to challenge and resist official advice to the contrary.

Labour's 1964–70 terms in office are commonly described as disappointing (Morgan, 1992; Shaw, 1996). The party's programme had two main aims. First, it sought to actively manage the economy through planning and prices and incomes policies to achieve growth and full employment. Second, it aimed to enhance equality and social justice through extending social welfare, health, housing and other public services. This was to be financed by economic growth, the aim being a 3.8 per cent per annum increase in output between 1964–70 (Shaw, 1996, pp. 68–75). Economic crises undermined these plans. Deflationary measures in mid-1966 led to increased unemployment and lethargic economic output.

Constant pressure on sterling led to devaluation of the pound in 1967, with the consequence of further deflationary policies, wage restraint and the need to negotiate credits from the International Monetary Fund (IMF). The effects were compounded by an ill-judged television address by Harold Wilson, which tried to downplay the seriousness of economic events. According to Bale (1999, p. 125) these events ended any reputation Wilson or his government had for economic competence. A White Paper, *In Place of Strife*, advocating reforms to trade union legislation to outlaw certain forms of industrial action met with resistance from the union movement. Wilson was forced to abandon the proposals, further undermining his authority. The 1964–70 Labour governments did introduce a number of key reforms in higher education, arts funding and in liberalizing measures from the Home Office. Nonetheless, the fact that unemployment had increased, economic growth was slower than when Labour took office and that little had been achieved in terms of redistribution underlined the failure of Labour to live up to its goals when in office (Shaw, 1996, pp. 92–105).

Labour returned to power in 1974 having stood on one of the most radical manifestos in its history (Webb, 2000, pp.112–13). The party made some initial progress, Chancellor Healey introducing, for instance, increased pensions and benefits. However, Labour again faced difficulties. A majority of four in the October 1974 election restricted the party's ability to legislate. This majority declined throughout the parliament, with Labour forced to rely on the Liberals and others for support towards the end of the term. There was a lack of clarity in some of the party's aims, for instance with regard to economic intervention (Shaw, 1996, p. 126). Harold Wilson resigned in spring 1976, being succeeded as premier by Callaghan. Like its 1964–70 predecessor, this Labour government was also beset by financial crises and pressure on the pound, perceived to be because of high levels of public spending and borrowing. This necessitated several rounds of extensive spending cuts and wage restraint, before the government was eventually forced to negotiate a loan from the IMF in 1976. The conditions of this loan involved further spending cuts of £2bn, although Callaghan eventually managed to have these terms reduced while also managing to steady confidence in the British economy after a major speech at the 1976 Labour Party conference. In retrospect, two additional factors necessitated this loan; the Treasury overstated UK borrowing by around £4bn; and the financial markets and US government were determined to force the UK to follow their economic orthodoxy (Shaw, 1996, ch. 6). While the unions had supported the government throughout much of these difficulties, by 1978 they were unable to get behind further wage restraint. Industrial unrest in the 1978–79 'Winter of Discontent' became widespread, affecting public services considerably. Although defeated by the Conservatives in 1979, the judgement of Labour's 1974–79 period of office has been of a government 'struggling to do its best' in extremely difficult circumstances (Shaw, 1996, pp. 157–8).

Scenes of industrial and financial unrest associated with earlier Labour governments were the stuff of nightmares for 'New' Labour. While political scientists rate Blair highly amongst Prime Ministers (Theakston and Gill, 2006, pp. 198–9), the longer term view of the 1997–2010 Labour governments is likely to be less favourable. Determined to reassure markets, the party committed itself to maintaining Conservative levels of public spending for two years after winning office in 1997. The party made some ambitious commitments when it took up office, such as abolishing child poverty within 20 years, and an end to 'boom and bust' economics. Significant reforms were implemented. These included devolution of power to Scotland, Wales, Northern Ireland and London, investing in public services like the NHS, the introduction of a national minimum wage, and New Deal and Sure Start programmes aimed at dealing with unemployment and supporting disadvantaged children. The party also appeared to be taking some redistributive measures, for instance, through tax credits. By 2001, commentators noted progress but saw the first term as disappointing while assuming that more would be achieved subsequently (Driver and Martell, 2002; Taylor, 2001; Toynbee and Walker, 2001). Indeed, Seldon (2007) notes that more extensive programmes of public sector reform began in the second term and continued into the third. Economically, the party presided over considerable apparent success between 1997–2008, with an extended period of economic growth, low inflation and prosperity (Coates, 2008).

On the debit side, from the events of late-2001 onwards, Labour's agenda increasingly became dominated by terrorism, policies impinging upon civil liberties, and most importantly, the Iraq war and its aftermath. Toynbee and Walker (2010) give the Labour governments of 1997–2010 a rating of six out of ten, arguing that despite many well-intentioned measures, the party was too timid both in challenging predominant ideas and interests, and in communicating the reasons for what it was doing. The surface economic success of 1997–2008 masked the fact that other economic indicators – productivity, manufacturing – had been less favourable (Coates, 2008). New Labour also failed to reduce inequalities in British society, including those related to child poverty (Dorling,

2010). Gordon Brown faced a number of difficulties after taking office in 2007. The major policy crisis related to the near-collapse of the banking system and the onset of recession in 2007–08. Brown gained credit for acting decisively to use public money to prop up the banking system and stimulating the economy, as well as for leading international efforts to ameliorate the worst effects of the recession. Nonetheless, the economic crisis represented the collapse of the political economy followed by Labour since 1997, led ultimately by Brown as Chancellor. This was based on the idea of economic growth led by public spending and consumption financed by both private and public sector borrowing, and some so-called 'stealth taxes' such as national insurance (Coates, 2008; Lee, 2008, 2009). The consequences of many of these measures were a sizeable public deficit, and the subsequent public sector cuts implemented by the Conservative–Liberal Democrat coalition, many of which would also have been necessary had Labour returned to office in 2010.

Conclusion

Labour's history is rooted in the attempt to represent the working class and the disadvantaged in society. To greater or lesser degrees, its ideological approach has been concerned with the pursuit of equality, redistribution, full employment and public ownership. These issues have been battlegrounds throughout the party's history as the tension between ideological principle and electability was fought out between the left and right of the party. Such internal conflict has impacted upon all aspects of the party's affairs – ideology, policy, leadership and candidate selection. The party has been led by some iconic political figures such as Attlee and Blair, but also for different and superficially less successful reasons, Kinnock and Foot. In office, Labour can point to one of the great reforming governments of British political history. The 1945–51 Attlee governments introduced the welfare state and the National Health Service, institutions which have remained central to British political debate ever since. Since then, Labour's performance has been less impressive, with the party failing to make a lasting impression on inequality and facing repeated financial crises when in government throughout the 1960s, 1970s and more recently under Gordon Brown until 2010. Despite its initial apparent economic success, the 1997–2010 Labour governments presided over the greatest economic crash since the great depression in the 1930s. The challenge under new leader Ed Miliband has been to redefine what Labour stands for. While the cuts imposed by the

Conservative–Liberal Democrat coalition had the potential to give sharper focus to Labour's criticisms and rhetoric in opposition, the party nevertheless found it difficult to distance itself from the claim that, in office, it was central to causing the economic crisis in the first place. Consequently, and contrary to the aims of 'New' Labour when it took office in 1997, the party has yet to decisively shake off the reputation for economic crisis that has dogged it every time it forms a government.

5

The Liberal Democrats

The Liberal Democrats (and predecessors) have been very much the third party in the Westminster party system. However, the party has dramatically increased its parliamentary representation in recent years, achieving 62 seats in 2005, and holding 57 seats in the 2010 parliament. This has been achieved by taking seats from both Labour and the Conservatives, and by being able to exploit popular issues not represented by the two main parties, for instance in opposing the 2003 Iraq war. The Liberal Democrats have consequently become an important area for study in their own right (Russell and Fieldhouse, 2005). Nevertheless, their ascent has not been problem-free and has variously involved the perception of internal ideological and policy conflict, and some high-profile changes of leadership. This chapter therefore examines developments in the Liberal Democrats. The first section sets out the key elements of Liberal Democrat ideology and policy through the lens of the two main ideological strands in the party, classical liberalism, and more interventionist social liberalism. The second part evaluates the leadership of the party, and outlines the party's procedures for selecting a leader. The third section sets out the party's candidate selection processes and assesses how representative the party's MPs are. Post-2010, the Liberal Democrats have participation in a coalition government alongside the Conservatives at Westminster to add to their record of holding office in the devolved institutions. The final section therefore evaluates the party's record in office.

Ideology and Policy

Liberalism has long ideological roots. All variants of liberalism ultimately aim to achieve individual liberty or freedom. Two main strands are traditionally identified: *classical liberalism* and *social liberalism*. Both can be traced in the ideological and policy approach of the Liberal Democrats. The primary concern of *classical liberalism* was to challenge

86

entrenched privilege through the extension of the electoral franchise, toleration of nonconformist religion and, most importantly, removing barriers to allow free economic competition to established elites. This latter concern with freeing up barriers to economic competition has led some writers, primarily in the media, to use the term 'economic liberalism' as a synonym for classical liberalism (Grayson, 2010). Importantly, the 'freedom from' various obstacles to achieving individual liberty that classical liberalism sought to achieve also extended to the state and a concern for protecting civil and political liberties from the state's potentially coercive apparatus.

From the late nineteenth century, the industrial revolution made liberals aware that inequality, poverty, disease and lack of education presented severe obstacles to individual development. The problem was that while individuals may have, at least nominally, various freedoms extended to them, these inequalities prevented them from fully realizing their potential in both economic and democratic terms. A second strand of liberalism therefore developed in an attempt to address these questions. As a general ideological trend, this is most commonly referred to as *social liberalism*, although the term 'new liberalism' has also been used particularly when talking historically about late nineteenth- and early twentieth-century developments. Social liberalism was an approach which saw the actions of the state not necessarily as a threat to individual liberty, but as something which might be able to help individuals to realize their potential. There are a number of different statements of social liberalism (Howarth, 2007; Jones, 1996, pp. 63–70). In one classic account, Hobhouse (1964, p. 126) argues that 'people are not fully free in their political capacity when they are subject industrially to conditions which take the life and heart out of them'. He argues for intervention in the economy and, in contrast to classical liberals, the need for the state to provide, where necessary, the means to live and realize people's potential. To Hobhouse (1964, p. 71) the state 'not only involves no conflict with the true principle of personal liberty, but is necessary to its effective realisation'. In practical terms, Hobhouse emphasizes the need for measures like a living wage to provide minimum living standards.

Social liberalism is therefore mainly concerned with providing social justice to allow individuals the 'freedom to' maximize their potential. Liberals were able to put such ideas into effect. In 1909, the Liberal government's budget sought to 'wage implacable war against poverty and squalidness' through redistributive taxation measures, while it also passed national insurance legislation in 1911 (Dutton, 2004, pp. 22–4). Although the Liberal Party was not in government for most of the twentieth century, social liberal thinkers were able to influence policy in later decades. The influential economist J. M. Keynes, for example, contributed to the Liberal Party publication *Britain's Industrial Future* in 1928, commonly known as the *Yellow Book,* which argued for increased government intervention in the economy. Keynes' later work on these themes provided intellectual arguments for government intervention in the economy, tax system and government investment to provide full employment and stimulate demand. Similarly, the introduction of the welfare state by the post-war Attlee government owed much to the work of another Liberal thinker, William Beveridge. The 1942 Beveridge Report aimed to deal with the five evils of 'Want, Disease, Ignorance, Squalor and Idleness'. Building on the National Insurance scheme introduced by the Liberal Government in 1911, this proposed a free National Health Service, and a range of social security benefits.

A key problem for liberal ideology and policy, and a vital strategic question for the Liberal Democrats more generally, has been that these ideas have either overlapped with other political philosophies, or have been adapted by other political parties. A central controversy has related to the relationship between social liberalism and social democracy. The key social democratic ideas are outlined in Chapter 4's discussion of Labour Party ideology and its 'revisionist' debates. The overlap with social liberal ideas should be evident. Indeed, Labour implemented the Beveridge report and Grayson (2007a, pp. 33–4) observes how Crosland's *The Future of Socialism* contains many ideas that social liberals could subscribe to. Some liberal ideas have also been traced in New Labour's so-called 'Third Way' (Beer, 2001). Ultimately, however, liberals prioritize the pursuit of freedom and tend to be more ideologically disposed towards decentralizing measures (Dutton, 2004, ch. 5; Grayson, 2007a). Both these aspects have distinguished liberal thought from overlaps with more state-centric social democrats.

Conservative politicians have also adopted liberal lines of argument. This was most evident post-1979 when, under Margaret Thatcher, economic liberal ideas gained credence. In particular, suspicion of the role of the state in the economy became an ideological driver of policy. This led, among other things, to privatization of a number of publicly owned utilities in the name of promoting competition in the market. This was accompanied by a related line of argument prioritizing individual freedom and responsibility and attempts to promote individual entrepreneurship over state intervention through welfare. Arguments for cutting taxes were emblematic policies for this strand of argument. More recently, some have detected a liberal conservatism which emphasizes tolerance of social difference and post-material issues such as the environment (Beech, 2009). These are all areas which overlap with Liberal Democrat ideas.

How might the modern Liberal Democrat approach be characterized? Most writers have consistently emphasized the social liberal nature of Liberal and Liberal Democrat policy. Meadowcroft (2000, p. 437) tracks the party's social liberal approach through Liberal party leader Jo Grimond in the late 1950s, to Charles Kennedy in 2000. Grayson (2007a, pp. 34–6) tracks the party's social liberal lineage through a range of Liberal Democrat policy documents from 1989 to 2006. Webb's (2000, p. 106) summary points to 'the continuation of the left-of-centre social liberalism which has been prominent in Britain for more than a century'. Such arguments have also been prominent in the party's manifestos, as in 2005 where then party leader Charles Kennedy argued that '[s]ociety is still scarred by inequality. Tackling that is a priority for the Liberal Democrats' (Liberal Democrats, 2005, p. 2). Building upon this, the 2006 policy paper *Trust In People* (Liberal Democrats, 2006, p. 8) continued to argue that 'Liberal Democrats want to create a much fairer society, which means a much less unequal one. A fair Britain is one where progressive national and local taxation, based on people's ability to pay, redistributes money from the richest to the poorest'. Importantly, such an approach is a 'precondition of freedom' (Liberal Democrats, 2006, p. 16).

Expert assessment of party manifestos has underlined these more qualitative assessments of Liberal Democrat policy. Benoit and Laver (2006) placed the Liberal Democrats to the left of Labour economically, while at the same time placing the party at the liberal end of the liberal–conservatism spectrum on social policy issues. Liberal Democrat members and voters can also be placed into broadly social liberal ideological categories. Liberal Democrat members are more likely to have liberal views about lifestyle issues, be in favour of redistribution and be pro-EU, although classical liberal 'free market' views are also well represented within the party (Bennie et al., 1996; Whiteley et al., 2006, ch. 3). Party members are often seen as more radical than party voters. However, this appears to be less the case with the Liberal Democrats. Whiteley et al. (2006, p. 66) point to 'a great deal of commonality in the attitudes of grassroots party members and Liberal Democrat voters'.

What does this mean in terms of policy? The Liberal Democrats initially emphasized five 'E's to encapsulate their policy priorities; economic policy, the environment, education, electoral and constitutional reform, and Europe (Brack, 1996). Often the party's tax proposals attract most attention. Grayson (2007a, p. 36) points to the party's

best-known policy being the 1992–2003 proposal to add 1p in the pound
to income tax to help improve education. In 2005 the party's manifesto
was mainly noted for its proposals for a 50p tax rate for incomes over
£100,000 and restoring the link between pensions and earnings
(Kavanagh and Butler, 2005, p. 74). However, the range of polices
offered were much wider (Liberal Democrats, 2005). In health, the party
proposed free personal care for the elderly, and a range of additional
measures designed to benefit patients. In education, the Liberal
Democrats proposed to abolish student tuition fees, and spend £1.5
billion on reducing class sizes. Staple commitments to electoral and
constitutional reform were also evident, while there was also an emphasis on curbing the power of the prime minister, especially after the Iraq
war. The party also argued for a local income tax to replace the council
tax, protecting the post office network and proposed giving pensioners an
extra £100 per month beginning with the over-75s. The Labour government's ID card policy would be cancelled and the money used to put more
police on the streets. Finally, environmental concerns were addressed by
commitments towards public transport and rural communities.
Environmental action was pledged in every policy area. The 2006 *Trust
in People* policy document further emphasized environmental issues as
an urgent area for government activity through a range of measures to
both raise environmental awareness and policies to address climate
change and environmental degradation (Liberal Democrats, 2006,
pp. 20–5).

A degree of ideological and policy change has been perceived in
recent years, with a move from the party's consistent social liberalism
towards an appeal which draws upon earlier classical and economic liberalism. A key text in this shift is *The Orange Book* (Marshall and Laws,
2004). Primarily the work of a small group of Liberal Democrat parliamentarians, this was perceived as a rightward shift in the party towards a
more tax-cutting, free-market approach. The authors address a combination of personal, political, economic and social aspects of liberalism.
They are quite clear about their approach. As Laws (2004a, p. 36) argues
'[a] key question for the Liberal Democrats is to what extent we can draw
on our heritage of economic liberalism to address some of the current
problems in public service delivery'. Rather than being an end in itself, he
portrays this move as being a means to social liberal ends (Laws, 2004a,
p.40). Similar themes are rehearsed through the book. In economic
policy, Cable (2004, ch. 5) argues for a 'new wave' of deregulation, prioritizing the role of markets over regulation, part privatization of the post
office, and cutting some areas of government activity. In health, Laws

(2004b) suggests bringing in competition through an insurance based system aimed at giving people choice in how they pay for their healthcare, while Clegg (2004, ch. 3) strikes a more Eurosceptic tone than might be expected from Britain's most pro-European party. Confirming these changes of emphasis in favour of economic liberalism, the party adopted policies during 2006 which, for instance, accepted the part-privatization of the post office and abolished the party's 50p tax rate on income over £100,000.

The Orange Book was far from universally welcomed. As then leader Charles Kennedy noted in his foreword, not all the 'hard-headed' ideas were party policy at the time (Kennedy, 2004). Randall (2007) sets out a number of criticisms of the *Orange Book*. First, by comparison with the earlier *Yellow Book* which its title alluded to, it was a less ambitious volume, and was much less willing to challenge the prevailing socio-economic order. Second, internally he argues that 'it ruffled liberal feathers and failed to win either a general acceptance or instill a sense of common purpose' (Randall, 2007, p. 42). Finally, he indicates that the book could have been bolder in relation to decentralization, and, most importantly, the environment.

The *Orange Book* motivated a response from social liberals. The subsequent volume, *Reinventing the State*, sought to restate how the social liberal approach aimed to deal with various inequalities and use the state to deal with issues where market-based approaches had failed (Brack et al., 2007; Grayson, 2010). A key argument was that social liberalism remained the party's main approach. What was required was not to reduce the size of the state but to reform it, in particular making public services more local and democratically accountable. For instance, Brack (2007a) argues that the Liberal Democrats needed to be more explicit about why equality matters, and why a commitment to redistributive taxation was necessary. Taylor (2007) suggests that Beveridge's 'five evils', although altered, remain an issue in the UK, and also at global levels. He adds a sixth, that of environmental degradation. Other contributions deal with the limitations to the market, how to reform the state to make it more local and discuss key public services such as health and education (Grayson, 2007b; Holmes, P. 2007; Howson, 2007; Huhne, 2007; Pack, 2007).

A central argument in *Reinventing the State* is that all Liberal Democrats are ultimately social liberal. Consequently, what is often taken for a split between social and economic liberals is actually a difference in the degree to which social liberals are willing to redistribute and use the state beyond the minimum required to achieve the necessary conditions for political freedom. These arguments can be quite nuanced and complex. Howarth (2007, p. 7) suggests that two types of social liberals can be found in the party. 'Maximalist' social liberals are those willing to go beyond creating the conditions for the exercise of political freedoms by, for instance, seeing a greater role for the state in economic intervention, redistributive taxation and decentralized public services. 'Minimalist' social liberals by contrast, as Laws (2004a, p. 40) suggests, see a lesser role for the state both more generally and in the delivery of public services.

To what extent has the *Orange Book* and subsequent policy changes marked a rightward shift in the party? Some commentators initially suggested that this had been overstated (Brack, 2007b, p. 86; Denham and Dorey, 2007, p. 35; Russell et al., 2007a, p. 95). While cutting the 50p top tax rate was actually a redistributive measure, it also began to mark a shift from being a tax-raising party to being a tax-cutting party (Grayson, 2007a, p. 36). To both Grayson (2007a, pp. 38–9) and Meadowcroft (2000) any shift could be explained by the political context. Since Labour had largely occupied social liberal policy space, while at the same time displaying many illiberal and statist attitudes, emphasizing classical liberal aspects of the party's ideology and policy was an obvious way to differentiate the Liberal Democrats from Labour.

'Maximalist' social liberals are much less sanguine under Nick Clegg's leadership. Grayson (2010) notes how the 2008 policy document *Make It Happen* contained a passage aiming to 'cut Britain's overall tax burden'. This was a major shift, committing the party to reducing the size of the state instead of using it to redistribute wealth and deal with inequalities. Despite an opposing amendment, this was approved at conference. A 'huge shock' to many, this showed the leadership that the party would go along with moves to reduce the state (Grayson, 2010). Maximalist social liberals have organized against this rightwards shift, winning motions at conference to keep some key commitments party policy. Nevertheless, this suggests that the leadership had indeed moved policy away from maximalist social liberal approaches, something that appeared to make agreement on coalition with the Conservatives after the 2010 election more possible than it might have been previously.

The 2010 Liberal Democrat manifesto demonstrated some continuities with past commitments (Liberal Democrats, 2010). Liberal Democrat philosophy was argued to be about distributing both economic and political power fairly. Discussion of equality appeared to be downplayed however in favour of the more amorphous term 'fairness' with four key themes: fair taxes; fair chances; a fair future; and a fair deal. In policy terms, the Liberal Democrats were presented as 'doing politics differently' from the other two main parties. Fair taxes were to be achieved by raising the tax threshold to £10,000 and by a mansion tax on properties worth over £2m. Equality of income was not an aim, but redistribution was mentioned, if not dwelt upon. There was discussion of the power both of politicians and big business, which led to 'a fragile society marked by inequality'. The manifesto included a promise to break up the banks and assorted commitments to political reform. It also included a promise to begin reducing the deficit in 2011–12 after a one-year economic stimulus. Much would be funded by cutting government programmes such as ID cards and expensive defence projects. Poorer pupils would be encouraged through a 'pupil premium', while university tuition fees would be scrapped saving students over £10,000 each.

However, the 2010 manifesto also differed in tone from previous policy programmes. There was no mention of progressive taxation and tax-cutting appeared a key aim; the party's commitment to increase tax thresholds was something that may benefit poorer workers, but ultimately benefited all. As the manifesto suggested, 'we propose the most radical tax reform in a generation, cutting taxes for millions, paid for by closing loopholes at the top' (Liberal Democrats, 2010, p. 9). It also promised to restrict some tax credits and scrap Labour schemes such as the Child Trust fund. Although not using the term directly, it also included a commitment to creating 'free schools', removing local authority control from education, a theme that only came to light after Clegg had been elected leader (Grayson, 2010). Finally, the party was no longer committed to free personal care for the elderly as in 2005, instead only offering to try to establish a cross-party investigation into the matter. In other words, while the manifesto showed some clear continuities, it also differed in important ways from previous Liberal Democrat policy programmes.

Leadership

Leadership is arguably even more important for the Liberal Democrats than the other major parties. As the 'third' party in the Westminster system, the Liberal Democrats have regularly struggled to have their voice heard. Consequently, Liberal Democrat leaders often record low recognition rates at the start of an election campaign, although these rates steadily increase because the party gets greater coverage during elections (Butler and Kavanagh, 2002, p. 103, pp. 248–9). Having a leader that is

Table 5.1   Liberal and Liberal Democrat leaders, 1945–2011

Term of office	Leader	Party
August 1945–November 1956	Clement Davies	Liberal Party
November 1956–January 1967	Jo Grimond	Liberal Party
January 1967–May 1976	Jeremy Thorpe	Liberal Party
July 1976–July 1988	David Steel	Liberal Party
July 1988–August 1999	Paddy Ashdown	Liberal Democrats
August 1999–January 2006	Charles Kennedy	Liberal Democrats
March 2006–October 2007	Menzies Campbell	Liberal Democrats
December 2007–	Nick Clegg	Liberal Democrats

both widely recognized and able to make the party's distinctive liberal position clear to voters is therefore a key issue for the party.

Table 5.1 lists Liberal Party and Liberal Democrat leaders from post-war onwards. The Liberal Democrats emerged out of a complex merger process between the Liberal Party and the SDP which was completed in 1988. The SDP was formed in 1981 after a split in the Labour Party (Crewe and King, 1995). While retaining their autonomy, from early on the Liberals and SDP co-operated, developing electoral pacts, parliamentary co-operation and joint policy statements. David Steel, then Liberal Party leader, favoured co-operation with the SDP, in what became known as the Alliance, and ultimately merger between the parties. Had Steel not pursued merger, it is unlikely that this would have been achieved and the history of the Liberal Party would have been very different.

The first elected leader of the Liberal Democrats was Paddy Ashdown, who led the party from July 1988 to August 1999. A former Royal Marine officer, his leadership is most regularly described as energetic and dynamic. Ashdown presided over a period of unprecedented success. Under his leadership the Liberal Democrats increased their number of MPs to 46 and also saw the number of Liberal Democrat councillors in local government increase by around 40 per cent (Alderman and Carter, 2000, p. 312). Brack (2007b) divides Ashdown's leadership into three phases. The first was between 1988–92 when the party was fighting for survival. The new party faced organizational challenges, with a lack of funding and members leaving the party among its problems. It also faced electoral challenges, such as former SDP voters returning to the Labour Party. Such challenges placed severe potential limits upon the prospects for the Liberal Democrats. Brack (2007b, pp. 80–1) is clear that Ashdown's energetic leadership style can take much of the credit for the party's survival in this period. The new party was positioned as 'equidistant' between Labour and the Conservatives. Ashdown was able to find high profile issues, often in foreign policy, where he could adopt a distinctive liberal position to differentiate the party from its larger competitors. He was also able to establish distinctive policy positions on constitutional matters, the environment and a penny on income tax for education.

The second period of Ashdown's leadership, between 1992–97, was based around the idea of realigning the left – Labour and the Liberal Democrats – in an anti-Conservative alliance. The Liberal Democrat policy of 'equidistance' between Labour and Conservatives formally ended in 1995. Ashdown had prefigured this idea in a speech at Chard in his constituency shortly after the 1992 election where he talked of the need for co-operation to create a 'non-socialist alternative' to the Conservatives. Liberal Democrat–Labour co-operation in the mid-1990s became known as 'The Project', shorthand for the attempt to work together to marginalize the Conservatives. The parties co-operated on constitutional issues prior to the 1997 general election, while Blair also appeared to offer Liberal Democrat participation in a Labour government (Ashdown, 2000, p. 560; Russell and Fieldhouse, 2005, pp. 41–2). Ashdown's pursuit of co-operation led the Liberal Democrats into a Joint Cabinet Committee (JCC) with Labour on constitutional issues. Brack (2007b, p. 82) argues that this second period under Ashdown must also be seen as a success, increasing Liberal Democrat levels of representation, bringing the party influence, while avoiding being 'squeezed' by New Labour in the anti-Conservative mood prior to 1997.

Ashdown sometimes led the Liberal Democrats into places the party was reluctant to go. For instance, the Chard speech led to conflict within the parliamentary party (Ashdown, 2000, pp. 160–6), and conference occasionally defeated the leadership on positions it disagreed with during Ashdown's tenure (Ingle, 1996, pp.120–1). Ashdown announced his resignation in January 1999 and stepped down after the European elections that year. Ashdown's diaries indicate that his resignation was preplanned (Ashdown, 2002, p. 12). However, it also coincided with rising discontent within the party about co-operation with Labour, not least since Labour had failed to deliver electoral reform. Indeed, the Liberal Democrat conference put stringent conditions on future attempts at coalition in 1998, the so-called 'Triple Lock' which necessitates approval of coalitions by the party's Federal Executive, parliamentary party, and approval from the membership. There was also a negative reaction within the party to the announcement of further JCC co-operation later that year. Brack (2007b, p. 83) characterizes this third period as a failure, largely because Ashdown tried to lead the party into a position that he could not deliver and the party did not want. Nevertheless, the Liberal Democrats both survived and prospered under Ashdown. Consequently, his dynamic leadership must largely be seen as a success, with Ashdown portrayed as 'the most significant Liberal leader since Jo Grimond'(Brack, 2007b, p. 79)

Ashdown was succeeded in August 1999 by Charles Kennedy. In contrast to Ashdown, Kennedy's leadership style was regularly described as relaxed and laid back. Kennedy had been seen as a possible leader and had a good public profile, appearing regularly on popular TV shows. The early period of his leadership involved a search for distinctive social liberal positions for the party in domestic policy which would give the party a clear identity (Alderman and Carter, 2000, pp. 325–7; Grayson, 2010). The 2001 general election appeared to play well; Kennedy was credited with principled interventions while the party achieved the best Liberal Democrat vote share since the Alliance in 1987 and elected 52 MPs (Brack, 2007b, p. 85; Butler and Kavanagh, 2002, p. 67). 2005 also appeared to be a success with Kennedy adopting an anti-Iraq war stance and further increasing the party's vote share to 22 per cent and the number of seats to 62. Consequently, Russell et al. (2007a, p. 92) highlight the perception that Kennedy's leadership 'was mostly characterized by good times for the party'.

Kennedy announced his resignation from the leadership in January 2006, due to a drink problem. This surprised many given the party's record under his leadership. There had nevertheless been considerable concern within the party for some time about Kennedy's leadership (Denham and Dorey, 2007, pp. 32–4). Despite record results in the 2001 and 2005 elections there was a sense that the Liberal Democrats underperformed in both (Butler and Kavanagh, 2002, p. 249; Kavanagh and Butler, 2005, p. 197). His relaxed style was perceived to be part of the problem; one memorable comment likened Kennedy to being more a chairman than a leader. Some public performances were erratic, notably the 2005 manifesto launch when Kennedy proved unable to answer a question about local income tax. Brack (2007b, pp. 85–7) dates these difficulties to after the 2001 election. He argues that Kennedy had no clear leadership agenda or direction for the party, that he did not manage the party and that his communication skills deserted him after this. In policy terms Kennedy is criticized as always opposing, not forwarding a positive liberal agenda and, in the case of the anti-Iraq war stance the party adopted, being lucky that this resonated with the public. Kennedy became increasingly isolated within the party before stepping down in January 2006. Contextually, David Cameron's election as leader of the Conservative Party in December 2005 also made the Liberal Democrats appear vulnerable to both Labour and the Conservatives at this point. According to Brack (2007b, p. 85) however, 'Kennedy's underlying problem was that he was a poor leader, drunk or sober'. Kennedy however remains a popular public figure and the party ultimately improved its performance in general elections while he was leader.

Kennedy was replaced by Sir Menzies Campbell in March 2006 after a leadership election which generated headlines more for its revelations about some of the candidates than for the policy differences between them. Campbell was a widely respected 'elder statesman' figure, both within the party, as deputy leader under Kennedy, and more broadly for his high profile contributions to debates about foreign affairs. Nevertheless, he was seen as a 'caretaker', holding the position until other more inexperienced candidates had built up their profile and experience to allow them to contest the leadership (Denham and Dorey, 2007). Although appearing hesitant in his early days as leader, Campbell is credited with making some organizational and managerial changes to the party (Russell et al., 2007a, pp. 93–4). His leadership became quickly embroiled in questions about his age – he was 64 when elected leader – and how this impacted upon his ability to lead the party into a general election and beyond. Indeed, Campbell had declined to stand for the leadership because of his age in 1999 (Alderman and Carter, 2000, p. 316). This became a major distraction, and Campbell resigned in October 2007, having led the party for just 19 months, citing his age as a key factor in preventing the party from getting its message across.

Nick Clegg became the party's fourth leader in December 2007. Clegg was elected by a very narrow margin, much lower than had elected any previous Liberal Democrat leader, achieving 50.6 per cent of the votes cast against Chris Huhne's 49.4 per cent. Clegg was a contributor to the *Orange Book* and therefore associated with the change of emphasis towards economic liberal issues within the party. As with other Liberal leaders before him, Clegg's key task was to forward a distinctive agenda setting the party apart from its larger rivals. Importantly in this regard *The Guardian* (19 December 2007) pointed out the day after his election that 'Mr Clegg must define himself as something other than a second Cameron. He will not get far by hoping that the Tory party is found out.'

Like Campbell, Clegg's leadership also began hesitantly. Early media performances were unconvincing, and Clegg seemed overshadowed by Treasury Spokesman Vince Cable during the 2008–10 economic crisis. The label of 'Calamity Clegg', used by leadership contender Chris Huhne in the leadership election, initially appeared to have stuck, particularly in relation to a split within the parliamentary party on the question of a referendum on the EU's Lisbon Treaty and a failure to answer a question about the state pension correctly. Through 2009 there were signs of Clegg having a sharper agenda and ability to get Liberal Democrat views across. For instance, he called for the abolition of the 2009 Queen's speech in favour of a broader programme of political and constitutional reform (Clegg, 2009). Clegg's approval ratings consequently rose from mid-2009, to being consistently above 40 per cent approval.

Under Clegg the Liberal Democrats' policy emphasis changed to become one of cutting back the state, although far from all in the party agree with this change of emphasis (Grayson, 2010). The major breakthrough for Clegg was appearing alongside the other two main party leaders in Britain's first-ever televised leadership debates. Clegg's technique in the first debate was highly effective, although less so thereafter. Perceived to have 'won' the first debate, the debates gave Clegg an important and immediate boost in credibility. His rating on an opinion poll question about whether he had clear ideas to deal with the important problems facing Britain jumped by 31 points between the first and last debates. Clegg's performance also gave the Liberal Democrats an important boost in the polls, placing the party ahead of Labour in many (Kavanagh and Cowley, 2010, pp. 250–1). Dubbed 'Cleggmania', this led to unprecedented scrutiny of the Liberal Democrats, previously all but ignored by many major newspapers (Yelland, 2010). Although achieving the second best Liberal Democrat performance in the party's short history and a percentage point increase in vote share, these poll ratings failed to hold up and the Liberal Democrats were disappointed to lose five seats.

Clegg subsequently led the Liberal Democrats into coalition with the Conservatives after negotiations that Liberal Democrats perceived to have given the party some major concessions (Laws, 2010). Notably, these included a referendum on electoral reform, a key Liberal Democrat issue but one that the Conservatives had traditionally opposed. In office however, Clegg became almost universally derided, associated with going back on many policies that the party stood for at the election, most notably university tuition fees, or failing to criticize other unpopular government policies implemented by Conservative ministers. One commentator, for instance, referred to Clegg's 'increasingly toxic reputation' (Harris,

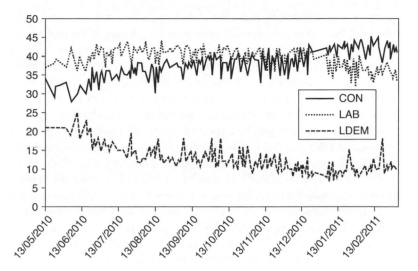

Figure 5.1   Voting intentions, May 2010–March 2011 (%)

Source: Data from UK Polling Report, http://ukpollingreport.co.uk/voting-intention, 9 March 2011.

2011). The party's poll ratings had plummeted to a low of around 8–10 per cent in early 2011 (see Figure 5.1). It was beaten into sixth place in the March 2011 Barnsley by-election behind the BNP and also suffered badly in the 2011 local and devolved elections. Clegg's approval ratings also fell precipitously. While polling company YouGov found that 72 per cent thought Nick Clegg was doing well in early May 2010, this had fallen to only 28 per cent in February 2011 with 62 per cent indicating that he was doing badly. Similar falls were evident when voters were asked about various leadership characteristics.

How do the Liberal Democrats select their leader? Although previous chapters highlight an opening up of the role of the membership in select-ing party leaders across mainstream parties, the Liberal Democrats and their predecessors paved the way in doing so. In contrast to the informal arrangements that existed before then, in 1976 the Liberal Party became the first major party to open leadership selection to an all-party ballot. David Steel was therefore the first mainstream British party leader elected in this way (Cole, 2009, p. 265; Denham and Dorey, 2007, p. 27). Liberal Democrat leadership elections are carried out by a postal ballot of all party members using the STV electoral system. An election can be triggered by a vote of no-confidence by a majority of the parliamentary party, or a submission by more than 75 local parties. Nomination papers for candidates must be proposed by at least 10 per cent of the parliamentary party and 200 other members in 20 or more local parties (Liberal Democrats, 2009). The all-member postal ballot may make the party seem highly participatory. However, it is important to qualify this. Alderman and Carter (2000, p. 325) suggest that less than 10 per cent of members attend leadership hustings. Turnout at such leadership elections can be lower than might be expected, with the turnout of members balloted in 1999 and 2007 being 62 and 64 per cent respectively. While the 2006 leadership contest had a turnout of 72 per cent, this still points to a party in which a sizeable proportion of members do not use the participatory rights granted them. Importantly, Russell et al. (2007a) point to the critical importance of the parliamentary party in the Liberal Democrats' leadership difficulties in 2005–2007. As they put it, 'the real power brokers did not seem to reside in the party at large ... but from a widely shared sentiment in the parliamentary party' (Russell et al., 2007a, p.93).

Candidate Selection and Representativeness

The Liberal Democrats claim to recognize the importance of being representative of the population at large; manifestos have highlighted the party's desire to have more women and ethnic minorities elected, while the party constitution also indicates the need for gender, socio-economic, ethnic and other considerations being taken into account when approving candidates (Liberal Democrats, 2005, p. 18; Liberal Democrats, 2009, Article 11). Since the party has historically been relatively small, achieving such representativeness has been less controversial than in other parties. Nevertheless, the party's success in recent general elections has served to put its representativeness under the spotlight.

Candidate selection is the realm of the local party in the Liberal Democrats. Although there are Candidates Committees which approve candidates, it is the local party executive that has the initial responsibility of shortlisting applications from potential candidates. Assuming that there are enough applicants from each sex, local shortlists are required to have some regard for gender balance. Shortlists of between two and four applicants are meant to have at least one member of each sex, while shortlists of five or more must have at least two members from each sex. Local parties are also supposed to have 'due regard for the representation of ethnic minorities' (Liberal Democrats, 2009, Article 11.5g). Having shortlisted applicants, local parties organize hustings where the potential candidates can present their case to local party members. Local party members then have a one-member-one-vote (OMOV) ballot to select their constituency candidate.

In the aftermath of the 2010 general election, the Liberal Democrat parliamentary party conceded its place as the youngest parliamentary party in the previous parliament to the Conservatives. The average age of the 57 Liberal Democrat MPs was 50, up somewhat from 46.5 years old in 2005 (Gay, 2009, p. 9): 22 per cent of the party's MPs were 60 or over, up from 10 per cent in 2005. The same proportion fell into the under 40 age group, down from the 31 per cent of the party's MPs under 40 in 2005 (Gay, 2009, p. 9; Kavanagh and Cowley, 2010, p. 322).

The middle-class nature of MPs has been highlighted in previous chapters. Table 5.2 demonstrates that of the 57 Liberal Democrat MPs elected in 2010, only one came from a manual work background, while the remainder were from solidly middle-class backgrounds (Kavanagh and Cowley, 2010, p. 327). Of the 22 MPs with professional backgrounds, 10 were involved in education, and four had been in the legal profession. Those with miscellaneous backgrounds included four from a white-collar background, five who had been journalists, and seven with a history as a politician or political organizer. Indeed, both contenders for the party leadership in 2007 had been MEPs. Cole (2009, p. 265) also points to the importance of previous local government experience to Liberal Democrat parliamentarians, while previous participation within the party is a criteria for becoming an approved candidate according to the party constitution (Liberal Democrats, 2009, Article 11.3). The same proportion of the 2010 cohort of Liberal Democrat MPs had gone to fee-paying school as in the 2005 group – 39 per cent – although this had decreased from the 55 per cent that had done so in 1979. During the same period, the proportion of university graduates among Liberal Democrat MPs rose from 45 per cent to 80 per cent in 2010. By contrast, the

Table 5.2   Occupation of Liberal Democrat MPs elected in 2010

	Number	*%*
Professions	22	39
Business	11	20
Miscellaneous	23	40
Manual workers	1	2
Total	57	100

Source: Data from Kavanagh and Cowley, 2010, p. 327.

proportion going to Oxbridge universities remained relatively steady at around 28–30 per cent (Gay, 2009, p. 12; Kavanagh and Cowley, 2010, p. 326).

Despite its commitment to increasing ethnic minority representation, like all parties the Liberal Democrats have struggled to achieve this. Despite standing 42 ethnic minority candidates in 2005 and 46 in 2010 (Kavanagh and Cowley, 2010, p. 320), the Liberal Democrats have never elected an ethnic minority candidate at a general election The party did succeed in having one ethnic minority candidate elected in a 2004 by-election, the candidate coming from third place to overturn a large Labour majority but failed to retain the seat at the subsequent 2005 general election (Gay, 2009, p. 12).

At one level, the Liberal Democrats have seemed to fare better in their attempts to increase the numbers of women representing the party. Indeed, the party has had the highest number of women councillors of the main three parties in local government (Evans, 2008, p. 590). Such progress has not carried through to Westminster. In both 2005 and 2010, around 20 per cent of Liberal Democrat candidates were women (Evans 2008, p. 598; Kavanagh and Cowley, 2010, p. 319). In 2005, the party elected 10 women, or 16 per cent of the parliamentary Liberal Democrats, while in 2010 it elected seven, representing 12 per cent of Liberal Democrat MPs. This is lower than the parliamentary average; the 2010 parliament had 22 per cent of women as MPs. The party appears to have done no better in Scotland, despite the semi-proportional electoral system, electing only two women in each of the 1999, 2003 and 2007 Scottish elections (Mackay and Kenny, 2007). The party fared slightly better in Wales, electing three women in each of the Welsh Assembly elections and accounting for half of the Welsh Assembly Party between 1999–2011. Since the election of Kirsty Williams in December 2008, the Welsh party has the first woman leader of any of the Liberal Democrat state parties.

Why have the Liberal Democrats not lived up to their aim to elect more women to parliament? One potential explanation is that in 2001 party conference voted against introducing all-women shortlists, on the grounds that they were essentially illiberal. Evans (2008) adopts a comprehensive supply and demand perspective to explain the party's lack of success in extending women's representation. She argues that the difficulty is not one of the potential supply of women candidates, noting that just under half of the party's membership consisted of women. In over half of the party's English regions, she indicates that there were women available to stand in more than 30 per cent of seats. Instead, Evans (2008) attributes responsibility to a range of demand-side factors. Firstly, she highlights attitudes within the male-dominated selection processes that exist at local level as placing unreasonable obstacles in female candidates' paths. Secondly, even when women candidates are selected, this is often in unwinnable seats. Indeed, the 'party's willingness to select women for winnable seats is debatable' (Evans, 2008, p. 599). Finally, although a Campaign for Gender Balance was established in the aftermath of conference rejecting all-women shortlists, it is underfunded, too Westminster-centric, and has little interaction with local parties to contribute effectively to having more women elected (Evans, 2008, p. 598).

In Office

A key jibe opponents used to make was that Liberal Democrats were never likely to form part of a government. Although the Liberal Democrats had not been in government at Westminster for close to a century, from May 2010 the party became the junior partner in a Conservative-led coalition government. The party has also experienced power in the devolved institutions in Scotland and Wales. Assessing the Liberal Democrats in public office is therefore an essential element of understanding how the party has adapted to its changed circumstances and additional responsibilities.

In both Scotland and Wales, Liberal Democrats were the junior coalition partner alongside Labour. In Scotland, Liberal Democrats participated in the Scottish Executive for two full terms of office between 1999–2003 and 2003–07. This is largely seen as having been a success for the Liberal Democrats. Assessing this period of devolved government, one former Labour Scottish First Minister suggested that 'the Liberal Democrats have probably gained more from devolution than any other party' (cited in Laffin, 2007a, p. 665). The Liberal Democrats delivered a range of key party policies which were not favoured by their Labour coalition partners. These included the abolition of up-front student tuition fees and their replacement with a 'graduate endowment' payable after graduation. They also included the extension of free personal care for the elderly and a more extensive Freedom of Information regime in Scotland than exists in the rest of the UK. Successes in the second term included electoral reform for Scottish local government and providing free dental and eye tests.

Roddin's (2004) assessment of the first Scottish coalition suggests that two-thirds of the policy initiatives in that period originated from the Liberal Democrats, and only a third from Labour. Similarly, Laffin (2007a, p. 665) suggests that Liberal Democrats achieved all their policy demands in 1999 and 2003. These successes were achieved partly because of policy overlaps and electoral compatibilities between the two parties. A further reason was that Liberal Democrats were more policy orientated in the coalition negotiations than Labour. In both negotiations, Liberal Democrats had a specific list of policies they wanted to achieve while Labour had more general aspirations. Being well prepared and having the results published publicly in lengthy coalition partnership agreements ensured that the Liberal Democrats were able to hold Labour to what had been agreed (Laffin, 2007a, 2007b). One issue for Labour during these coalitions was that Liberal Democrat backbenchers in the Scottish parliament occasionally rebelled against the coalition and its Liberal Democrat ministers. Such rebellions helped ensure that the Liberal Democrats kept a separate identity from Labour during these coalitions. They also occasionally helped deliver policy outcomes; free care for the elderly was delivered after Liberal Democrats made clear they were willing to vote against Labour on the issue.

In Wales, Liberal Democrat participation in coalition only happened in 2000 after Labour's first attempt to govern as a minority failed. This coalition lasted until Labour assumed office on its own in the aftermath of the 2003 election. As in Scotland, the Liberal Democrats are perceived to have done well in their brief period in Welsh office; analysts agree that Labour conceded to almost every Liberal Democrat demand (Deacon, 2007; Laffin, 2007a). Despite only being in government briefly in Wales, participation in both devolved administrations was widely seen as having enhanced the party's credibility (Holmes, A., 2007; Laffin, 2007a).

The party agreed a controversial coalition with the Conservative Party in the aftermath of the 2010 Westminster election. The leadership-led shift towards cutting the state, discussed above, ensured there were potential areas of overlap with the Conservatives. A couple of other points are pertinent. In parliamentary votes, the Liberal Democrats had increasingly voted with the Conservatives from 2001 onwards. By the end of the 2001 parliament, the Liberal Democrats were more than twice as likely to vote with the Conservatives as they had been in 1997. While this was not necessarily because the party agreed with the Conservatives, Cowley and Stuart (2008b) nevertheless observe that such parliamentary behaviour seemed 'a long way from any stance of equidistance'. Moreover, the party believed that had it not agreed a coalition, a second general election was only a matter of time. In addition to having little money to contest such an election, it feared being blamed for the failure to form a stable government and consequently punished heavily at the ballot box. It also felt pressured by the financial markets (Laws, 2010). Finally, having argued in the past for coalitions as a better form of government, it was felt that this would make it extremely difficult to plausibly defend failing to take part if a coalition could be agreed (Grayson, 2010).

A coalition was the Liberal Democrats' priority, with a looser arrangement giving the Conservatives parliamentary support always seen as second best. The party's Scottish experience fed into its approach to coalition negotiations with intra-party discussions about the party's negotiating position beginning well in advance of the election (Laws, 2010). Parliamentary arithmetic meant that the only possible majority coalition was with the Conservatives. While the Conservative–Liberal Democrat negotiations appear to have been conducted in good faith, Liberal Democrat perceptions were that Labour did not seriously want an agreement (Laws, 2010). The end result was a coalition agreement which contained 434 pledges. Liberal Democrat parliamentarians and Federal Executive voted overwhelmingly for the coalition agreement (Laws, 2010, p. 198). There have been various estimates of which party did best out of the negotiations. One early account suggests that 164 of these pledges originated in either the Liberal Democrat or both parties' manifestos (Norton, 2011, p. 256). *The Guardian* newspaper has tracked the coalition pledges comprehensively. Its data (available at www.guardian.co.uk) showed that 82 (or 19 per cent) of the pledges originated from the Liberal Democrat manifesto, 183 (42 per cent) originated from the Conservative manifesto, while 66 (15 per cent) came from both manifestos. A further 102 (24 per cent) originated in neither party's manifesto. There appeared to be some notable 'wins' for the Liberal Democrats. These included, for example, commitments to fixed-term parliaments, a referendum on changing the Westminster electoral system to the Alternative Vote, several civil liberties measures, and the raising of the tax threshold to £10,000.

Many were however at best mixed wins, and seemed to fall short of what the party was aiming for. The Liberal Democrats' favoured electoral system is the more proportional Single Transferable Vote (STV), not the majoritarian Alternative Vote (AV), and the referendum on changing the electoral system to AV was lost in May 2011 by a considerable margin. Raising the tax threshold was to be phased in gradually over the whole parliament, instead of immediately. Moreover, the party abandoned its more measured approach to cutting the deficit, signing up instead to the more aggressive approach favoured by the Conservatives. Most notable was the party's volte-face on university tuition fees, for which it has suffered considerable criticism. It is therefore hard to disagree with Russell's (2010, p. 516) observation that 'it is tempting to see that the actions of the coalition government have leant much more heavily on the Conservatives than on Liberal Democrats' policy arenas'.

The Liberal Democrat leadership calculated that it had to see the coalition agreement through to the end of the parliament. It is clear that there was considerable disquiet at some of the measures Liberal Democrats were being asked to support. Business secretary Vince Cable was openly critical about issues such as the government's immigration policy, while senior party figures such as Shirley Williams and Lord Oakeshott have spoken out against Conservative-led government health and banking reforms. Others have pointed to the coalition agreement being 'woefully inadequate' in many areas (Grayson, 2010, p. 12), while conference defeated the party leadership in its support for Conservative-driven NHS reforms in March 2011. Some suggest that the Liberal Democrats have somehow tempered the Conservatives' policy ambitions. Given the many radical reforms to the state the Conservatives have embarked upon, it is far from clear that this has been the case. The Liberal Democrats have therefore suffered accordingly at the polls for their participation in government with the Conservatives.

Conclusion

The history of the Liberal Democrats can be summed up as being about the search for two crucial resources in party politics: distinctiveness and credibility. The Liberal Democrats have certainly forwarded distinctive policy positions, primarily originating from the party's social liberal approach which emphasizes the pursuit of freedom through issues such as education, economic policy and the environment, but also from its efforts to defend traditional liberties. As the 'third party' in the Westminster party system, the party has regularly been subject to incursions from both Labour and the Conservatives on its territory; both parties have been associated with policy positions which overlap with traditional Liberal Democrat concerns in recent decades. The problem for the Liberal Democrats has been remaining distinctive despite being squeezed by the two main parties. Leadership has been crucial to the party in attempting to do so. Indeed, Liberal Democrat leaders from Ashdown to Clegg are regularly described as embarking on a search for a distinctive liberal agenda for the party, albeit each in their own particular way. Ashdown, in typically energetic style, ensured the survival of the party and brought it close to power with some impressive results. Kennedy also recorded record results despite his laid back style, and Clegg deployed a sharper, economic liberal edge to distinguish the party, taking it into national government for the first time in nearly a century. While the Scottish and Welsh Liberal Democrats gained respectability as parties of government in the devolved institutions, it is far from clear that the Liberal Democrats have repeated this feat at national level in coalition with the Conservatives. Russell and Fieldhouse (2005, p. 6) have argued that 'the biggest single obstacle to Liberal Democrat success is electoral credibility … Credibility is … the key to third and minor party success.' The Liberal Democrats steadily built such electoral credibility. The difficulty for the party has been maintaining that credibility as the junior party in a coalition government alongside a Conservative-led attempt to cut back public services and the state, things which many Liberal Democrat voters, representatives and members hold dear. Survival as a party under Ashdown may have been the party's greatest challenge. It is surely not overstating matters to suggest that maintaining credibility in the challenging circumstances the party found itself in post-2010 was a challenge of no less magnitude.

6

Beyond the Mainstream

Although small parties have not historically been seen as significant actors in the UK, recent years have been marked by a rise in the number of small parties both seeking election and winning office at various levels (Copus et al., 2009; Rasmussen, 1991). In early 2011, a total of 382 so-called 'political parties' were registered with the Electoral Commission. Moreover, an increasing number of voters are casting a vote for such minor parties. In the 2005 general election, minor party candidates, excluding the Nationalist parties, secured over one and a quarter million votes in Britain, a 4.6 per cent vote share which represented an increase of 1.5 per cent on 2001 (Butler and Kavanagh, 2002; Kavanagh and Butler, 2005). In 2010, this continued to rise, small parties achieving almost 1.9m votes, and a vote share of around 6.4 per cent (Kavanagh and Cowley, 2010). Small parties often achieve more spectacular results outside Westminster elections. In the 2007 and 2008 English local elections, small parties and non-partisan candidates achieved around 10 per cent of the vote and in 2009 votes for non-mainstream candidates increased to around 18 per cent. In the 2009 European Parliament elections, small parties received around 6 million votes; a 39.8 per cent vote share and an increase of around 6 per cent on the previous 2004 European elections.

Consequently, some small parties have become noteworthy actors with the Green Party, the UK Independence Party (UKIP) and the British National Party (BNP) achieving representation in the European Parliament, and the Greens, Respect and the BNP also winning seats in local government and contesting parliamentary seats. This chapter therefore examines the role of small parties in the UK. Discussion proceeds in two main parts. The first section introduces some of the key small parties active in British politics. These include the Green Party, UKIP, the BNP and Respect. Their ideological and policy positions are set out, their electoral record tracked over time and challenges facing individual parties identified. The second section assesses the systemic impact of such minor parties upon British party competition, and the collective challenges they face. Minor parties often enable new political issues to be highlighted, while also offering alternative means through which people can participate in politics. Such a role in part depends upon the perceived failure of the mainstream parties to represent particular policy issues and interests. Small party success often also depends upon their ability to utilize so-called 'second-order' elections as an avenue for protest and the extent to which the mainstream parties react to the new issues raised by the minor parties. This second section therefore critically assesses the complex interplay between minor parties and political participation, the competitive relationship between the minor parties themselves, and the ability of the major parties to co-opt, poach, and adapt to the new issues raised by their smaller competitors.

Small Parties in the UK

A major difficulty facing any analysis of small party politics is definitional. How can small parties be identified and defined? This is not as easy as it seems, and there are numerous ways of doing so. One solution is to set a threshold, with parties falling below that being classified as small. Mair (1991) suggests a threshold of 15 per cent. However, this is problematic with a party like UKIP, which has no representation in the House of Commons yet achieved 16.5 per cent in the 2009 European elections. The Scottish National Party (SNP), Plaid Cymru (PC) and the Northern Irish parties may also be small parties viewed from a Westminster perspective (Webb, 2005). However, they are major parties in each of the devolved political systems and cannot be considered small parties in those party systems, nor in the UK as a whole. Consequently, they are discussed in Chapter 7. Setting a threshold also involves thinking about setting a lower barrier to inclusion. This is necessary to exclude the purely ephemeral groups – most of the 382 parties registered with the Electoral Commission – that register as parties yet achieve little electorally. Mair (1991) sets this at 1 per cent of the national vote. Inevitably the decision involves a degree of arbitrariness. In the discussion that follows, the parties discussed are those parties, outside the three mainstream parties, that either have representation in the European Parliament, or have otherwise achieved significant levels of representation in local government. These include UKIP, the Greens, the BNP, and Respect. Each has to some degree impacted on party competition in their political environment in recent years.

UKIP

The United Kingdom Independence Party (UKIP) claims to be Britain's fourth largest political party. UKIP was formed in late 1994. The impetus for the party came from members of the Anti-Federalist League, a cross-party group opposed to increasing levels of European integration. UKIP's central issue is opposition to the European Union (EU). It is placed on the right and the party's ideological core revolves around nationalism, free-market economics and populist anti-establishment beliefs (Abedi and Lundberg, 2009). UKIP argues primarily for the withdrawal of the UK from the EU, claiming, in the 2009 European elections, that EU member-ship is anti-democratic, costs the UK £40 million per day, impinges upon parliamentary sovereignty and means that the UK cannot follow its own policy priorities. Under UKIP, a 'free, democratic, independent Britain' would replace EU membership with free trade and co-operation agree-ments with other countries and re-emphasize links with the Commonwealth. The party would freeze immigration, deport illegal immigrants and permit immigration only from those needed for the British economy. Economically, the party argues for cutting corporation taxes, introducing flat-rate taxes starting at £10,000, encouraging UK manufacturers to trade globally, and opening UK farmers to fair compe-tition. In public services, the NHS and pensions would be paid for through insurance schemes, while police, schools and hospitals would be under local control. The party would also promote the use of referenda at local and national levels.

UKIP has experienced its greatest level of success in European Parliament elections. Table 6.1 documents how the party's vote and representation has grown in European elections. Both 1999 and 2004 were threshold elections for the party, winning three seats in 1999 and increasing this fourfold to 12 in 2004. While the number of votes cast for the party was slightly down in 2009, UKIP nevertheless consolidated its

Table 6.1   UKIP European election results

Year	Number of votes	Vote share (%)	Number of MEPs
1994	150,000	1	0
1999	696,000	7	3
2004	2,661,000	16	12
2009	2,498,000	16.5	13

Sources: Data from Tetteh, 2008; Mellows-Facer et al., 2009.

vote share and added an additional MEP to its European representation. From 2009, UKIP sits in the Europe of Freedom and Democracy group in the European Parliament. The European focus and the proportional electoral system used for European elections undoubtedly benefits UKIP. It has had less success in Westminster elections, achieving only 3.1 per cent in 2010. There, the issues are less favourable and the first-past-the-post electoral system is a considerable obstacle for non-mainstream parties. Little comprehensive data is available on who votes for UKIP. The few studies that exist suggest that UKIP voters come from areas with lower levels of both educational attainment and ethnic minorities, and higher levels of older people. UKIP is likely to draw support from more affluent workers in these areas than the more working-class oriented BNP, and also has the potential to appeal to discontented Conservative voters (Borisyuk et al., 2007; John and Margetts, 2009).

UKIP faces a number of challenges. Abedi and Lundberg (2009) observe that success often leads to organizational difficulties within UKIP. In 2004, the party made a considerable leap forward partly because it had a well-known, outspoken former TV presenter – Robert Kilroy-Silk – among its candidates. This helped to communicate its anti-EU, anti-establishment message to a broader audience. Post-election, Kilroy-Silk made a bid for the party leadership. He was rebuffed by UKIP members and left to found his own short-lived party, Veritas. Similar organizational difficulties followed in 2009: then party leader Nigel Farage stood down to unsuccessfully contest the seat of the Leader of the House of Commons in the 2010 general election, while internal conflict at senior levels also led to the party treasurer standing down. Farage's successor as leader, Lord Pearson, proved short-lived, resigning nine months into his leadership, being once again replaced by Farage in late 2010. Secondly, despite having UK in its title, the party needs to appeal beyond its core English electorate. The party has no Scottish representation and policies aimed at replacing Scottish parliament, Welsh and Northern Irish assembly MSPs/AMs/MLAs with MPs are unlikely to win the party favour outside England. Finally, UKIP have a strategic problem in that their main issue – Europe – is not a major issue at Westminster elections. Consequently, voters are more likely to turn to the Conservatives, who also have Eurosceptic views, but are much more likely to form the government. Abedi and Lundberg (2009) suggest that UKIP's efforts to broaden their policy agenda should help the party. In general elections, however, UKIP tends to be noteworthy more for its general anti-political establishment stance than for its policy initiatives.

Respect

According to Denver and Bochel (1994, p. 403) 'flash parties experience rapid rises in support followed by rapid declines'. Respect are a good recent example of a 'flash party' in British politics. Respect emerged in 2004 out of the anti-Iraq war movement (Galloway, 2005, ch. 11). Respect was a coalition of disparate elements. As if to underline this, the party's subtitle was 'The Unity Coalition'. In addition to its peace wing, there were three other identifiable strands to the party. These included a spectrum of active Muslim political opinion, ranging from the moderate to the highly radical, and activists from a range of far-left organizations. Added to this, and using his considerable political entrepreneurial skills to advance Respect's prospects, was the party's best known figure, former Labour MP George Galloway. Respect's ideological approach was rooted in far-left politics. The party favoured the extension of public ownership across large sections of the economy, including public utilities such as water, gas, the railways, electricity and the North Sea oil industry. The party was for a substantial increase in corporate taxation to fund public services, and aimed to deal with issues such as discrimination, poverty and the dispossessed. Internationally, Respect was both anti-EU and anti-globalization, seeing both as exploiting the working classes while also lacking democracy (Clark et al., 2008).

For a small, newly formed party, Respect had considerable initial levels of success. George Galloway was elected to Parliament for Respect in the 2005 General Election after an intensive local anti-establishment campaign against the incumbent Labour MP in Bethnal Green and Bow in London. Although the party only averaged 6.9 per cent in the constituencies where it stood, other Respect candidates also polled well with some achieving upwards of 17 per cent of the vote (Webb, 2005, pp. 769–70). The party also had success in local government in inner cities, most notably in Tower Hamlets in East London where it won 12 seats and became the official opposition in the 2006 council elections. The party was particularly effective at appealing to Muslim sentiment. In this sense, Briggs (2007, p. 95) argued that Respect had been 'more skilful than Labour at navigating and working community dynamics to its own political ends'. An analysis of voting for small parties at the height of Respect's success indicated that higher levels of support for the party were drawn from areas with larger proportions of both religious minorities and the economically deprived (Borisyuk et al., 2007; Webb, 2005, pp. 769–70).

Such levels of success led to severe intra-party conflict over the direction of the party. This suggested that there were limits to the party's populist approach towards campaigning (Clark et al., 2008). Tensions between the radical left, Muslim activists and George Galloway came to a head in late 2007 when Respect: The Unity Coalition split. This split impacted not only on the party's leadership, but was felt all the way through the party in its local organizations and also splitting the party's representatives in council chambers. A central difficulty for Respect was that the issue which it rose to prominence on, anti-Labour sentiment drawn from the anti-war movement, is no longer as salient. Combined, these factors mean that Respect has struggled to survive as a party and, at best, is likely to be confined to the left-wing margins of British politics.

The Green Party

The UK has three separate Green Party organizations, one for England and Wales, and one each in Scotland and Northern Ireland. The Green Party of England and Wales began life in 1973 known as 'People', before changing its name in 1975 to the Ecology Party and in 1985 to the Green Party. The Scottish Greens also trace their development to the late 1970s (Bennie, 2004, ch. 2), while the Northern Irish Greens began to develop in the 1980s. The primary aim of the Green Party is the promotion of policies intended to deal with environmental degradation. A key difficulty for all Green parties however is the danger of being portrayed as a single issue party, only interested in environmental issues often at the expense of current economic practices. While the party had a relatively narrow 'ecological' focus in its early years, the Greens have more recently made efforts to avoid the 'single-issue' trap by stressing that this is a false choice and that environmental protection is perfectly compatible with economic growth. As Carter (2008, p. 234) notes, the Greens have now developed a broadly left-libertarian policy profile which combines environmental policies with themes such as social justice, equality, public services, and international co-operation. In particular, in its 2009 European election campaign it proposed a 'Green New Deal' which sought to create one million jobs through investment in renewable energy, housing, transport and social care.

Table 6.2 outlines Green performance in Westminster, European and Scottish parliament elections. At Westminster, the Greens have struggled to make an impact achieving at best just over 1 per cent of the national vote in 2005. Although the party does not have the organization that would allow it to contest all constituencies, the number of Green candidates has increased from 95 in 1997 to 335 in 2010. Where they stood, Green candidates also steadily increased the party's average vote share in those

Table 6.2   Green Party electoral performance

Westminster	Share of vote (%)	European Parliament	Share of vote (%)	Scottish Parliament	Share of vote (%)
1974 (F)	0.01	1979	3.7	1999	3.6
1974 (O)	0.01	1984	2.6	2003	6.9
1979	0.13	1989	14.9	2007	4.0
1983	0.18	1994	3.2	2011	4.4
1987	0.30	1999	6.3		
1992	0.56	2004	6.1		
1997	0.23	2009	8.6		
2001	0.72				
2005	1.04				
2010	1.00				

Note: Vote share for the Scottish parliament relates to regional list seats, since the Greens do not contest constituency seats in the Scottish electoral system.
Sources: Data from Carter, 2008; Tetteh, 2008; Kavanagh and Cowley, 2010.

constituencies between 1997 and 2005 from 1.4 per cent to 3.4 per cent, although this fell back to 1.8 per cent in 2010 (Birch, 2009; Carter, 2008; Kavanagh and Cowley, 2010). In some constituencies Green candidates perform very well, particularly where the party has some local representation already. Thus, in 2005, the Green candidate in Brighton Pavilion achieved 22 per cent of the constituency vote partly because of his service as a local councillor. In 2010, party leader Caroline Lucas became the party's first MP by building on this to achieve 31.3 per cent of the vote in Brighton Pavilion. The Greens have also had impressive performances in elections to other institutions. The party's most spectacular European result was 14.9 per cent in the 1989 European parliament contest at a time of heightened concern about the environment, although the Greens failed to have an MEP elected under the first-past-the-post electoral rules used at the time. The move to proportional representation in European elections from 1999 onwards enabled the Greens to convert their steadily rising support into seats with two MEPs elected in each election from 1999. The party has also achieved some success in the proportional regional list element of the Scottish parliament, electing as many as seven MSPs in 2003 although this fell back to two in both 2007 and 2011. The Greens also had six members elected to the London Assembly in 2008, representation on 42 councils across England and Wales in 2010 and became the largest group on Brighton and Hove council in 2011.

While Green votes are often cast out of expressive motives, the party's electorate is typically drawn from young, well-educated voters, who often work in the public sector, are concerned about post-material issues and also on the left of the political spectrum. Birch (2009) argues that the party has a considerable pool of potential support amongst those who vote for other parties that it may be able to draw upon as it develops. This latent support is mainly among well-educated and centre-left voters who have not yet voted Green. The key challenges for the Greens are twofold. First, having won a Westminster seat, the party will have to balance the tension between remaining true to its principles while also trying to advance electorally in such a way that does not frighten the party's potential pool of voters. The 2008 decision to elect a leader to replace the previous 'collective leadership' arrangements represents one organizational step in such a direction. Second, the environment is seldom a key election issue even if the mainstream parties do compete on environmental matters between elections. The Green Party therefore needs to find a way of making its voice heard effectively in order to highlight its policies and unique approach to politics. Its Westminster seat certainly helps in raising the party's profile. At the same time it must try to avoid its policies being copied by the party's mainstream competitors.

The British National Party

A considerable amount has been written about the British National Party (BNP) in recent years (for instance: Copsey, 2008; Copsey and Macklin, 2011; Eatwell and Goodwin, 2010; Goodwin, 2011). The BNP was founded in 1982 as the result of splits in an earlier far-right movement, the National Front. The BNP is regularly described as being on the far or extreme right and has been identified as evolving from both Nazi and Fascist tendencies (Carter, 2005, p. 51; Copsey, 2007; Eatwell, 2000; Renton, 2005, p. 34). Fascism and Nazism are however catch-all terms comprised of different elements and consequently disagreggation of what the party stands for is required. First, the BNP emphasizes British nationalism and race as key issues. This nationalism is exclusionary. The party campaigns for 'rights for Whites' and sees the British people as being exploited by immigrants, asylum seekers and foreigners (BNP, 2005; Eatwell, 2000, p.184; Hainsworth, 2000, p. 11). Asylum seekers are 'bogus' and the party favours deporting illegal immigrants and asylum seekers (BNP, 2005, p. 14). It argues for 'voluntary resettlement' where legal immigrants will be given 'generous financial incentives' to leave Britain. Second, the party is highly authoritarian. It demands a stronger police force and the reintroduction of both corporal and capital punishment for certain offences. It favours strong leadership and government and wants the Prime Minister to be elected for an indefinite period. Third, in economic policy, the BNP's approach derives from left- not right-wing economics. Protecting disadvantaged British workers is a key theme. The party argues for worker shareholder and co-operative schemes, and would prioritize British citizens' welfare claims over those from immigrant groups. It is also anti-globalization, argues for greater British self-sufficiency and is in favour of withdrawing from the EU.

While the BNP's left-wing economic approach renders the common description of the party being on the extreme right at least partially problematic, its appeal nevertheless appeared to be effective. For many years it was confined to the electoral sidelines. The party has never won a Westminster seat, and averaged around 4 per cent in the 2005 and 2010 elections. It nevertheless performed well in certain seats, with its best result being 16.9 per cent in Barking in 2005. The party has achieved more than 10 per cent of the vote in three constituencies in each of the three general elections held between 2001 and 2010. These results have been built through efforts at local level to adopt a populist 'community politics' approach which sees the party gaining support through local activity (Clark et al., 2008; Copsey, 2008, chs 6–7). Indeed, the seemingly banal nature of much of this local activity legitimizes voting for the BNP in the eyes of some voters (Rhodes, 2009). Consequently, the BNP experienced some success in local government. It formed the official opposition in Barking and Dagenham council after the 2006 elections and in 2008 had 58 councillors in England and a representative in the London Assembly (Wilks-Heeg, 2009). The BNP made a further major breakthrough by having two MEPs elected in the 2009 European parliament election. BNP support tends to be concentrated in post-industrial areas of North West England, Yorkshire, the West Midlands and parts of London. BNP voting is closely correlated with low formal educational qualifications, larger proportions of manual workers and low status employees, and in the North and Midlands, larger non-white and Asian populations (Borisyuk et al., 2007). Some studies suggest that the party has broader levels of latent support than those who have actually cast a vote for it (Ford, 2010; John and Margetts, 2009).

The BNP nevertheless faces a number of challenges. First, the BNP's approach achieved success, but its anti-establishment 'outsider' rhetoric has been difficult to maintain when the party has seats in the European parliament and English councils. This put the party under a greater level of scrutiny, particularly in relation to its attitudes towards race. Many of the party's policy positions have been unrealistic and its MEPs and councillors unlikely to be able to deliver the policies that voters elected them on (Clark et al., 2008). This risks alienating those who have already voted for the party in the longer term. Indeed, the BNP performed poorly in the 2010 local elections, losing all its seats on Barking and Dagenham council. Its results were also poor in the 2011 local elections. Second, its, as yet unfulfilled challenge, has been to start converting its latent support into votes if the party is to regain any momentum, appealing to more affluent and higher-status workers without alienating its core vote in the North, the Midlands and London. Third, a further electoral breakthrough for the BNP would be to win a Westminster seat. Nevertheless, it is still some way from this and the main parties have campaigned vigorously to prevent the BNP from doing so. The electoral system also poses a considerable hurdle for the BNP. Finally, the BNP has regularly suffered from bouts of severe internal conflict which limit its appeal. For instance, party leader Nick Griffin only narrowly survived a leadership challenge in July 2011. While some authors have suggested that the BNP presented a considerable threat to mainstream British politics (John and Margetts, 2009; Wilks-Heeg, 2009), developments post-2009 have, on the contrary, suggested that the BNP may be in decline as an electoral force.

Explaining the Rise of Small Parties in the UK

Implicit in many theoretical discussions about small parties is the idea that they contribute in a variety of ways to the conduct of democratic politics. Copus et al. (2008, p. 254) suggest that small parties 'provide new channels of citizen engagement, political activism, participation and new avenues for political accountability'. Such a discussion is intimately entwined with examining why small parties have experienced some success in the first place. A number of factors have been suggested to explain the rise of small parties in advanced democracies. Earlier chapters have noted how attachment to mainstream British parties amongst voters is declining. This process of dealignment has been evident from the early 1970s and is the key backdrop against which small parties have achieved some success. Indeed, the vote for non-mainstream party options, often just referred to collectively as 'others', have increased in general elections from 1.5 per cent in 1970 to 6.4 per cent in 2010 as mainstream party support has gradually declined. Weakening loyalties mean that voters are often now more willing to cast a vote for small parties, or even not turn out to vote at all.

A second potential explanation has also been encountered previously. This is the failure of mainstream parties to represent certain issues important to voters. In other words, the mainstream parties have been decreasingly able to aggregate and articulate interests from certain sectors of the electorate. As outlined in Chapter 2, there are three key ideas here. The first relates to the rational choice arguments of Downs (1957) about party competition. In short, it is rational for mainstream parties to follow centrist policies since this is where most voters are clustered. Following from this, mainstream parties compete around a relatively narrow policy framework, acting almost like a cartel and actually choosing not to compete on some issues (Blyth and Katz, 2005; Katz and Mair, 1995). Finally, changing values have broadened the range of political issues of salience to voters. A key divide that cuts across left–right issues is that between material and post-material politics (Inglehart, 1990a, 1990b). While this certainly provides opportunities for mainstream parties (Kitschelt, 1994), the concentration of mainstream parties in a centrist position also provides small parties with the space on both left–right and material–post-material issues to articulate a distinctive policy position.

This suggests that the key small parties will have distinctive policy platforms that they are able to articulate in such a way as to distinguish themselves from their mainstream counterparts. Indeed, Herzog (1987, p. 318) argues that small parties play a role in setting the boundaries of political debate. There are few assessments of British small parties' policy placement on either the left–right or material–post-material spectra. Nevertheless, it is possible to draw some conclusions about the contribution of small parties to political and policy debate in the UK. Each of the small parties outlined above has a distinctive ideological and policy approach which draws upon the material–post-material divide. While the environment is perhaps the post-material issue *par excellence*, the Greens also draw heavily upon other 'quality of life' issues such as equality and social justice that are equally important to those with such 'post-material' values. This is a distinctive agenda which differentiates the Greens from the mainstream parties who only address such issues to a limited extent (Carter, 2006). By contrast, the BNP's concern with the rights of the supposedly indigenous British, the protection of British jobs and welfare, repatriation of immigrants and arguments for authoritarian policy measures are all classic materialist issues.

Material–post-material issues are sometimes combined with the left–right spectrum in unique ways in small parties' policy platforms. In articulating populist anti-war sentiments, environmental, and multicultural issues, Respect drew upon strands of thinking which have been key post-material issues. However, parts of Respect's programme of economic renationalization also came from the far-left and had considerable elements of economic authoritarianism, while its concern for the dispossessed was a classic materialist concern (Clark et al., 2008). UKIP by contrast have taken a distinctive right-wing approach to economics which distinguishes them from the main parties and also from the anti-EU BNP. Small parties therefore can and do introduce a range of issues which sets them apart from the main parties.

Some have pointed to the role of the minor parties and their leaderships in spotting an electoral opportunity and weighing the costs and benefits of standing for election (Hug, 2000; Katz and Mair, 1995; Pedersen, 1982; Tavits, 2006). Some argue that a key point in this is understanding what motivates a small party to form in the first place (Hug, 2000; Pedersen, 1982). Nevertheless, many so-called 'political parties' form, but few experience the levels of success achieved by the small parties discussed above. It is therefore more important to explain why some succeed in getting their voice heard in the crowded political arena. One common factor partially explaining the appeal of UKIP, the BNP and Respect has been their ability to deploy a 'populist' approach towards politics which resonates with anti-politics and anti-party sentiments amongst voters. A number of attempts have been made to outline the characteristics of populism (Abts and Rummens, 2007; Taggart, 2000). There are four key elements. First, central to populism is an antagonistic relationship between the 'people' and the 'elite'. Second, populism claims to be able to give power back to the people and restore 'popular sovereignty'. Third, populism conceptualizes the people as a homogeneous body. In this conception, the key analytical units are the 'people' and the 'elite', with the people's interests in some way or another harmed by the decisions of the governing elites. Fourth, Schedler (1996, p. 294) adds a further element, the 'populist' or 'anti-establishment' party. The populist or anti-establishment party aligns itself with the people or citizens against the political class which sits above them making what are perceived to be decisions going against the 'common sense' wisdom of the people.

Populist parties portray themselves as being 'victims' of a political system that does not address the political needs of ordinary people (Schedler, 1996: p. 300). Much work on populism has concentrated on small and radical European parties. These dynamics are also evident in the UK. George Galloway's expulsion from the Labour Party and the ignoring of the anti-war movement that Respect grew out of, combined with the BNP being accused of inciting racial hatred are each good examples where this perception of victimhood is exploited by small parties. Similarly,

Abedi and Lundberg (2009, p. 76) observe that, in relation to the EU and other constitutional matters, 'UKIP constantly invokes populist appeals to show how it stands up for "the people's" interests while the other parties support the same old status quo'. All three parties' election literature is replete with populist references to the failings of the British political class (Abedi and Lundberg, 2009; Clark et al., 2008). Importantly, populist approaches are compatible with either radical right, or left, ideology. The paradigmatic cases set out by Abts and Rummens (2007, p. 409) could almost be modelled on the BNP and Respect. The BNP uses ethnicity and nationalism to identify the people it claims to represent, while Respect did the same with the 'disenfranchised and dispossessed' (Respect, 2006, p. 4). In Mudde's (2007, pp. 48–9, 308) terms, Respect would be classed as 'social populists' combining socialism and populism, whereas the BNP would be placed on the populist radical right.

The populist approach has not, however, been the only template for small party success in the UK. By contrast, the Greens have been able to sustain and improve upon their levels of success without such populist tactics. Although the Greens may benefit from anti-establishment sentiments amongst voters, Birch (2009, p. 54) argues that Green support has gradually built up because of a greater awareness of environmental issues and more favourable opinions of the party amongst voters than exist for the other small parties.

Proportional representation electoral systems are commonly perceived to be more conducive to small party success than the first-past-the-post system used for Westminster (Harmel and Roberston, 1985). Related to this, small parties are often more successful in what are known as 'second-order' elections (Reif and Schmitt, 1980). These are elections which are not for a country's national parliament, Westminster in the UK case, but to institutions perceived to have less power such as the European Parliament and local government. Such 'second-order' elections tend to be marked by declining support of major parties, low turnout and an increased level of votes for small parties. Indeed, as Tables 6.1 and 6.2 above demonstrate, both UKIP and the Greens have had success in European elections held under proportional rules, while the Greens have also been successful under the Scottish Parliament's proportional regional list element of the electoral system. Similarly, the BNP succeeded in 2009 in having two MEPs elected under proportional rules to the European Parliament. The Labour Party's creation of new institutions since 1997 has also been helpful to small parties, leading to new opportunities for them to be elected. The Scottish parliament has already been noted, but the London Assembly and the eleven directly elected mayors across England have also seen non-mainstream candidates achieve some success.

The relationship between electoral systems and small party success is not quite as straightforward as this might seem however. Proportional electoral systems have thresholds of support which parties must pass before they can be elected. These thresholds can be either formal, where a party has to achieve a certain proportion of the vote to win seats, or informal, resulting from the specific features of the electoral system in use and the turnout in the area concerned. Thus, in 2004 the BNP were confident of winning a European seat in the North West region of England. The party polled around 135,000 votes and 6.4 per cent of the vote yet failed in their ambition. In 2009, the BNP polled fewer votes, around 132,000 in the North West. This represented a share of 8 per cent, and party leader Nick Griffin was elected as an MEP. A similar dynamic also led to the BNP winning a European seat in Yorkshire and the Humber region in 2009.

First-past-the-post electoral systems have not always proved the insurmountable handicap to small parties that some suggest. If a small party can muster enough geographically concentrated support, then they can do well. The examples of Respect's George Galloway winning a parliamentary seat in 2005, and three separate Independent candidates also winning Westminster seats between 1997 and 2010, underline this even if such parliamentary success is notable because it is extremely rare. First-past-the-post is less of a hurdle at local government level. Electorates in local council wards are smaller than those found in parliamentary constituencies. Small parties therefore need far less support in local elections to gain representation. Although they still face the considerable difficulty of overcoming opposition from mainstream party candidates, recent experience has demonstrated that it can nevertheless be possible for small parties to win seats regularly under first-past-the-post rules in local elections (Copus et al., 2008). Indeed, Respect, the BNP, and the Greens have all adopted 'community politics' approaches in an attempt to increase their representation in local government and use that as a springboard to contest parliamentary seats (Birch, 2009; Clark et al., 2008; Wilks-Heeg, 2009). UKIP have also shown signs of adopting such an approach, albeit to a lesser extent.

Problems Maintaining Small Party Success

The idea that small parties go through a lifespan of growth and decline has been central to the study of such parties (Müller-Rommel, 1991;

Pedersen, 1982). With the exception of Deschouwer's (2008) model of small parties in government in Europe, the general assumption in such debates is that small parties will ultimately decline. Small parties face a range of challenges that can make consolidating their position difficult. While some of the party-specific challenges are mentioned above, there are a number of more generic challenges faced by all small parties.

That small parties often raise distinctive policy issues has already been demonstrated. What can be decisive is the interaction between the mainstream and small parties. Small parties are particularly vulnerable to some of their ideas and policies being copied by mainstream parties. As Copus et al. (2009, p. 12) note, issues raised by small parties can cause 'introspective policy reassessment by the main parties, seeking to address the issues raised, and to reassure the voters that their concerns are recognised, that they need not support the small party'. For example, Carter (2006, pp. 752–3) highlights the role of the Green Party achieving 14.9 per cent in the 1989 European elections in forcing all the mainstream parties to 'scramble onto the environmental bandwagon'. Similarly, in the 2005 general election a key policy emphasis for the Conservative Party was to argue for restricting immigration and asylum. This was the most important issue for Conservative voters and the issue had risen in salience since the previous election in 2001. UKIP's success in the 2004 European elections, on an anti-immigration platform, highlighted the threat that UKIP posed to the core Conservative vote. Indeed, where UKIP does well, the Conservatives have been the most likely to suffer (Curtice et al., 2005, p. 246). Cowley and Green (2005, p. 62) therefore indicate that the Conservatives' adoption of strong immigration and asylum policies was designed with one key aim in mind: to stem the challenge that UKIP posed to the Conservative vote. The Conservatives have also actively campaigned in some areas of BNP strength on the issue of immigration and asylum (Renton, 2005, p. 35).

There are a number of conditions under which the so-called 'poaching' by mainstream parties of small parties' policies takes place. First, the policy area has to have some degree of broader *salience* with the wider electorate than the relatively small number of people who vote for small parties. Cowley and Green (2005, p. 64) demonstrate how immigration and asylum rose from being an issue of minor importance in 1997 to becoming an issue viewed as more important than education and almost as important as health by 2005. Second, small parties need to have achieved some degree of *success* with the issue, thereby demonstrating its electoral appeal. Thus, in the examples given above, the Greens, UKIP and the BNP had all been able to achieve some degree of electoral success, whether at local or European levels, which made the main parties take notice of the issue they were reacting to. Third, the mainstream parties must see the issue as *a threat to their support*. Some Labour Party policy emphases have clearly seen the BNP as a threat and have been developed in an attempt to head off that threat, while the Eurosceptic UKIP presents an alternative which disillusioned Conservative voters may potentially find credible. Finally, the mainstream party must set out and *compete on these policies*. It is important to note however that mainstream parties only tend to encroach on particularly salient small party policies. While some socio-economic policies may have been adapted by Labour to target the BNP and the Respect vote, no mainstream party has adopted the anti-globalization policies that both small parties have espoused. As Carter (2006) notes, the mainstream parties are limited by their own ideologies in the extent to which they can adopt policies raised by small parties.

Another difficulty for small parties is that it is not just the mainstream parties that they are competing against; they are often competing amongst themselves. This is most apparent between parties with obvious overlapping policy ideas. For instance, while the BNP and UKIP may differ on economic policy, they nevertheless both advocate withdrawing from the EU and taking a hard line on immigration and asylum, using British symbols such as the Union Flag to underline their appeals. Both parties are competing for similar voters. Borisyuk et al. (2007) point to the social and political overlaps between UKIP and BNP supporters. Moreover, both parties' voters tend to have favourable views of each other (John et al., 2006, p. 9; John and Margetts, 2009, pp. 508–10).

There can also be interesting patterns of competition between parties which initially seem to be almost diametrically opposed. While there are many areas of considerable policy differences between the BNP and Respect, Clark et al. (2008) demonstrate how there were also some overlaps in the types of policy appeals made by both parties, particularly in relation to economic policy. Both claimed to be standing up for workers against influences such as globalization and the EU, both argued for worker involvement in the economy and for publicly funded public services. On the other hand, both parties draw strength not only from opposing the 'political classes', but also from opposing each other and the communities they claim to represent. The BNP has campaigned against local plans to build Mosques for instance, while Respect has attempted to 'fight the particular terror of the resurgence of the BNP' (Galloway, 2005, p. 206). As has happened elsewhere in Europe, competition between parties of the extreme left and right, Respect and the BNP in the British

Table 6.3   Small party membership, 2002–09

	UKIP	BNP	Greens	Respect
2002	9,000	3,487	5,268	
2003	16,000	5,737	5,858	
2004	26,000	7,916	6,281	3,751
2005	19,000	6,008	7,110	5,674
2006	16,000	6,281	7,019	5,739
2007	15,800	9,784	7,441	2,472
2008	14,600	9,801	7,553	500
2009	16,252	12,632	9,630	1,085

Source: Data from party accounts registered with the Electoral Commission, various years (http://www.electoralcommission.org.uk/), 2 March 2011.

case, has gained them support and legitimized their views in the eyes of their supporters (Clark et al., 2008; Talshir, 2005).

Whether or not small parties can follow up successes depends considerably upon whether or not the party in question can muster the resources to do so. Having members able to campaign for the party both between and during elections is a key aspect of building up a small party's vote. Discussion above has noted that the BNP, Greens and Respect have been active in community politics, often exploiting local weaknesses amongst the mainstream parties. Nevertheless, small parties' overall levels of membership are suggestive more of organizational weakness than strength. Table 6.3 tracks the memberships of the main small parties in the UK from 2002 onwards. UKIP claims the highest levels of membership, peaking at around 26,000 during the European election year of 2004, before falling to around 16,000 in 2009. Green Party membership appears to show the steadiest growth without the fluctuations evident with the other parties; Green membership has risen from around 5,250 in 2002 to around 9,600 in 2009. That Respect was essentially a 'flash party' is underlined by its membership figures, with just under 4,000 new members at the party's formation in 2004, rising to a peak of around 5,700 in 2004–2005 and falling to as low as 500 in 2008. BNP membership has fluctuated from around 3,500 in 2002 to 7,900 in 2004. This fell back to around 6,000 in 2005–06, before rising again to around 9,800 in 2007–08 and 12,600 in 2009. Respect's reports to the Electoral Commission highlight a difficulty faced by all small parties; members who join in their initial enthusiasm for the cause often let their membership lapse, whether because of poor retention efforts on the part of the party, or because the member has lost interest (Bennie, 2004; Respect, 2006, p. 3). Such low levels of membership mean that small parties are unlikely to be able to do much more than target a few constituencies with active local campaigns in general elections.

A final difficulty for small parties is the ability to raise enough money to allow them to operate effectively. Assuming a small party is formed and has some degree of success, a much bigger challenge however is to raise enough finance to allow it to consolidate its position and to continue to prosper electorally. The lack of state subsidies for political parties in the UK is a particular hindrance for a small party as they attempt to grow, not least since the requirement for candidates to pay £500 deposits to stand in general elections give small parties a considerable financial hurdle to overcome if they wish to stand a large number of candidates (Birch, 2009, pp. 66–7; Carter, 2008, p. 228). Figure 6.1 highlights the fact that the four small parties discussed have relatively small incomes with which to conduct their activities. The only small party to break the £1 million barrier between 2001–09 was UKIP with income of just over £1 million in 2001 and just over £1.7 million in the European election year of 2004. UKIP's income has fluctuated widely however, with the party surviving on just over £250,000 in 2002 and just over £600,000 in 2008. Both the BNP and the Greens demonstrate an upward trend in income from 2001. Both have also been subject to fluctuations, albeit not so sharp as those UKIP has experienced in that period. From 2004, BNP

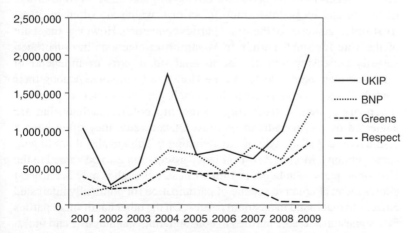

Figure 6.1   Small party income, 2001–09

Source: Data from party accounts registered with the Electoral Commission, various years (http://www.electoralcommission.org.uk/), 2 March 2011.

income varied between around £611,000 and £726,000, while Green Party income has varied from a low of around £366,000 in 2007 to a high of £546,000 in 2008. The Greens, UKIP and BNP all show steep increases in income in 2009 in the run up to European and general elections in 2009–10. Both UKIP and the BNP break the £1 million mark, with the BNP in particular having income of just under £2 million due to the level of donations almost doubling between 2008–09 and income from membership subscriptions more than tripling. Respect's income has been in sharp decline since the party's formation from just under £500,000 in 2004 to around £32,000 in 2009. Despite the increases in small party incomes in 2009, all four small parties have limited finances, certainly by comparison with their much larger mainstream competitors (see Chapter 9). This means that small parties in the UK 'usually endure a "hand-to-mouth" existence, unable to contest most seats and having little money available to fund professional marketing and campaigning activities' (Carter, 2008, p. 228).

Conclusion

Although party politics in the UK is dominated by the Conservatives, Labour and the Liberal Democrats, small parties have nevertheless become increasingly important actors in British politics in recent years. This has been most immediately obvious in so-called 'second-order' European and local government elections, which are often in effect 'first-order' contests for the small parties concerned. However, the share of the vote for small parties in Westminster elections has also been steadily increasing with the occasional small party or Independent candidate even being elected to the House of Commons. Among their contributions to party competition, small parties can act as a sort of 'boundary system' introducing issues into political debate that are neglected by the mainstream parties. Of necessity, they often have a distinctive 'populist' style of campaigning which enables them to gain some publicity. Moreover, if political participation is to be valued in the UK, small party membership, limited in size though it may be, at least allows for an alternative avenue of participation for politically interested citizens to that found in the main parties. On the other hand, small parties face some considerable hurdles to consolidating, maintaining and building upon their successes. Mainstream parties can 'poach' their policies if these policies resonate with a large enough section of the electorate. Infighting between small parties competing for similar voters can also present unwelcome competition. The small parties must also overcome the combined difficulties of the electoral system, low levels of membership and income if they are to prosper and make the breakthrough at Westminster. While some individual small parties will persist and others will decline under such circumstances, declining levels of party loyalty mean that Copus et al.'s (2009) suggestion that small parties in general are likely to have 'fluctuating fortunes but a permanent presence' in British politics is likely to be apposite for many years to come.

7

The UK's 'Multi-Level' Party Systems

Writing just after the 2004 European elections, Dunleavy (2005) criticized the Westminster focus of much debate on British party politics, arguing that this failed to take account of the increasingly complex and multi-level patterns of party competition that now occur across the UK. Indeed, Scotland, Wales and Northern Ireland have a number of different parties, which means that party competition in these regions has operated in a significantly different manner from the UK norm. This has had a varied impact upon Westminster politics over the years, with, on occasion, parties such as the Scottish National Party (SNP) and Ulster Unionist Party (UUP) holding the balance of power. Since devolution, these parties can no longer be considered 'minor' parties in the UK system, but also as significant parties operating in distinct devolved party systems. Moreover, it is not just in the devolved institutions that party competition varies from the Westminster norm, but also in competition for the London Assembly, local government and the European Parliament.

Discussion of Britain's 'multi-level' party systems is oriented around two main sections. The first introduces the distinctive parties found in Scotland, Wales and Northern Ireland, each of whom are significant actors in their own party system. In Scotland, the pro-Independence Scottish National Party (SNP) led a minority government in the Scottish Parliament from 2007, and in a stunning result in 2011, now leads a majority administration in Edinburgh. Similarly Wales has a large Nationalist party, Plaid Cymru (PC), which participated in the Welsh government alongside the Labour Party between 2007–11. Northern Ireland has a completely different party system to the rest of the UK, with the main cleavage being attitudes towards a united Ireland and union with Britain. The main parties of Northern Ireland – the Ulster Unionists (UUP), Democratic Unionist (DUP), Social Democratic and Labour Party (SDLP) and Sinn Féin – are introduced and their positions also set out. The second part places the UK's 'multi-level' party systems in theoretical and comparative perspective. Institutional change since 1999 has led to party system change in each of the devolved territories. The 'effective number of parties' (ENP) in each system is set out, and a classification made of these systems in light of the work of Sartori's (2005 [1976]) influential models of party systems.

Parties and Territorial Politics in the UK

The Scottish National Party

Formed in 1934, the SNP's core aim is to achieve Scottish independence. Brand (1978, pp. 8–18) reduces the core of Scottish nationalism to two sets of arguments: a 'spiritual' appeal based on the right of national communities to govern themselves as independent states; and a more pragmatic appeal which suggests that self-government would result in better and more responsive government. These arguments can be traced historically through intra-party disagreements between independence 'fundamentalists', an argument currently in the minority, and those who have adopted a more 'gradualist' approach, seeing independence only being achieved through gradually increasing the powers of the current devolved political structures. In attempting to achieve its aims, the party has successfully adopted a 'populist' rhetorical approach (Brand, 1978, p. 33; McEwen, 2002, p. 57) which characterizes its competitors as parties who take orders from a distant government or party machine in London (SNP, 2010).

The SNP has historically had a centre-left approach. Its conception of citizenship is inclusive, not exclusionary and, particularly from the mid-1970s, the party adopted centre-left socio-economic policies with Levy (1994, p. 158) noting the party's 'socialist orientation'. In 1999 the party asked the electorate to forego a one penny tax reduction offered by Labour nationally in order to improve public services. In 2003, although the party argued for cutting corporation tax, the argument was that this would stimulate investment, create jobs and, consequently, provide greater tax revenue to be spent on public services (SNP, 2003). More recently some indicate that an emphasis on tax-cutting measures equates to a shift to the right. Leith and Steven (2010, p. 268) suggest that this can be detected in party policy and in the pronouncements of party spokespersons. Others argue that the SNP is following neo-liberal economic policies, albeit with the aim of achieving some social democratic outcomes in the field of social policy (Cuthbert and Cuthbert, 2009; Maxwell, 2009). Lynch (2009, p. 632) suggests that rather than abandoning social democratic aims, the pragmatism necessary to challenge seriously for office means the party no longer feels the need to compete on ideological grounds. Finally, the SNP has also been consistently pro-European, as exemplified by its policy of 'independence in Europe'.

Two events heralded the SNP's breakthrough to becoming a prominent actor in Scottish politics: a shock 1967 by-election victory in Hamilton; and achieving more than 30 per cent of the Scottish vote in October 1974. From the early 1990s, the party has polled close to a fifth of the Scottish electorate in UK general elections, most recently achieving 19.9 per cent in 2010. Since devolution, the main electoral focus of the SNP has been the Scottish parliament. The party has performed considerably better in Scottish elections than in those for Westminster (Table 7.1). In the first devolved elections in 1999, it achieved 28.7 per cent in the constituency section of the Scottish parliament's mixed member proportional (MMP) electoral system and 27.3 per cent in the proportional regional list section. Under the brief leadership of John Swinney, this fell in 2003 to 23.8 per cent in the constituencies and 20.9 per cent in the regional lists. Led again by Alex Salmond from 2004, a major breakthrough came in 2007, with the SNP polling close to a third of the Scottish vote and forming a minority government in Edinburgh with one more seat than Labour. This was followed by an extraordinary result in 2011, when the SNP won an outright majority of 69 seats on around 45 per cent of the vote.

A constraint for any minority administration is that it must rely on the

Table 7.1 Scottish Parliament results, 1999–2011

	1999		2003		2007		2011	
	Share of vote %	*Seats*	*Share of vote* %	*Seats*	*Share of vote* %	*Seats*	*Share of vote* %	*Seats*
Labour	36.2	56	32.0	50	30.6	46	29.0	37
SNP	28.0	35	22.3	27	32.0	47	44.7	69
Con	15.5	18	16.1	18	15.2	17	13.2	15
Lib Dem	13.3	17	13.6	17	13.7	16	6.6	5
Other	7.0	3	16.0	17	8.4	3	12.1	3

Note: these results combine both constituency and regional list elements of the Scottish parliament electoral system.
Sources: Data from Tetteh, 2008, p. 52; Herbert et al., 2011, p. 3.

support of other parties to enact its programme. The SNP has in the past played this supporting role, its 11 MPs playing a key role in maintaining the Callaghan-led Labour government in office at Westminster until the failure of the 1978 devolution referendum and consequent withdrawal of support in the 1979 vote of no confidence. Minority governments are regularly perceived in the UK to be an unstable form of government. The 2007–11 SNP minority administration in Edinburgh nevertheless appeared relatively stable. It gained support from other parties for some of its popular proposals, such as a 'freeze' on council tax, saving some hospital emergency provision, removing tolls on the Tay and Forth Bridges and abolishing prescription charges. Particularly notable given the historical antipathy between the parties – SNP policy rules out coalition at national level with the Conservatives – has been the support of the Conservative Party for many SNP measures, including the 2008 budget. However, the SNP has been defeated by the other parties working together to oppose other measures, such as dropping a promised tram system for Edinburgh. It was also defeated on the initial 2009 budget when two Green MSPs voted against SNP proposals, the budget being passed at the second attempt after concessions to Labour and the Liberal Democrats. On other issues the SNP were also unable to get the necessary support to pass legislation; for example, the party was unable to replace the council tax with a local income tax. Nevertheless, the way in which the SNP conducted itself in office has been given as a key reason why the party was able to win by such a large margin in 2011. The SNP's extraordinary success in 2011 meant that it no longer had to compromise with other parties to get its measures through.

Importantly, between 2007–11 the SNP was unable to get its way on a referendum on Scottish independence which it had originally promised for 2010. In recent Scottish elections, the SNP has separated independence from broader questions of policy by promising a referendum after the election (Leith and Steven, 2010). Scottish public opinion has tended not to favour independence. At best, around a third consistently support independence, with only 24 per cent saying they did so around the time of the SNP's success in 2007 and 23 per cent in 2010 (Curtice and Ormston, 2011). What does have traction are arguments for more powers to the Scottish parliament. The SNP appear to have recognized this. Its so-called *National Conversation* exercise conducted during the 2007 parliament outlined, in addition to independence, a range of options to give the Scottish parliament more powers for raising revenue and deciding public spending priorities. In 2011, the SNP sought to neutralize independence as an electoral issue by promising again to hold a referendum sometime after the elections. The party's landslide performance means that such a referendum is now virtually inevitable and likely to be held sometime towards the end of the 2011–16 Scottish parliament. Given scepticism among the electorate as to the merits of independence, it appears that a multi-choice referendum will be put to voters with options for more powers for the Scottish parliament, the so-called 'devolution max' option, as well as a vote for independence.

Plaid Cymru

Plaid Cymru (PC) was formed in 1925. Its roots can be traced to cultural nationalist circles in North Wales based around the defence of the Welsh language. For much of its history, Plaid has oscillated between, on the one hand, acting as a pressure group for the defence of Welsh interests, and, on the other, as a party seeking power and influence through contesting elections (McAllister, 2001). According to a major in-depth study of Plaid, its key aim is 'a new Wales with sufficient powers and authority to make its own decisions as to political organization and economic and social priorities' (McAllister, 2001, p. 129). This is not necessarily the same as independence for Wales. While some argue the party does favour independence (Price, A. 2010), secession from the UK has been a source of some controversy within PC (McAllister, 2001, pp. 142–3) and the somewhat ambiguous formulation 'full national status for Wales within the EU' tends to be most often used to describe Plaid's position (Price, A. 2010, p. 16).

PC can be characterized as being left of centre, with diverse influences deriving from utopianism, anarcho-syndicalism, guild socialism and environmentalism. It committed itself in 1981 to policies which were 'nationalist, decentralist and socialist', and, while there was considerable debate within the party as to the merits of describing itself socialist, this description persists with Plaid adopting a position of 'community socialism' in an attempt to distinguish itself from the Welsh Labour Party while at the same time allowing it to emphasize its concern for Welsh interests (McAllister, 2001, ch. 6). Despite Elias (2009) suggesting that Plaid has moderated its ideological approach in order to become more electable, the party's position was still summarized in the 2010 election as being 'left of centre, decentralist, socialist, green, nationalist and internationalist, with a healthy dose of scepticism about free markets and globalisation' (Price, A. 2010, p. 15).

Plaid started to break out of its North Wales strongholds in 1959, gaining support in the Labour heartlands of South Wales in that year's general election. Its first MP was elected in 1966 after a high profile by-election in Carmarthen, described as a 'momentous' breakthrough which changed both internal and external perceptions of the party being a serious Welsh political actor (McAllister, 2001, pp. 114 15). This was followed with large swings from Labour to Plaid in two by-elections in 1967–8. From 1970 onwards, Plaid has contested every Welsh seat, winning three seats in the October 1974 election on 10.8 per cent of the Welsh vote. Although falling back in the 1980s, in the 1990s Plaid won four seats in both 1992 and 1997 on 9–10 per cent of the Welsh vote. More recently, Plaid achieved 12.6 per cent in 2005 and 11.3 per cent in 2010, winning three seats in both general elections.

The key catalyst for party, policy and ideological change in Plaid has been the devolution of powers to the National Assembly of Wales (NAW) (Elias, 2009; McAllister, 2001, p. 123). Like the SNP, Plaid performs better in devolved elections than in those for Westminster. Table 7.2 tracks PC's results in NAW elections between 1999–2011. The party achieved well over a quarter of the vote in both tiers of the electoral system in the first devolved elections in 1999, notably polling more than 30 per cent in the regional lists and becoming the main opposition in the NAW. It has declined somewhat since, its 21–22 per cent in 2007 winning three more seats but falling 'far short of a serious breakthrough across Wales' (Elias, 2009, p. 544). This fell further to around 19 per cent of the vote and 11 seats in 2011. Nonetheless, this is still better than the party achieves at Westminster, underlining the fact that Plaid now competes in a complex multi-level electoral environment. While it must focus its resources on devolved elections, it must also take care to avoid momentum being lost in Westminster contests.

Table 7.2   National Assembly of Wales results, 1999–2011

	1999		2003		2007		2011	
	Share of vote (%)	Seats	Share of vote (%)	Seats	Share of vote (%)	Seats	Share of vote (%)	Seats
Labour	36.5	28	38.3	30	30.9	26	39.6	30
PC	29.5	17	20.5	12	21.7	15	18.6	11
Con	16.2	9	19.5	11	21.9	12	23.8	14
Lib Dem	13.0	6	13.4	6	13.3	6	9.3	5
Other	4.9	–	8.3	1	12.2	1	14.7	0

Note: these results combine both constituency and regional list elements of the Welsh Assembly electoral system.
Source: Data from Tetteh, 2008, p. 50; www.bbc.co.uk, 9 May 2011.

Plaid's performance in 2007 was sufficient to ensure that it did make one major breakthrough. It became a party of government for the first time, agreeing a 'One Wales' grand coalition with Labour after an initial attempt to co-operate with the Liberal Democrats and Conservatives collapsed. Many of the party's manifesto commitments were included in the coalition agreement, including provisions for developing the Welsh language, and a promise to hold a referendum on further powers for the NAW. The party held three ministerial posts and had one further deputy minister. Then party leader Ieuan Wyn Jones also combined his ministerial role with that of Deputy First Minister. Elias (2009, p. 544) argues that Plaid's performance in office between 2007 and 2011 was essentially concerned with presenting itself as a serious and competent party of government, a continuation of the party's vote-seeking efforts to be seen as more acceptable to voters through policy moderation and pragmatism from 2005 onwards. This has had the consequence of neutralizing its radical image and has led to some disquiet within the party when efforts to promote Welsh culture have failed to meet expectations (Elias, 2009, p. 544). While the 'One Wales' coalition was relatively stable, tensions with the larger Labour Party were evident over issues relating to Welsh culture and schooling. Plaid Cymru has now made the transition from being a party of protest, via a period of being the main opposition in the NAW, to now holding office and defending a record in the 2011 devolved elections. Its performance depended on two things: whether it convinced its core nationalist voters that it had done its best to defend Welsh interests and develop Welsh culture; and the extent to which it received credit, or blame, more broadly for the coalition's performance in office. While the extent to which it received credit or blame is unclear, the decline in the PC vote in 2011 suggests that the party failed to convince voters that it had been able to deliver fully on some of its promises.

The Northern Irish Parties

Aside from an ill-starred electoral alliance between the Conservative Party and the Ulster Unionist Party (UUP) in the 2010 general election, the main British parties have tended not to contest elections in Northern Ireland. Instead, Northern Ireland has its own party system, where the dominant cleavage revolves around attitudes towards a united Ireland and union with Britain. Table 7.3 sets out the results for Northern Ireland Assembly elections between 1998 and 2011.

Table 7.3 Northern Ireland Assembly results, 1998–2011

	DUP		UUP		Alliance		Sinn Féin		SDLP	
	Share of vote %	Seats	Share of vote %	Seats	Share of vote %	Seats	Share of vote %	Seats	Share of vote %	Seats
1998	18.1	20	21.3	28	6.5	6	17.6	18	22	24
2003	25.6	30	22.7	27	3.7	6	23.5	24	17	18
2007	30.1	36	14.9	18	5.2	7	26.2	28	15.2	16
2011	30.0	38	13.2	16	7.7	8	26.9	29	14.2	14

Note: Vote share refers to first preference votes.
Sources: Data from www.ark.ac.uk/elections/, 25 November 2010; www.bbc.co.uk, 9 May 2011.

The Democratic Unionist Party

The Democratic Unionist Party (DUP) was formed in late 1971 out of dissatisfaction with the direction of unionist politics. The DUP has historically positioned itself as the staunchest defender of the union with Britain. This has led it to adopt an oppositional approach, opposing developments such as the 1985 Anglo Irish Agreement, and the breakthrough 1998 Good Friday Agreement (GFA). Until 2008, it was led by one of the most imposing figures in UK politics, the Rev. Ian Paisley. Accounts of party organization emphasize the leadership-dominated nature of the party, with one even referring to the DUP as 'Paisley's fan club' (Bruce, 2009, p. 104; Tonge, 2004, p. 65). Party members appear essentially loyal to the party, with activists drawn in large numbers from Paisley's Free Presbyterian church (Bruce, 2009, pp. 297–9). While Paisley stood down as leader in 2008, replaced by his former deputy, Peter Robinson, the party's coalition of support remains concentrated among what Tonge (2004, p. 61) calls urban loyalists and rural evangelists.

With the left–right cleavage virtually absent, constitutional politics has dominated DUP policy, although this is noticeably changing. The dominant issues in its 2007 Northern Ireland Assembly manifesto related to the GFA, opposition to holding office with Sinn Féin (SF) prior to SF recognizing the Police Service of Northern Ireland (PSNI), and differentiating the party from the more moderate UUP. Discussion of economic policy only begins halfway through the manifesto, with the DUP adopting a right-wing stance, arguing for lower taxes, building a competitive economy, protecting rural communities and maintaining academic selection. Where the party is interested in social policy and deprivation, this is conceived of as protecting disadvantaged unionist communities (DUP, 2007). Albeit in more moderate language, in 2010 the party still underlined its ability to block aspects important to SF, such as an Irish language act, while at the same time emphasizing unionist culture and proposing changes to how Stormont works (DUP, 2010). Sharing power with Sinn Féin from May 2007 has nevertheless led to a greater focus on 'bread and butter' economic and social policy issues. Indeed, there is little explicit mention of constitutional issues in the DUP's 2011 Assembly manifesto, which mostly emphasizes policy issues such as the economy, education, health, crime and government reform (DUP, 2011).

Electorally, the DUP overtook the UUP in the 2003 Assembly elections, cementing that result in the 2005 general election where the UUP was left with only one MP. In both the 2007 and 2011 Assembly elections, the party achieved 30 per cent of first preference votes, more than double the share of its UUP competitors. Although the 2010 general election saw party leader, Peter Robinson, lose his Westminster seat, the DUP nevertheless was post-2010 the only Northern Irish unionist party represented in the House of Commons with eight seats. The DUP held the position of Northern Irish First Minister in a power-sharing executive from May 2007 after SF agreed to support the PSNI, and continued to hold it post-2011. Mitchell et al. (2009) argue that the DUP became the largest unionist party because voters perceived it to be strongest at defending unionist interests, showing a blend of intransigence and pragmatism in its doing so. The 2011 Assembly election suggests that this approach continues to be successful and that the DUP are unlikely to be eclipsed as the main unionist party for some time.

Sinn Féin

Sinn Féin can trace its history through various splits and developments in the Irish republican movement. The Troubles in Northern Ireland from the late 1960s led to an increased role for Sinn Féin because of its relationship with the Provisional IRA (Murray and Tonge, 2005, chs 1–4). SF's main policy is the pursuit of a united Ireland and the end of British rule in Northern Ireland. It organizes on an all Ireland basis, making it, uniquely among the parties considered in this book, active in two separate sovereign state jurisdictions. Many SF policies have an all-Ireland aspect, such as proposals for an all-Ireland economic development plan contained in the party's 2007 Assembly manifesto (Sinn Féin, 2007). Such policies were repeated in SF's 2011 manifesto, alongside policies designed to increase the economic powers of the Northern Ireland Assembly in the first instance (Sinn Féin, 2011). In addition to arguments for Irish independence, in recent decades SF's ideological influences have included the 'new left' that emerged in the late 1960s, while during the 1970s and 1980s SF made links with more radical elements of the British left (Bean, 2007, ch. 2). SF now draws upon communitarian and egalitarian thinking which prioritizes identity politics, with a discourse of 'equality, diversity and respect' achieved through 'rights based governance' becoming increasingly the party's dominant theme (Bean, 2007, chs 4 and 5; Sinn Féin, 2007; Tonge, 2004, p.121).

The most significant shift for Sinn Féin has been its move away from immediate demands for a united Ireland and the ending of British rule, to a position where, after acceptance of the GFA in 1998, these are seen as longer-term goals to be achieved by participation in the institutions of the Northern Irish state whose very existence the party used to challenge.

This shift has had a number of sources. Tonge (2004, p. 102) points to party leader Gerry Adams' 1983 development of a concept of Irish self-determination as a crucial step, while also highlighting the importance of talks with John Hume of the SDLP, then the dominant nationalist party in Northern Ireland, in 1988. Bean (2007) notes the crucial experience gained by SF members in working in local government in Belfast as an example of how SF began to accept that working within institutions might benefit the nationalist community. He also points to the impact of changing social structure and a changed international context offering examples of conflict resolution that SF could emulate.

One of SF's aims is to become the largest party in Northern Ireland (Tonge, 2004, p. 120). In the 2003 Assembly elections, it built upon becoming the largest nationalist party in the 2001 general election by doing the same at Stormont, with 23.5 per cent of first preferences and 24 seats. It improved on this in 2007 to achieve 26.2 per cent and win 28 seats, the party's performance increasing again in 2011 to 26.9 per cent and 29 seats. The 2009 European elections saw SF overtake the unionist parties to win most first preferences and the first Northern Irish seat in the European Parliament, a first for the party and the province. SF also polled more votes in total than any other Northern Irish party in 2010 when it succeeded in having five MPs elected to Westminster, although the party does not take up its seats there. With infighting between the unionist parties, there was concern that the more disciplined SF would become the largest party in the Assembly in the May 2011 elections, although in the event SF came second behind the DUP. After agreeing to support the PSNI, SF held the post of Deputy First Minister at Stormont from May 2007, along with four other ministerial positions. Relations between the DUP and SF were relatively cordial when Paisley was First Minister but became notably cooler when he was replaced by the DUP's Peter Robinson. As Bean (2007, p. 215, pp. 258–69) observes, the difficulty participation in office presents is that SF effectively become constitutional nationalists and get drawn into technocratic matters of governance which do little to further its eventual aim of a united Ireland.

The Ulster Unionist Party

The Ulster Unionist Party (UUP) was founded in 1905 as a reaction to Irish nationalism. Its key aim has been to preserve the union with Great Britain, manifested through loyalty to its conception of Britishness and to the monarchy. These are still key issues for the UUP. Even if its policy agenda has broadened due to devolution, Walker (2004, p. 286) nevertheless observes that the UUP 'remains essentially the one-issue organization of its inception and formative years'. The UUP has been internally fissiparous, with much power deriving from constituency associations, the affiliated protestant Orange Order (albeit now disaffiliated since 2005) and in the party's ruling 858-member Ulster Unionist Council (Kaufmann and Patterson, 2006; Walker, 2004). The UUP's internal structure has, on numerous occasions, made it difficult for the party's leaders to follow an unpopular line towards constitutional issues. Under the leadership of David Trimble, the UUP entered the talks which led to the GFA, albeit without IRA decommissioning. At the same time, the party began to attempt to modernize its political approach, discussing a new 'civic' and pluralist unionism which sought to broaden the party's appeal. Evans and Tonge (2005) argue that this modernization process is hardly what would have been expected of a rational-actor model of party development given that most unionist voters and party members were not in favour. Given this, the UUP needed to instil confidence in Unionist voters that it was standing up for their interests.

This modernization process failed when the DUP overtook the UUP in 2003 to become the largest Unionist party. Since 2003, the UUP has suffered numerous election setbacks. Party leader David Trimble lost his Westminster seat in 2005, subsequently standing down as leader, and the party was reduced to one MP. It polled the smallest share of first preferences of the four main Northern Irish parties in both the 2007 and 2011 Assembly contests. In 2010, Reg Empey, Trimble's leadership successor, failed to win the seat he contested. An alliance with the Conservative Party, the Ulster Conservative and Unionists – New Force (UCUNF), also failed to win a seat after the party's sole MP resigned the whip in protest and subsequently held her seat as an Independent. The UUP elected another new leader in late 2010, Tom Elliott. Early commentary noted his relative inability to get the party noticed and Elliott came under pressure after a poor election result in 2011. Consequently, the UUP has looked unlikely to break the domination of the DUP and regain its previous pre-eminence of the unionist bloc in future Northern Irish elections.

The Social Democratic and Labour Party

The Social Democratic and Labour Party (SDLP) can trace its roots to the Northern Irish civil rights movement of the late 1960s. Formed in 1970, the early emphasis was on broad socialist principles in relation to economic and social matters, with policy documents and the party's constitution describing it as being socialist (Tonge, 2004, p. 105; Murray and Tonge, 2005, pp. 11–12). While the SDLP was committed to Irish unity, this was not its primary aim. Indeed, an early aim was to utilize its labourist and social democratic origins to appeal across Northern Ireland's sectarian divide (Tonge, 2004, p. 103), although the SDLP's electoral support – predominantly drawn from catholic communities – demonstrated that that aim was not achieved. From 1974, emphasis on socialist issues was eclipsed by a 'greening' of the party which saw a greater focus on the nationalist agenda with the party arguing for greater involvement of Dublin in the affairs of Northern Ireland. Division between the socialist and nationalist elements of the party's membership remains, although there is 'evidence that the red section of the party has been marginalized' (Tonge, 2004, p. 106). The SDLP's analysis of the constitutional question involved an acceptance that the unionist community was the majority population in the North. Talks between the leaders of Sinn Féin and the SDLP – the 1988 Hume–Adams dialogue – helped lay foundations for changing SF attitudes towards the political process. That the SDLP's thinking on the future of Northern Ireland informed much of the eventual GFA can be seen as a 'vindication' of the party's thinking on the constitutional issue (Tonge, 2004, p. 110), and more than two-thirds of SDLP members view the power-sharing institutions as more important than Irish unity (Murray and Tonge, 2005, p. 204). In policy terms, the SDLP ultimately remains focused on social and economic inequalities and reforms.

Electorally, the party was overtaken by SF in the 2001 general election and has been in decline against its republican competitor ever since. The strategic difficulty is that SF has occupied much of the SDLP's political territory. SF is perceived as the party standing up most strongly for nationalist interests (Mitchell et al., 2009), and is seldom interested in co-operation. This leaves the SDLP with the option of going it alone, a strategy of apparently diminishing returns, or attempting to forge a centrist space alongside the UUP and smaller non-sectarian Alliance party, where lower vote preferences may transfer between them (Tonge, 2004, p. 115). Like the UUP, the SDLP has also had leaders perceived not to have made much of a mark since John Hume stood down in 2001. The incumbent from 2010, Margaret Ritchie, failed to make much impact with her initial pronouncements, and the party's declining vote and seat share in 2011 also put her leadership under the spotlight.

Assessing the UK's Multi-level Party Systems

While Northern Ireland is a case apart, the other devolved party systems in Scotland and Wales also involve the Scottish and Welsh organizations of the main three British parties – the Conservatives, Labour and the Liberal Democrats – as well as in some cases smaller parties like the Greens. The presence of the territorially-based political parties introduced above means that the interactions between parties in these systems differ from those found at the Westminster level. But to what extent and what impact does this have?

The first question to address in assessing the parameters of these party systems is how many parties are 'relevant' in each system. Sartori (2005 [1976]) argues that parties are relevant if they have either blackmail or coalition potential. A greater number of parties have had coalition potential in the devolved settings than at Westminster. Plaid Cymru's participation in the 'One Wales' coalition indicates the broader relevance of the Welsh nationalists, while the Liberal Democrats' participation in coalition in both Scotland and Wales predated their participation in coalition at Westminster. However, this focus at the parliamentary level needs to be complemented by an assessment of how many parties are also relevant in the electoral arena. This is important because the SNP and Plaid Cymru, not to mention the Northern Irish parties, bring specific arguments to the electoral arena which both affect party competition, and differentiate the systems from the Westminster system.

Assessing how many parties are 'relevant' to electoral competition in each system provides some indication of the fragmentation or concentration of a party system. A widely used measure of party system fragmentation is the Effective Number of Parties (ENP). Derived from a simple mathematical formula, this can be calculated in relation to parties either in the electorate or in parliament thereby giving a sense of the number of relevant parties at both levels (Lijphart, 1999, pp. 67–9). Table 7.4 outlines the effective number of electoral parties (ENEP) and the effective number of parliamentary parties (ENPP) in elections held to the devolved institutions from 1998–99 onwards. The equivalent figures for Westminster elections are set out in Chapter 1 (Table 1.2, p. 12). There has been a small increase in ENEP at Westminster since 1997, but over the equivalent period the average ENEP has been 3.46, suggesting that elections at Westminster have revolved around interactions between just over three relevant parties. The equivalent measures for the devolved institutions are considerably higher, Scotland having an ENEP average of 4.56, Wales with 4.32 and Northern Ireland 5.14.

Table 7.4   Effective number of parties, devolved institutions

Year	Scottish Parliament		National Assembly of Wales		Northern Ireland Assembly	
	ENEP	ENPP	ENEP	ENPP	ENEP	ENPP
1998/9	4.36	3.34	3.82	3.03	6.06	5.41
2003	5.64	4.23	4.38	3.00	4.91	4.54
2007	4.71	3.41	5.08	3.33	4.81	4.30
2011	3.51	2.55	3.98	2.93	4.81	4.16
Mean	4.56	3.38	4.32	3.07	5.14	4.60

Note: Figures for the Scottish Parliament and Welsh Assembly are based on the regional list vote. Figures in the 1999 row for Northern Ireland refer to the 1998 Assembly elections.
Sources: Data from Gallagher, 2010.

Proportional electoral systems used for the devolved institutions help to ensure this electoral diversity is carried through to the parliamentary arena. ENPP for Westminster is just over two, ending at 2.57 in 2010 providing evidence to support the idea that the UK is gradually becoming a two and a half party system (see Table 1.2, p. 12). In Scotland, ENPP peaked at 4.23 in 2003 when seven Green and six Scottish Socialist MSPs were elected, and, post-2011, averages just over three relevant parliamentary parties across the four Scottish elections. Wales has had a lower ENPP of around 3 in each NAW election, largely due to the lower number of seats in the Assembly. Finally, while Northern Ireland has declined from 5.41 to 4.16 since 1998, its unique party system still records an average ENPP of around 4.6 across these four elections. In other words, in both the electoral and parliamentary arenas, devolved party politics is considerably more diverse than that found at Westminster and this impacts upon the dynamics of competition in each party system.

Understanding the nature of these party systems however also requires an assessment of the ideological distance and direction of competition evident in each (Sartori (2005 [1976]). A number of authors have assessed the ideological polarization of the Scottish and/or Welsh party systems (Bennie and Clark, 2003; Dunleavy, 2005; Massetti, 2008; Webb, 2000). The most comprehensive and recent assessment is provided by Massetti (2008). In terms of the left–right dimension, party competition is centripetal. In Scotland, the SNP and Labour are slightly centre-left with the Liberal Democrats positioned just to the right but in a position equating to the centre of the spectrum. The sole representative of the right is the

Scottish Conservatives, while the Greens can be found further to the left. These assessments are echoed by Dunleavy (2005). Welsh politics is slightly different, with Plaid and Labour further to the left, the Liberal Democrats just to the right of centre and the Conservatives again the main pro-market representative of the right. In both countries, the Liberal Democrats have moved rightwards from their positioning pre-devolution (Webb, 2000, ch. 1). Two further dimensions are assessed by Massetti (2008). These are the extent to which the party favours environmental protection or economic growth and the extent to which the parties are either libertarian or authoritarian. In all three dimensions in both Scotland and Wales, the direction of party competition is towards the centre. While the Scottish and Welsh Liberal Democrats are more pro-environment and libertarian than Labour, the Conservatives remain on their own as being the most authoritarian and pro-growth party in both countries.

To understand how parties' ideological positioning impacts on the Scottish and Welsh party systems, it is necessary to revisit the theoretical models of party systems introduced in Chapter 1. To recap, Sartori's (2005 [1976]) classification identifies four main types: pre-dominant party systems; two-party systems; moderate pluralism; and extreme or polarized pluralism. That the direction of ideological competition in both Scottish and Welsh systems is centripetal, and there are more than two relevant parties in each, suggests that both systems have had a form of moderate pluralism in their first three terms.

The situation is however somewhat more complex. In Scotland, the structure of party competition is not only bi-polar on the left–right spectrum. It is also cross-cut by attitudes for and against Scottish independence. While the SNP and Greens are pro-independence, the other three parties are in favour of maintaining the union albeit with further powers to the Scottish parliament. Ideological overlaps between potential partners are crucial in coalition formation (Laver and Schofield, 1990). This means that while the SNP, Labour, Liberal Democrats, and Greens can all be found on the centre-left, there is little overlap between the SNP and Labour and the Liberal Democrats on Scottish independence (Bennie and Clark, 2003; Massetti, 2008). The Conservatives' positioning on the right means that they are unlikely to have enough of an overlap with the other parties on the left–right spectrum to become part of a governing coalition (Bennie and Clark, 2003). Moreover, the SNP's decision to form a minority government in 2007 questions the idea that in moderate pluralist systems, parties cannot govern alone, although, as noted above, the SNP had to rely on the support of other parties to remain in power during that parliament. Whether the SNP can sustain its post-2011 majority in future elections remains to be seen however. Assuming Labour can regroup in Scotland after its large losses in 2011, the key parties in government formation are likely to remain the two largest parties, Labour and the SNP. Consequently, Scotland still has a potentially multi-polar form of moderate pluralism with the left–right and constitutional dimensions both playing an important role. Nevertheless, the nature of the SNP's victory indicates that Scotland's party system is in a period of transition and will need to be reassessed by commentators after the 2016 elections.

While the constitutional question has been important in Wales, it has tended to be less acute than in Scotland, as demonstrated by the participation of Plaid Cymru in the 'One Wales' coalition alongside Labour from 2007. Massetti (2008) suggests that it is unclear whether overlaps on the left–right or constitutional dimension formed the basis for this coalition. Despite historical enmities between the two parties, both cleavages seem to have contributed. Overlaps on the left–right dimension have coincided with broad agreement about the need for further powers for the NAW on the constitutional dimension. Another important difference between the two devolved institutions is that while Scotland has now experienced a change of government under the SNP, in Wales the post-devolution governments have reflected experience in pre-devolution Wales, where party politics was traditionally dominated by Labour. Despite attempts to form a broad Plaid–Liberal Democrat–Conservative administration in 2007, Labour has been central to every Welsh executive since 1999, either as a minority government or in coalition. Arguably Labour's pre-eminence both before and after devolution means that Wales has had a dominant party system (Webb, 2000, pp.27–8). However, Massetti (2008, p. 20) suggests that the inclusion of the Liberal Democrats (2000–2003) and Plaid Cymru (2007–2011) in coalition with Labour means that the Welsh party system is something of a hybrid falling somewhere between a predominant party system and what he calls 'limited pluralism'.

Party competition in Northern Ireland revolves around the constitutional question, instead of the left–right dimension, with competition taking place within two blocs, the Unionist and the Nationalist. On the face of it, the recent predominance of the DUP and Sinn Féin in Northern Ireland's party system would appear to classify it as a case of polarized pluralism. Both parties have historically demonstrated either anti-system or consistent oppositional behaviour and have been ideological opposites on the Irish question. In standing up for their communities, the DUP and Sinn Féin were historically the most intransigent parties in the Northern Irish system. Their overtaking the SDLP and UUP might therefore be seen as a case of irresponsible outbidding on constitutional and ethnic issues putting a squeeze on more moderate centre-placed parties in a manner similar to that outlined by Sartori (2005 [1976]).

In explaining the rise of the DUP and Sinn Féin, Mitchell et al. (2009) make a compelling case for why such an assessment is mistaken. Their argument is that the increase of support for these two parties has not been accompanied by a polarization of public opinion regarding constitutional issues, but by a convergence of opinion in support of Northern Ireland's institutions. Because the power-sharing institutions create incentives for parties to co-operate, they argue that voters compensate for the inevitable compromises such co-operation involves by voting for the parties with a record of standing up for their communities most vociferously. What appears to be polarization is therefore a case of voters wanting the strongest party to stand up for their interests, with the DUP and Sinn Féin ultimately filling the role of 'ethnic tribune parties' in Northern Ireland.

London, Mayors and Local Government

A range of other party systems exist at the sub-national level. These include in London, for the Greater London Authority (GLA), for a number of directly elected Mayors in England, and in local government across the UK. Different structures of competition are often evident in each of these levels.

Table 7.5 provides results for GLA elections between 2000–2008. Set up in 2000, the GLA was another institution created as part of Labour's early devolution of power. The three mainstream parties have dominated representation since the GLA was established. Nevertheless, party competition has been more diverse in the GLA. Small parties have been able to use the GLA to build their profile with the Greens, UKIP and the BNP all winning seats. The ENP figures demonstrate that there have been upwards of four effective parties active in the electoral arena, rising to more than five in the 2004 elections held concurrently with the European parliamentary elections.

As part of the Local Government Act 2000, English localities were also given the option to hold referendums to consider whether or not they wanted to have directly elected Mayors run their council. Twelve cities initially voted in favour of such a directly elected position. Mainstream parties have faced a range of diverse competition in these Mayoral elections. Five of the eleven contests held in 2002 were won by Independent candidates. Four of these Independents held their positions in the subsequent 2009 elections, which also saw a small party, the English Democrats, win the Mayoralty in Doncaster. The most famous

Table 7.5   Greater London Authority results, 2000–2008

	2000		2004		2008	
	Share of vote %	*Seats*	*Share of vote %*	*Seats*	*Share of vote %*	*Seats*
Con	29.0	9	28.5	9	34.6	11
Lab	30.3	9	25.0	7	27.6	8
Lib Dem	14.8	4	16.9	5	11.4	3
Green	11.1	3	8.6	2	8.4	2
BNP	2.9	–	4.8	–	5.4	1
UKIP	2.1	–	8.4	2	1.9	–
Other	9.8	–	7.8	–	10.7	–
Total	100.0	25	100.0	25	100.0	25
ENEP	4.52	–	5.15	–	4.34	–

Note: Vote share based on London-wide vote shares.
Sources: Data from Tetteh, 2008; Young, 2008.

Independent insurgency was however former Labour MP Ken Livingstone becoming London Mayor in 2000, having been rejected by Labour as its London candidate in 2000 and winning as an Independent, although he subsequently rejoined Labour. In 2008, Conservative candidate Boris Johnson won the London Mayoralty from Livingstone.

Despite being much more established than the new and devolved institutions, local government also highlights the diversity of party systems throughout the UK. Party fortunes often appear to fluctuate with the popularity of the party at national level. Thus, Labour in power from 1997–2010 lost many councillors and control of councils due to the unpopularity of the then Labour government (Leach, 2006, ch. 1; Rallings and Thrasher, 2009). Table 7.6 outlines developments in local party politics across Britain between 1979 and 2010. In 2010, the Conservatives had just under half of the total number of councillors, and controlled around half of all councils, not dissimilar proportions to that held in 1979. By contrast, Labour's 23 per cent of councillors fails to achieve a proportionate amount of power in town halls. In 2010 Labour controlled only 14 per cent of local administrations, a pattern also similar to that found in 1979 (Webb, 2000, p. 33; Tetteh, 2010, pp. 7–9). While a hung parliament and coalition at Westminster has caught the attention of analysts, such developments are increasingly likely in local government, with 28 per cent of councils having no overall control (NOC), an increase from 15 per cent in 1979.

Table 7.6   Party politics in local government, 1979–2010

Party	April 1979		May 2010	
	Councils controlled	Share of vote %	Councils controlled	Share of vote %
Conservative	257	49.2	202	50.0
Labour	78	14.9	55	14.0
Liberal Democrat	1	0.2	25	6.0
Nationalists	5	1.0	0	0
Independent/Other	102	19.5	12	3.0
NOC	79	15.1	112	28.0
Total	522	99.9	406	101.0

Note: percentages do not total exactly 100 due to rounding.
Sources: Data from Webb, 2000, p. 33; Tetteh, 2010, pp. 7–9.

These raw figures mask the diversity of party systems found in local government. Labour representation and control in local government tends to be based around urban London and metropolitan boroughs, while Conservative representation tends to be situated in more rural county and shire district councils as well as in English unitary authorities (Tetteh, 2010, p. 7). There are a number of classifications of local party systems (Webb, 2000, pp. 32–4; Wilson and Game, 2006, ch. 14). These classifications vary on the degree to which parties dominate local representative politics. Thus, Wilson and Game (2006, ch. 14) propose six potential categories. *One-party monopolistic* systems have 75 per cent or more seats held by one party. *One-party dominant* systems have between 60–75 per cent of seats held by one party. *Two-party* systems have 80 per cent or more of seats held by two parties, with neither having more than 60 per cent. *Multi-party or fragmented* systems have 20 per cent or more seats held by third parties. *Weakly partisan* systems have between 20–59 per cent of seats held by Independents. Finally, *non-partisan* systems have 60 per cent or more seats held by Independents. All of these party systems can be found somewhere in British local government, rendering party political competition in councils considerably more varied and complex than at national level.

European Elections

UK parties compete not only for sub-national institutions, but also for election to a supra-national institution, the European Parliament. This is

Table 7.7   European election results in Britain (percentages)

	Con	Lab	Lib Dem	UKIP	Green	SNP	PC	BNP	Others	ENEP
1989	35	40	6	–	14.9	3	1	–	–	3.23
1999	35.8	28	12.7	7	6.3	2.7	1.9	1	4.6	4.26
2009	27.7	15.7	13.7	16.5	8.6	2.1	0.8	6.2	8.5	5.99

Sources: Data from Tetteh, 2008; Mellows-Facer et al., 2009.

elected every five years, by closed-list proportional representation. European elections are 'second-order' elections *par excellence*, marked by low turnout and small parties making advances against their larger counterparts (Reif and Schmitt, 1980).

Table 7.7 outlines parties' vote share for three of the European elections between 1989 and 2009. From 1999, the trend has been for the Conservatives to 'win' the European elections, standing on the Eurosceptic platform which the party tends to have a lead on. A major trend in European contests however is the decline in the combined vote share of the three main parties. The combined vote share for the Conservatives, Labour and Liberal Democrats was 89 per cent in 1994, but has declined steeply since to just over 57 per cent in 2009 (Tetteh, 2008; Mellows-Facer et al., 2009). Indeed, the mainstream parties have struggled to maintain their position in the face of challenges from small parties. The Greens' 14.9 per cent of the vote in 1989 put the environment on the party political map, beating the post-merger Liberal Democrats into fourth place. More recently, UKIP achieved a higher share of the vote in both 2004 (16.2 per cent), overtaking the Liberal Democrats, and in 2009, coming second on 16.5 per cent, behind the Conservatives but ahead of Labour. The Liberal Democrats again came fourth in 2009, with the Greens and BNP both returning two MEPs each. The increasing diversity of European elections is underlined by the ENEP figures, with around three relevant parties in the 1989 and 1994 elections, rising sharply to a figure of almost six in 2009. Dunleavy's (2005) assessment of the 2004 European contest shows that this diversity extends all the way down to the electoral regions used for European Parliament elections in Britain.

Partisan dealignment and the second-order nature of the elections both contribute to the diversity of European elections. A further explanation can be found in the dynamics of party competition. UKIP and its anti-EU stance has already been introduced in Chapter 6. UKIP can be seen as an anti-system party in European elections since their main aim is for the

UK to withdraw from the EU. UKIP therefore engage in what Sartori (2005 [1976]) calls 'irresponsible outbidding'. This has the effect that UKIP rhetoric in European contests contributes considerably to delegitimizing any positive debate on European issues, in the manner that Sartori (2005 [1976]) predicts of anti-system parties. Given an already largely Eurosceptic electorate, this is difficult for mainstream parties to deal with, since none fundamentally challenges the UK's place in the EU, even if they may otherwise adopt a Eurosceptic stance. Moreover, the success of UKIP in these elections can act as an example to other small parties; in addition to UKIP, the BNP and the Greens, six other mainly Eurosceptic minor parties fielded enough candidates to qualify for a party political broadcast in the 2009 European campaign. European elections therefore create an increasingly diverse pattern of party competition, which is difficult for mainstream parties to respond to effectively.

Conclusion

Party politics in the UK is considerably more varied than a focus on Westminster might suggest. Both Scotland and Wales have nationalist parties that have graduated from being parties of protest to becoming parties of government. While the constitutional question is still a major issue in Scotland, Plaid Cymru's participation in a coalition government between 2007–11 suggests that this cleavage has declined in importance in the Welsh context. Northern Ireland has a *sui generis* party system which has been based around competition over the Irish question, with parties unique to the province but which have occasionally commanded some influence at Westminster when there were weak majorities.

ENEP figures demonstrate that the diversity of electoral competition increasingly extends across other tiers of government. The UK therefore now has a number of party systems at multiple levels of government – local, devolved and European – in all of which the dynamics of party competition are somewhat different. The outcomes of elections in each of these systems are not only important in their own right, but have implications for how parties campaign and present themselves at other levels. Intuitively, the differences between election results at Westminster and each of these different levels suggests that some voters split their vote depending on the institution. Electoral evidence supports this idea. Some people vote on the basis of local rather than national factors in local elections, and ticket-splitting behaviour also occurs when multi-level elections are held concurrently (Heath et al., 1999; Rallings and Thrasher,

1997, 2003). Less is known about how the UK's political parties are adapting to these complex conditions, both in relation to party competition, but also in relation to the proportional electoral systems used for the devolved and European institutions. Some have attempted to analyse how parties campaign at different levels when multi-level elections are held concurrently (Clark, 2012), and how the new devolved structures have impacted upon party organization more generally (Hopkin and Bradbury, 2006). These advances notwithstanding, two points remain pertinent. First, 'like it or not, party leaders in every part of the UK must now think strategically in multi-party terms. When they have forgotten or ignored this key imperative the results have been disastrous' (Dunleavy, 2005, p. 529). Second, the multi-level nature of UK party politics has created a 'complex network of influences which we still imperfectly understand' (Dunleavy, 2005, p. 522). Further research is therefore required to establish how parties are adapting to these complex multi-level environments in the UK, and assess how competition at one level of party system impacts on dynamics at different levels.

8

Parties and the Media

Most people experience party politics indirectly through the lens of the media. Parties have long recognized the importance of media management and their efforts to do so have included, for instance, the appointment of so-called 'spin doctors' such as Peter Mandelson, Alastair Campbell and Andy Coulson. Such efforts at media management extend well beyond the traditional campaigning period immediately preceding elections. Moreover, parties have also sought to expand their communication activities by exploiting the new media opportunities offered by the Internet. This chapter looks broadly at the relationship between parties and various media. Discussion revolves around five sections. The first provides a theoretical grounding by briefly outlining models of political communication. The second part introduces the structure of the press and broadcast media and assesses how this impacts upon partisanship. The third section evaluates the professionalization of political communication activity within the parties, both in government and opposition. The parties are convinced of the importance of the Internet in communicating to electors. The fourth part therefore examines parties' efforts to communicate via the Internet. The final section evaluates the success of parties' attempts to communicate and influence the media by briefly assessing whether or not the media impact upon voting behaviour. Only limited effects on voting will be highlighted. Often parties' efforts appear counterproductive, becoming a story in their own right. Parties may try hard to communicate with voters via the media. It is not always clear that they do so successfully.

Approaches to Political Communication

There are numerous theories of political communication (McNair, 1995; Watts, 1997). To have some conception of how parties interact with the media, it is useful to have an overview of some of these approaches. Kuhn (2007, ch. 1) sets out five functions of the media in relation to politics.

First, the media act as an *information provider*, providing their readers, viewers and consumers with a wide range of information on politics. Second, the media have an *agenda-setting* role. What they choose to include prominently in their coverage is likely to impact on how important those issues are in public debate. This also means that the media have a 'gate-keeping' role. Since they cannot cover everything equally, they must prioritize between different stories and issues. Third, the media *hold politicians and public figures accountable* in a way that citizens are rarely able to do. Fourth, the media can serve as an *agent of political mobilization*, with coverage of some issues serving to engage citizens to act politically. Fifth, the media help to *socialize* people into political life and support for the institutions of governance. Others provide a similar list of functions (McNair, 1995).

Watts (1997, ch. 1) highlights three approaches to political communication. The first is the *pluralist* model. This suggests that media outlets, their owners and journalists compete with each other for readers and viewers. The public are consumers who actively seek out media content and views that suit their opinions and interests. Consequently, many different views and opinions can be found and media outlets adapt their coverage to suit demand from their readers and viewers. The second has variously been labelled the *mass manipulative, direct effects* or *hypodermic needle* approach (Denver, 2007, ch. 6; Watts, 1997, p. 18). This is a direct, top-down model of communication. In short, political elites consciously seek to influence the public by presenting their views in the most favourable way through a particular channel of communication. The public are essentially passive recipients of such messages, accepting them and becoming indoctrinated into the beliefs of the political elite. This view has two difficulties. In modern democracies, there are few direct lines of communication between the elite and the public. Political messages must be placed in various outlets whether in the press or broadcast media. How the media present such an elite-driven message is therefore important and the political stance of the outlet itself of relevance to how messages are filtered to the public (Norris, 2000, ch. 1). Similarly, recipients have their own opinions which they use as a 'perceptual screen' to filter out unwelcome messages (Denver, 2007, ch. 6).

The third model combines these two positions. Watts (1997, p. 21) labels this the *interactionist* position. In short, the media do indeed seek audiences and tailor their coverage to suit market demands, as in the pluralist model, but they also play a role in helping to create and mould public opinion more generally, thereby lending some qualified support to top-down models of political communication. Crucially, this model provides the framework within which actors such as political parties must operate and behave. McNair (1995, p. 4) stresses three factors, which, adapted to focus more narrowly on parties than the original, serve to frame the following discussion. These are that:

1. all forms of communication undertaken by politicians and political parties are for the purpose of achieving specific objectives;
2. communication is also addressed *to* those actors by non-politicians such as voters and newspaper columnists;
3. communication can be *about* parties, politicians and their activities, as contained in various reports, editorials and media commentary on politics.

Instead of political communication between parties and citizens being a direct process, it is therefore a two-way process where the views of citizens can also feed back to parties and political elites via a third actor, the media. Each group – parties, citizens and the media – have 'perceptual screens' through which opinions they do not agree with or think important are filtered.

This can be presented schematically by the framework set out in Figure 8.1. This allows for a continual two-way process of communication and dialogue between parties, the media and citizens as highlighted by McNair (1995). In short, parties, whether in government or opposition, endeavour to communicate their policy programmes through speeches, appeals, and their advertising and public relations activities. These are reported, commented upon, and analysed by the media. This

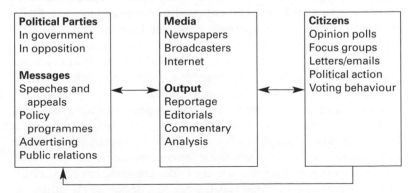

Figure 8.1   Party communication: a model

Sources: Adapted from McNair, 1995, p. 5; Norris, 2000, p. 14.

acts as immediate feedback to parties, but also goes on to provide the basis for what most voters see and hear about the party's message. Citizens' views feed back to media outlets either through participation in opinion polls, writing to editors, but also by taking part in political action and voting in elections. All of these are reported and commented upon, thereby underlining how the media can reflect citizens' views back to parties. Moreover, citizens can feed their opinions back directly to parties and politicians through political action and voting, but also by writing to their MPs and councillors, and contributing to the increasing levels of opinion research undertaken by parties as they seek to hone their message. This is represented by the direct feedback loop between citizens and parties.

The centrality of the media means that its agenda-setting role is central to how political communication works in a democracy such as the UK. While the media does not necessarily tell people what to think about a topic, through highlighting certain issues over others it can certainly have an influence on what topics enter the political agenda in the first place. Kuhn (2007, p. 26 emphasis added) characterizes how parties deal with this by noting that:

> Political actors are constantly trying to shape the media agenda for their own partisan purposes: a process known as *agenda-building*. They try to use (or exploit) the media to persuade (or manipulate) the public. Frequently, therefore, the media reflect and transmit agendas largely set by other political actors, such as political parties.

This does not always work. As Figure 8.1 highlights, messages, however favourably presented, are often criticized in media commentary. Often the media have their own agenda to pursue in doing so. This is particularly so with a partisan press which often sets the agenda for broadcast media. Both present themselves as self-styled watchdogs in doing so. Consequently, scandal, wrongdoing, conspiracy and controversy are prioritized as news values, over good public service and reporting occasions where parties and their policies have benefited citizens. As Norris (2000, p. 11) notes, this means that an adversarial relationship exists between politicians and the media. The former try to craft their message to fit journalistic norms, while the latter concentrate on exposing what politicians and parties are really trying to do. The result has been argued to be a 'media malaise' which contributes to a decline in the quality of public debate, and increasing levels of political disengagement among citizens (Blair, 2007; Lloyd, 2004; Norris, 2000).

Partisanship and the Structure of the Media in the UK

The main constituent components of the media are the press and the broadcast media. The press – daily and Sunday newspapers, and weekly news magazines – are highly partisan. Different newspapers have different readerships. Broadsheets such as the *Times* or *Sunday Times* are likely to have better educated and white-collar readerships than tabloids such as *The Sun* or the now closed *News of the World*, despite all four having had the same owner. The press often claim to have played a considerable role in helping decide election outcomes. Examples include 1992's famous *Sun* front covers which argued in an anti-Labour headline on election day 'If Kinnock wins today will the last person to leave Britain please turn out the lights', then going on to claim when the unexpected Conservative victory was known 'It's the *Sun* wot won it'. *The Sun* is not alone; other papers also use their front covers and their coverage to argue the case for and against various parties.

Wring and Deacon (2010) show that between 1992–2010 the party that wins most votes is the party with most press support. There is some debate as to whether the press leads public opinion in this regard, or whether the press is merely following behind and jumping on the bandwagon of public opinion. This notwithstanding, the partisanship of the press is thought important and the support of popular newspapers eagerly sought by party leaders. Election studies have often simply highlighted which party the paper has recommended (Butler and Kavanagh, 2002; Kavanagh and Butler, 2005; Kavanagh and Cowley, 2010). However, newspaper endorsements are often more nuanced. *Guardian* columnist Polly Toynbee famously advised readers to vote Labour in 2005, 'holding their nose' while they did so because of the party's many unpopular decisions. An editorial might suggest readers vote one way, but columnists and other reportage may have contrary views. Editorial endorsements can therefore be qualified considerably. Deacon et al. (1998) suggest that instead of an either/or classification of partisanship, a means of recognizing such qualifications is necessary. This involves a six-point scale of party support, indicating whether the newspaper has very strong, strong, moderate, weak, very weak or no partisanship (Denver, 2007, p. 140; Deacon et al., 1998; Wring and Deacon, 2010; Wring and Ward, 2010).

Table 8.1 sets out patterns of press partisanship for daily and Sunday newspapers between 1992 and 2010. From the party's foundation, Labour has always felt disadvantaged since most of the press has been Conservative-minded (Price, L. 2010). Conservative bias is clearly evident in the 1992 election, with five of the daily newspapers endorsing

Table 8.1 Press partisanship in Britain, 1992–2010

	1992	1997	2001	2005	2010
Dailies					
The Sun	Conservative Very strong	Labour Weak	Labour Weak	Labour Weak	Conservative Strong
Daily Mirror	Labour Very strong	Labour Very strong	Labour Strong	Labour Strong	Labour Strong
Daily Star	None	Labour Very weak	Labour Moderate	None	None
Daily Mail	Conservative Strong	Conservative Weak	None	Conservative Strong	Conservative Strong
Daily Express	Conservative Very strong	Conservative Moderate	Labour Moderate	Conservative Strong	Conservative Very strong
Daily Telegraph	Conservative Strong	Conservative Very strong	Conservative Strong	Conservative Strong	Conservative Moderate
The Times	Conservative Moderate	None	Labour Very weak	Labour Weak	Conservative Weak
Financial Times	Labour Very weak	Labour Very weak	Labour Very weak	Labour Very weak	Conservative Very weak
The Guardian	Labour Weak	Labour Strong	Labour Moderate	Labour Weak	Lib Dem Moderate

The Independent	None	Labour / Moderate	None	Lib Dem / Moderate	Lib Dem / Moderate
Sundays					
News of the World	Conservative / Very strong	Labour / Very weak	Labour / Moderate	Labour / Very weak	Conservative / Very strong
Sunday Mirror	Labour / Very strong	Labour / Very strong	Labour / Strong	Labour / Strong	Labour / Strong
The People	Labour / Very strong	Labour / Very strong	Labour / Very strong	Labour / Moderate	None
Mail on Sunday	Conservative / Strong	Conservative / Weak	Conservative / Strong	None	Conservative / Strong
Sunday Express	Conservative / Very strong	Conservative / Moderate	Labour / Very weak	Conservative / Very strong	Conservative / Very strong
Sunday Times	Conservative / Very weak	Conservative / Weak	Labour / Very weak	Conservative / Weak	Conservative / Strong
Sunday Telegraph	Conservative / Moderate	Conservative / Very strong	Conservative / Strong	Conservative / Strong	Conservative / Strong
The Observer	Labour / Weak	Labour / Strong	Labour / Strong	Labour / Moderate	Lib Dem / Strong
Independent on Sunday	None	Labour / Moderate	None	Lib Dem / Weak	None

Sources: Adapted from Wring and Deacon, 2010.

the Conservative Party to varying degrees and five Sunday newspapers also supporting John Major's party. Of these, *The Sun* and *News of the World*, and the *Daily* and *Sunday Express* were all strongly Conservative. A Conservative press was also evident in 2010 with six dailies and five Sundays supporting the party to varying degrees. However, this support appeared more qualified than in 1992, the last election where the Conservatives had dominated press endorsements. Only the *Daily Express* was classified as very strong Conservative among the dailies, as were the *News of the World* and *Sunday Express* among the Sundays. Even the normally staunchly Conservative *Daily Telegraph* only gave the party moderate support in 2010 with some of its commentators notably critical of the party (Wring and Deacon, 2010). This notwithstanding, readers of *The Sun* and *News of the World* demonstrated swings to the Conservatives considerably beyond that found amongst the electorate as a whole (Wring and Deacon, 2010; Wring and Ward, 2010).

Labour has had reliable support from fewer newspapers over the last five elections. In 1992 its support was confined to three dailies, and three Sundays. While the *Mirror, Sunday Mirror* and *People* were very strong Labour, the other Labour papers offered somewhat qualified support. In 2010, the situation was considerably worse, with only the *Mirror* in both its daily and Sunday editions strongly endorsing the party. Prior to 1997 however, Labour made representations to News International, parent company of *The Sun*, the *News of the World*, *The Times* and the *Sunday Times*. All had previously been Conservative-oriented. While *The Times* recommended no party and the *Sunday Times* remained Conservative in 1997, the two highest circulation papers in the UK, *The Sun* and the *News of the World*, endorsed Labour. This means that around 8.6 million people, the combined circulation of both newspapers at the time, were exposed to pro-Labour views, opinions not previously encountered in these publications (Butler and Kavanagh, 1997). This was a considerable coup, Tony Blair having famously flown to Australia in 1995 to address News International executives in an attempt to achieve such an outcome. Six dailies supported Labour in 1997, alongside five Sundays. In 2001, this increased to seven dailies and six Sundays with *The Times, Sunday Times* and *Daily* and *Sunday Express* all coming out for Tony Blair's party. In 2005, Labour's press support was beginning to wane, but still totalled five dailies and four Sundays. Importantly press support for Labour between 1997 and 2005 was considerably more qualified than that normally found for the Conservatives. *The Sun's* endorsement was only ever classified as weak, while the *News of the World* varied between very weak and moderate support. Much of this support was also directed towards Tony Blair's leadership, rather than the party itself.

Press partisanship has traditionally been dominated by the two main parties. The Liberal Democrats have found it hard to obtain press support, with one former *Sun* editor pointing out that newspapers belonging to the News International group had effectively ignored the third party (Yelland, 2010). However, 2005 saw the Liberal Democrats get endorsements from both the daily and Sunday versions of the *Independent*. In 2010, Liberal Democrat supporting papers still included *The Independent*, but grew to include *The Guardian* and *The Observer*. The Liberal Democrats have not been alone in finding it difficult to gain press support. In Scotland, despite brief support from *The Sun* in the early 1990s, the SNP have often found itself outgunned in endorsements because the dominant Scottish tabloid, the *Daily Record*, favoured Labour. This changed in 2011; while the *Daily Record* still supported Labour, the SNP's unprecedented victory was achieved with support from a number of Scottish newspapers, including the Scottish editions of *The Sun* and *News of the World* and the two main Sunday broadsheets, *Scotland on Sunday* and the *Sunday Herald*. Smaller parties can also suffer from the perception that only the main parties are likely to form a government. Thus, although the *Express* praised UKIP in 2010, it nevertheless still gave the Conservatives a very strong recommendation (Wring and Deacon, 2010).

Some have suggested that the increased tendency of the press to swing between the two main parties means that there has been a 'partisan dealignment' of the press in Britain (Deacon and Wring, 2002; Scammell, 2000). However, certain papers – *The Mirror* and *The Telegraph* for instance – did not change their support. It may be more accurate to argue that what Deacon et al. (1998) call the 'corridor of uncertainty' of press partisanship expanded between 1992 and 2010 to include titles previously loyal to one party or another, such as *The Guardian* or the *Express*. Ultimately high circulation titles such as *The Sun* have been central to these changes. As Wring and Deacon (2010, p. 451) put it, '*The Sun* has demonstrated that it is more politically promiscuous than other newspapers and keen to be seen to support the winning party at election time.' By 2010 most of the press had returned to its historical position of support for the Conservatives, while Labour support declined to the lowest level the party had experienced in five general elections.

The News International group, which owns *The Sun*, *Times* and *Sunday Times*, has been central to understanding the close relationship between politicians and the press in recent decades. This was put under the spotlight in 2011 after allegations about illegal phone hacking at the now closed *News of the World*. This called into question the role of the press in political life, briefly even put Prime Minister David Cameron's position under scrutiny, and led to the announcement of a number of public inquiries to be conducted from 2011 onwards into press practices both in general, and in particular the role of News International and titles such as the *News of the World*. The appearance of the senior News International executives, Rupert and James Murdoch and Rebekah Brooks, before a House of Commons Select Committee in July 2011 appeared to suggest that the News International press might in future have less influence over British party politics than it had previously enjoyed.

The broadcast media is perceived to be more trustworthy than the press (Denver, 2007, p. 132). Since newspaper circulation is declining, television is also the most important source of information for most people. During election periods, the broadcast media is obliged to provide balance between the parties in their reporting. Even between elections, it is legally obliged to be impartial. This contrasts sharply with the partisanship of the press, and such balance is closely monitored by parties. The broadcast media environment has however changed considerably in recent decades. At the time of the 1979 general election, there were three terrestrial TV channels – BBC1, BBC2 and ITV. From the early 1990s, cable channels challenged terrestrial broadcasters, although their popularity only spread slowly. Multi-channel broadcasting got a considerable boost with the Labour government's decision to switch from analogue to digital broadcasting across the UK between 2009–2012. This is now the norm for most households. At the time of the 2010 general election, there were literally hundreds of channels, some broadcasting free-to-view terrestrial digital services, others requiring some form of subscription.

Table 8.2 tracks audience share figures in the months of the 2001, 2005 and 2010 elections. In 2001, the BBC had a 36.6 per cent share of total viewing, a figure which had declined to 27.5 per cent in 2010. By contrast, the 'other' category, which includes the assorted cable and digital broadcasters, more than doubled in the same period. While the BBC remains a major actor, and has adapted to this new environment with channels such as BBC News 24 and BBC Parliament, other broadcasters, notably ITV, have found it more difficult to do so. BSkyB is also a major actor, providing popular programming and the rolling 24 hour Sky News channel. Of the two main 24 hour news channels, the BBC has greater viewer share averaging around 1.2 per cent during the 2010 election period, by comparison with Sky News's approximately 0.7 per cent.

Table 8.2   Percentage share of TV channels' total viewing

	2001	2005	2010
BBC1/BBC2	36.6	33.1	27.5
ITV1	27.2	21.9	15.9
Ch.4/S4C	10.9	9.1	6.2
Five	5.8	6.6	4.7
Other	19.5	29.3	45.7

Source: Data from Broadcasters' Audience Research Board (BARB), www.barb.ac.uk, 10 February 2011.

One consequence of this broadcast media fragmentation is that viewers can increasingly avoid political coverage on TV should they wish to do so. Increased competition in the broadcast market means that what political coverage exists is perceived to have been 'dumbed down' (Scammell, 2000). Even serious programmes such as *Newsnight* regularly engage in stunts to try to attract viewers' attention to their political coverage. That no mainstream news programmes were extended in 2010 to carry election coverage, as had happened in previous campaigns, and that election coverage was low-key is indicative that this trend continues, despite the fact that 2010 was likely to be a close run campaign (Blumler and Gurevitch, 2002; Kavanagh and Cowley, 2010). Where political coverage is prominent it tends to focus on four things: 'horse-race' issues regarding who is ahead in the polls; personalities and leadership; the hidden motives of political actors; and how events have damaged the various actors involved.

Parties have often been criticized for tailoring their messages to television audiences. A two-minute news slot will often contain brief 'soundbites' designed to convey the party's message in just a few seconds. Speeches are written with various soundbites in mind, in the hope that these will be the key phrases and messages that are picked up by broadcasters and subsequently conveyed to viewers. Until recently, parties were seldom able to speak directly to voters except through their Party Political Broadcasts (PPBs). The onset of rolling 24 hour news means that it is now not unusual for some major speeches and campaign events by party leaders to be broadcast in full. Such speeches and events are carefully managed and scripted with the potential TV impact in mind.

Scammell (2000) observes that the fragmentation of the broadcast media means that parties would be less able to control the rolling news agenda and its increasing demands. Tony Blair reportedly had four times the amount of interview requests than his immediate predecessor in Downing Street (Select Committee on Public Administration, 1998), and characterized the media as a 'feral beast' towards the end of his premiership (Blair, 2007, p. 479). Under such circumstances, Scammell (2000) indicates that parties would be likely to respond with an intensification and professionalization of their political communication activities as they attempt to get their message across.

Parties and Political Communication

It is now commonplace for parties to appoint former journalists to head their communication activities, the so-called 'spin doctors' of much political debate. Labour appointed former *Mirror* and *Today* journalist, Alastair Campbell, as press secretary in opposition, and he continued to fulfil such a role for the party in government between 1997–2003. Similarly, the Conservatives under William Hague appointed Amanda Platell, formerly editor of the *Sunday Express*, as his head of press. David Cameron followed suit in 2007 with the appointment of Andy Coulson, former editor of *News of the World*, as Head of Communications, a role he carried into government for several months before leaving in 2011 after allegations that he had been implicated in authorizing systemic phone hacking activity while editor of *News of the World*. The professionalization of the communication process is not confined to the two major parties; most parties have now undergone some degree of professionalization in relation to their communication activities (Evans and Sanderson-Nash, 2011; Lynch, 1996).

It is useful to make a distinction between communication strategies while parties are in opposition and when they are in government. The key objective of a communications strategy in opposition is that it is characterized by campaigning which aims to build support both amongst the press and broadcast media, but also among voters (Price, L. 2010, p. 342). A mix of techniques is necessary, and parties need both proactive and reactive communications strategies. Briefings can be either off- or on-the-record, and information can also be leaked to journalists which may damage opponents. Parties attempt to build up some stories, and play down others. They aim to build relationships with certain correspondents in outlets that are perceived as crucial, while initially excluding other outlets. One example of such activity is how Labour's communications team actively cultivated the tabloid press, particularly *The Sun* and the *Mail*, with exclusive stories in the run up to 1997. Similar efforts were undertaken by the Conservatives in 2010, Andy Coulson proving crucial to building support among the press prior to the election (Butler and Kavanagh, 1997; Kavanagh and Cowley, 2010). Labour's Excalibur rapid rebuttal database, introduced for the 1997 campaign, provides a good example of reactive communications activity. This allowed the party to reply to any charges made against it, and to do so in the same news cycle. Its introduction was 'a sign of Labour's new professionalization' (Butler and Kavanagh, 1997, p. 59).

The aim is also to build up an image of a leader and party that conveys competence, integrity and decisiveness. Thatcher famously was advised to adapt her tone of voice and dress sense to appeal to a wider audience. Blair, instead of focusing solely on the news media, was often to be found in less formal settings, appearing for instance on chat shows where he could expect to both reach more voters and be less likely to face critical questioning. This helped complement the image of decisive leader with that of an ordinary family man that voters could understand. Parties have often attempted to bypass the national media in favour of courting the less critical regional and local media to underline such an impression. More recently, Cameron's Director of Strategy, Steve Hilton, is credited with providing the impetus for presenting David Cameron as a liberal conservative interested in green issues, cycling to the Commons and flying to Norway to see glacier erosion for instance. From 2007 this strategy acquired a harder edge with Coulson's tabloid experience helping craft a message that would appeal to the C1 voters crucial to election victory (Kavanagh and Cowley, 2010). There is however a fine line between decisiveness and ineffectiveness, particularly if contradictory messages are sent or the leader looks uncomfortable. William Hague's efforts to portray a more down-to-earth image, for instance appearing at the Notting Hill Carnival or at a fun fair wearing a baseball hat, were undermined by intra-party divisions, contradictory statements about immigration and media advisors who were more focused on day-to-day tactics rather than any longer-term strategy (Bale, 2010).

In government, parties also have the impact of policies and of government activities to communicate. This is more problematic as the media and voters begin to be disappointed by how the party has performed in office (Price, L. 2010, p. 342). Historically, the prime minister's press secretary gave twice-daily briefings to the 'lobby', composed selectively of political correspondents from important media outlets. These briefings were unattributable, conducted on an off-the-record basis in order to give journalists an insight to the government's thinking. Press secretaries were civil servants and therefore obliged to represent the government and prime minister, but not engage in party politics in their briefings. This changed when Labour took office in 1997. They appointed Special Advisors, who were able to give orders to civil servants, and who were able to take a more party political line than their predecessors. This has continued under the Conservatives. Both Alastair Campbell and Andy Coulson were Special Advisors in their roles as Head of Communications. There is an inevitable tension in such a role, between the neutral civil service presentation of government and prime minister on the one hand, and the political representation of party and party leader on the other. Campbell was often accused of crossing this line when representing Blair as prime minister between 1997–2003. However, even civil service press secretaries can be perceived as being more political than their role permitted. Mrs Thatcher's press secretary, Bernard Ingham, was closely associated with her, regularly seeking to emphasize her personal leadership role instead of that of her government.

Kuhn (2007, p. 188) highlights seven techniques associated with Labour's news management practices in office. In reality, these techniques are generic and can be used by any party. First, diversions from potentially damaging stories can be created, through highlighting other information to put journalists off the scent (Price, L. 2010, p. 339). Second, pre-empting headlines by getting an embarrassing story out before journalists are able to reveal it. Third, milking a story by making drip-by-drip revelations about a policy prior to its official announcement. Fourth, kite-flying controversial proposals in the media in order to gauge potential reaction. Fifth, managing expectations is also important, particularly in relation to budget matters where typically expectations are played down in advance. This allows chancellors to appear to have exceeded expectations, and thereby get favourable coverage, when they are able to announce beneficial tax cuts or spending programmes. Sixth, the rapid rebuttal of any criticisms. Finally, 'pre-buttal', meaning that the party gets their response to anticipated criticisms out before such criticisms are voiced, thereby shaping the subsequent news agenda.

These were arguably however just tactics in Labour's broader communications strategy. Labour brought a campaigning approach into its government communications, something that had not been seen under their predecessors (Price, L. 2010, p. 362; Scammell, 2000, p. 181; Select Committee on Public Administration, 1998). This was complemented by a centralization of activity. MPs and Ministers were expected to be 'on message' at all times, major interviews had to be cleared with Downing Street, a Strategic Communications Unit was established to co-ordinate departmental announcements and former journalists were employed as press officers in place of civil servants, thereby leading to accusations of politicization of government communications. This initially appeared successful, but was undermined by internal competition between Blair, Brown and their respective press teams where internal rivalry saw these communications teams briefing against each other. 'Spin' became increasingly covered in the media, contributing to a suspicion of Labour's communications activities. This success was also clearly driven by the personalities involved, media relations becoming less central to Labour after Alastair Campbell's resignation in 2003 (Price, L. 2010, p. 371). The early period of Conservative–Liberal Democrat government from 2010 appeared much less disciplined than the equivalent period under Labour. This was partly because of the unusual circumstance of having a coalition government. In part however it was because the party appeared to have a more laissez-faire attitude, with ministers often making announcements that either appeared to contradict one another, or had to be retracted when details were found to be incorrect.

A consequence of the competitive media market and party responses has been to focus attention on party leaders. This was given a major impetus in 2010 with three live televised debates between the three main party leaders. Debates had often been suggested, but had never happened. In 2010, the interests of all three party leaders coincided and, after lengthy negotiations which led to 76 strict rules for their conduct, a series of three debates was agreed with ITV, Sky and the BBC all hosting one each at different regional venues in England. The novelty of the debates mean that they have been commented upon extensively (Allen et al., 2011; Chadwick, 2011a; Kavanagh and Cowley, 2010).

Each debate was in two halves. The first focused around a specific theme, while the second part opened debate up for the leaders to answer questions from the audience. The first debate covered domestic affairs, followed by international affairs in the second and the economy in the third. Each broadcaster pre-selected suitable questions for their debate. Leaders were given the chance to make an opening statement of one minute, and could make a closing statement of a minute and a half. Each leader was given a minute to respond to questions, and an additional minute to respond to other leaders' answers. Free debate of no more than four minutes was then permitted. The audience were not permitted to applaud except at the start and end of each debate, and broadcasters were not allowed to 'cut away' to show audience reaction during the debates.

These were expected to be high profile events. The first debate attracted 9.7 million viewers, while the third reached 8.6 million. The second debate attracted fewer – 4.2 million – but all three were also broadcast live on Radio 4 and shown later on other channels. The parties put in considerable efforts to prepare, with full-scale rehearsals, testing responses to the lines they expected opponents to take, as well as taking advice from experts who had experience of such debates elsewhere (Kavanagh and Cowley, 2010). The Conservatives had called for these debates as early as 2005, expecting that they could outperform their expected Labour opponent, Gordon Brown. Labour hoped that the debates would allow Gordon Brown to portray himself as the serious policy-oriented leader direct to the public, although he traditionally came across poorly on television. For the Liberal Democrats, the equation was simple: this would give them a public platform that they had never had before and therefore increased the party's exposure vastly.

In the first debate, Nick Clegg performed best with a technique which saw him addressing the TV audience directly, while also being able to present the Liberal Democrats as the party of change. YouGov polls showed that 51 per cent thought he performed best, by contrast with 29 per cent for Cameron and 19 per cent for Brown (Allen et al., 2011, p. 190). The subsequent 'Cleggmania' saw the Liberal Democrats rise sharply in the polls, becoming the second placed party, above Labour, in many of them before falling away just before polling day. In subsequent debates, Clegg received a harder time from Cameron and Brown, and the Liberal Democrats also faced considerable scrutiny from the pro-Conservative press. In both subsequent debates, David Cameron was perceived to have performed best, ahead of both Nick Clegg and Gordon Brown. This notwithstanding, many now attribute the Conservatives' failure to win an overall majority to the inclusion of the Liberal Democrats in the debates, giving them vital publicity which undermined Conservative support (Ashcroft, 2010).

The 2010 leaders' debates had a number of consequences. They impacted considerably upon how the campaign was reported. Commentary began in advance with expectations for each debate. This was followed up by analysis of each debate, with immediate commentary often being given by party elites and media advisors who were on hand at the debates in what became known as 'spin alley'. Further analysis was then devoted to reporting polls and research conducted on each debate. Campaign coverage was therefore dominated by media expectations and reactions. This had implications for party campaigns; traditional modes of activity such as daily press conferences were heavily curtailed because of the need to prepare for the debates (Kavanagh and Cowley, 2010). Assessing the first debate, Chadwick (2011a) also highlights the growing influence that new technology has in political communication. While the parties had live Twitter and comment facilities on their websites, he argues that the real-time commentary from a multitude of services and users, including the instant polling, texts and messages highlighted by the media, framed an even more quickly-changing political environment that parties now need to respond to. He therefore suggests that the news cycle has evolved into what he calls 'the political information cycle'.

Parties and the Internet

Over the past decade and a half parties and citizens have both had to adapt to the Internet. A number of claims have been made for its political impact. First, that its increasing use will allow smaller parties to communicate directly with voters in a way that enables these parties to close the gap to the major parties who dominate traditional modes of political communication (Ward, 2005). Second, some have suggested that the rise of the Internet will aid parties in their fundraising, membership recruitment and electioneering activities (Norris, 2001, ch. 8). Third, others have argued that the increasingly wide range of information on the Internet means that the new technologies would lead to both a deepening and a widening of democracy, not least because they would allow new, often harder to reach, social groups to participate. Finally, such arguments were undermined to some degree by the finding that Internet participation essentially replicated and reinforced the profile of those who were already politically active. While the Internet may aid the flow of information, parties were essentially 'preaching to the converted' on the web (Gibson et al., 2005; Norris, 2003).

In assessing parties' websites, a number of distinctions are useful (Norris, 2001, Ch. 8). The first is the extent to which the website is used to provide information. This might be quite basic, but may also include more detailed accounts of party history, the party's constitution, its policies and leadership. This can be thought of as a 'top-down' effort to communicate with website visitors. The second is the extent to which the website encourages some degree of interactivity. Examples include whether or not there are feedback forms, or discussion boards, and whether voters can contact the party, its leaders, candidates and organizations via the information on the site. Such facilities allow feedback from voters, and might be conceptualized as a 'bottom-up' form of communication to parties. A distinction can also be made about parties' internal use of the Internet and new technology. This can be used vertically, as a form of communication between leaders and members, or horizontally as a tool for members and activists to organize with each other to campaign across constituencies.

Since the Internet became widely available to users from the mid-1990s, every UK general election has been dubbed '*the* Internet election' (Coleman, 2001; Ward, 2005; Wring and Ward, 2010). Online enthusiasts have looked to campaigns in the USA, where Presidential hopefuls have utilized the Internet to great effect to mobilize supporters. Wring and Ward (2010, p. 811) suggest that high expectations of the Internet's role boiled down to three factors in 2010. The Internet would dominate the news agenda and parties would consequently lose control of the campaign agenda. Parties and candidates would use new technology extensively in their campaigns, thereby making them more interactive. Finally, the Internet would prove important in shifting voters' opinions and in mobilizing support, not least among the young. Such inflated expectations about the role of the Internet have been disappointed however. While the Internet has proved an important communication tool, it has not provided large scale mobilization, nor notably changed the tenor of campaigns in the UK (Coleman, 2001; Ward, 2005; Wring and Ward, 2010).

UK parties began to develop their web presence in the mid-1990s. By today's standards, these were unsophisticated sites, and were essentially bolt-on extras to parties' main campaign activities. Ward (2005, p. 192) notes that Labour's 1997 website was run by junior staff not related to the party's main communication efforts, and received less than 100,000 hits. Traffic to all main parties' websites increased in 2001, and one account suggested that during the election the hits to party websites were four times that experienced outside of the election period (Butler and Kavanagh, 2002, p. 226). In 2005, Ward (2005, p. 194) highlights the similarities among party websites and points to a

> well established pattern of: news and policy, including audio-video clips of party broadcasts and campaign speeches; about us – basic aims, organizational structure and key people; how to get involved – volunteering, joining and donating online; get in touch/keep in touch – email contacts and campaign diaries.

Most parties, including smaller parties such as the SNP and DUP, also offered website visitors the chance to subscribe to an email newsletter (Jackson, 2006). Increasingly, data from such subscribers is being used to target voters directly, not just with emails but also with direct mail.

In the run up to 2010, there had been some high profile developments, mainly involving more interactive Web 2.0 technology which the parties had begun to experiment with in 2005 (Ward, 2005). At the end of September 2006, the Conservative Party launched 'Webcameron' on its website. This involved regular Internet-based video content, centred around new party leader David Cameron. While the initial video was somewhat derided, it was part of the party's rebranding efforts and claimed to be an attempt to communicate directly with voters, giving them an insight into what the Conservative Party was thinking. Party websites have now evolved to include mobile alerts, YouTube and Twitter feeds and Facebook links. Prominent figures in the parties have used these new media to communicate with voters. During the 2010 campaign, both the Conservatives and Liberal Democrats had around 83–84,000 Facebook followers, while Labour had around 38,000 (Wring and Ward, 2010, p. 814). With the Liberal Democrats, the party therefore had a greater number of Facebook followers than paid-up members. All mainstream parties now include some type of feedback or contact form for website visitors, although this is seldom a high-profile link on the website. Consequently, much online party communication remains of the 'top-down' rather than the 'bottom-up' variety.

Smaller parties' websites tend to have similar content. The BNP, Green Party and UKIP websites all contain links to Twitter and Facebook as well as video content often hosted on YouTube, in addition to other downloadable content. The BNP have links to their two MEPs' blogs, while UKIP have an iPhone application available for download. Supporters can also download posters and other campaign material from the Greens and UKIP, while most small party sites also contain links to things such as petitions for various campaigns. While smaller parties' limited resources may mean they find it difficult to compete in traditional media, the Internet does therefore provide a space for them to communicate their views directly. Small parties' earlier sites may have lacked sophistication. However, given the increasing ubiquity of web technology and knowledge, a more level playing field is now beginning to exist in the relative sophistication of small party websites (Gibson and Ward, 2000; Ward, 2005).

Early candidate and local party websites were quite rudimentary, even if these have since increased in number and quality (Ward and Gibson, 2003; Wring and Ward, 2010). Most party websites now include member-only sections where activists can find information about local campaigns that they may be able to help with. Consequently, the web also helps erode geographical constituency boundaries, building 'horizontal' links between activists. Whether the web has increased this is unclear; parties

Table 8.3   Voters' Internet activity at the 2010 General Election

	%
Visit news sites	78.4
Visit FaceBook or MySpace	12.3
Watch Candidate or Party Videos	12.3
Exchange emails and text messages	11.9
Visit Political Blogs	11.7
Post Comments	4.8
N	862

Source: Data from the British Election Study 2010, http://www.bes2009-10.org/ 24 January 2011.

have always highlighted such opportunities, and activists build links at conferences and party meetings. Lusoli and Ward (2004) have nevertheless noted a small potential for the Internet to increase levels of activism, although this tends to be of the 'low intensity' variety such as reading party literature and renewing membership. Where websites have appeared to increase communication among activists, this has been away from the main party website on blogs such as ConservativeHome.com, Liberal Democrat Voice (libdemvoice.org) and LabourList (labourlist.org).

Table 8.3 reports voters' use of the Internet in the 2010 general election. Although more voters used the Internet in 2010 than in any previous election (Wring and Ward, 2010), by far the most popular activity was visiting traditional news sites, although typically less than half an hour per day was spent on this by those who did so. Far smaller proportions watched candidate or party videos, visited political blogs or posted comments. Gibson et al.'s research (2010, p. 8) also points to the main activity being accessing mainstream news websites, with only 15.5 per cent accessing official sites, 4.6 per cent signing up as a party supporter or for an e-newsletter, and 3.3 per cent using online tools to promote parties. Between elections, between 5–8 per cent visited party websites or sought information about politicians (Di Gennaro and Dutton, 2006; Gibson et al., 2005). Patterns of online participation tend to replicate those found in political participation more generally. However, younger age groups appear to be more inclined to use the Internet to participate, and evidence has also pointed to its potential to mobilize harder to reach groups (Gibson et al., 2005). In 2010, the most e-literate and Internet-active voters tended to be those who identified with the Liberal Democrats (Gibson et al., 2010).

The 2010 general election did not live up to its billing as *the* Internet election. Although the Internet certainly became more important, the tendency to seek out news from the main news organizations means that the Internet continues to follow traditional media. Nonetheless, a web presence is clearly important for parties, allowing them to communicate with voters directly, disseminating information such as manifestos, party news and videos. Moreover, the two types of media are increasingly becoming intertwined. Chadwick's (2011a, 2011b) notion of the 'political information cycle' highlights the interaction between new and old media and how this serves to drive debate on. This is likely to intensify, and parties' communication activities will have to continue to adapt to ensure their message gets across effectively.

Media Effects

What difference does all this make? Whether the media has any effect on party choice and voting behaviour is a topic that has been extensively researched. However, the results have been largely inconclusive. Given the power the media are regularly assumed to have, this might appear surprising. For instance, *The Sun's* readers showed a disproportional swing towards the Conservatives in 2010 after the paper switched allegiances (Wring and Deacon, 2010). Others have suggested that the pattern of coverage in the broadcast media can make a difference to how voters perceive parties (Gavin et al., 1996; Mughan, 1996). Increasing voter dealignment potentially makes the media's role even more influential.

Yet, some note the difficulty of disentangling the impact of the press or television from other influences such as friends, family, and the socio-economic context (Denver, 2007, p. 139; Newton and Brynin, 2001, p. 266). As Cowley's (2001) study of newspaper efforts to encourage tactical voting shows, even where the media does set out to change behaviour, it is far from clear that it is successful in doing so. Similarly, *The Guardian's* 2010 support for the Liberal Democrats was undermined by the fact that most of the paper's readers continued to vote Labour (Wring and Deacon, 2010). With the press, the consensus view tends to be that voters choose their newspaper because of already held beliefs and opinions. Consequently, the main newspaper effect is to reinforce readers' opinions, rather than to change them. More generally, most authors now argue that any media effects are long term in nature (Newton and Brynin, 2001; Norris et al., 1999; Norris, 2000).

Innovative research continues into these issues. In one of the most comprehensive studies, Norris et al. (1999) undertook extensive research into potential media effects in the 1997 general election, examining both the press and television using panel and experimental techniques. Their findings were modest. Their panel study suggested that the short-term effect of the news media had been exaggerated since different patterns of media use and attention were not associated with changes in political attitudes or participation. They also found that the agenda-setting role of the news media was limited, since it failed to divert voters' attention from areas they already felt strongly about, such as jobs, health and education. Their experimental research suggested that voters' party preferences could be influenced by positive television news coverage of parties (Sanders and Norris, 1998). However, they highlighted that positive coverage for one party tended to be cancelled out by positive coverage for another (Norris et al., 1999). Finally, the press was also found to have limited impact upon changing voters' behaviour in 1997. Instead, they underlined the argument that the press reinforces pre-existing attitudes and behaviour, but suggest that the press may make a difference by mobilizing their more loyal readers.

Newton and Brynin (2001) examined press effects on voting in the 1992 and 1997 general elections by comparing those whose views were reinforced by their newspaper; those whose views were different to those of their newspaper; and those who did not regularly read a paper. Their findings suggested that there were statistically significant newspaper effects in these elections, and that they were stronger in 1992 than 1997. The effects were highest for those with no partisan identification, and also for those with Labour sympathies. While the effects were small, Newton and Brynin suggested that they may have been large enough to make a difference in some tight election races. Moreover, they highlight the imbalance of press partisanship by speculating that the outcome of some post-war British elections may have been different had there been a more even balance of newspaper circulation between parties.

These arguments are unlikely to be resolved conclusively in the near future. If anything the limited media effects that have been found are likely to become weaker since declining newspaper circulation and the fragmentation of the broadcast media mean that voters can increasingly avoid political news and information should they want to do so. The Internet seems more likely to reinforce, rather than challenge, such a dynamic. Where the media have a considerable effect is upon party – not voters' – behaviour. Parties feel it is important to try to set the media agenda and thereby communicate to voters. Hence the professionalization and media management techniques discussed above. However, it is not always clear that this is effective either. Both Alastair Campbell and Andy Coulson resigned after they had both become a major story in their own right, Campbell in the aftermath of controversy over the Iraq war, Coulson after controversy about what he knew about his former newspaper engaging in illegal phone-hacking activity while he was editor. Parties therefore find it difficult to control the media, who will often concentrate on stories that parties would rather ignore. In a passage that continues to ring true, Norris et al. (1999, pp. 181–2) observe that:

> In the 1997 campaign the party and the news agendas remained worlds apart ... No party was consistently more successful than any other in setting the news agenda across different media outlets. It appears as though parties are trying ever harder to set the agenda, but that the rise of a more autonomous news media may have undermined the ability of politicians to get their message across.

Conclusion

The media is central to the conduct of party politics in modern democracies. While the media are market driven and seek audiences, they also help shape public opinion. Political communication is a two-way process in such a situation. Parties direct their communication efforts towards specific goals, targeting specific media outlets which they hope will be favourable. However, such messages seldom feed through to voters directly. Media coverage often provides parties with important and swift feedback about their message. It is these mediated versions which are mostly received by citizens, who in turn can feed their own views back to parties either directly or via the media. The highly partisan bias of the British press means that newspapers present certain messages in particular ways, depending on their party allegiances at the time. However, the broadcast media are perceived, and required, to be more impartial. Nevertheless, how the media report party politics is important for analysts to understand, as are parties' efforts to manage and influence media coverage. Typically, parties have attempted to do so by professionalizing their media operations, and by diversifying their communications activities to include new technologies such as the Internet. This is not always effective. The Internet has consistently failed to live up to the claims made for it in the last three general elections. Similarly, it is not always evident that there is much in the way of an electoral effect from either parties' media management efforts, or even from press endorsements. If they exist, such effects are modest at best and are only evident in the longer term. As often as not, parties' efforts to manipulate the political agenda end up being counter-productive, with regular debates about the perceived negative consequences of 'spin' placing parties in the media dock. Parties are caught in an 'arms race' dynamic here; efforts to gain an advantage in political communication by one party are reacted to by others fearful of falling behind in their presentation efforts. The increasing fragmentation and interaction of both old and new media outlets means that such efforts are likely to become more, not less, important to parties. With a disinterested electorate, the diversity and pluralism of the various media suggest however that parties' efforts are likely to have no more effect in the future than they have had previously.

9
Developments in Party Organization and Funding

To fulfil their democratic functions, parties must have a degree of organization and be able to fund their activities throughout the electoral cycle. Organization helps parties to debate and decide upon policy, recruit members, activists and potential candidates, and to campaign for election. Nevertheless, the study of organization and funding is often overlooked since it involves looking at aspects of parties' internal affairs conducted behind closed doors. Yet party organization and funding are key issues, and important conflicts over political power often occur not in the broader political system, but within parties. To be able to form any view on how political parties in the UK are working, understanding organization and funding is imperative. This chapter therefore introduces and evaluates key developments in party organization and funding in the UK in recent years. The chapter focuses on the main three parties at Westminster: the Conservatives, Labour and the Liberal Democrats. These issues however also apply to the smaller and non-UK-wide parties and indicative examples are provided to enable some comparison between different party types. Discussion revolves around three sections. The first section provides an assessment of the parties' organizational structures. Having a sizeable and active local membership is often seen as a key indicator of party strength and the second section therefore discusses levels of membership and activism. The final section introduces key aspects of the funding of political parties and assesses recent attempts to reform the system of party funding in the UK.

Organizational Structures

Five main elements of party organization can be identified. These are the *party leadership*, the *parliamentary party*, the party's *policy-making process*, the *grassroots party organization*, and the *professional wing* of the party. These elements have different degrees of importance within different parties.

Debates on party organization have historically revolved around the question of whether or not parties can be internally democratic or are instead leadership dominated. In his famous 'Iron Law of Oligarchy', Michels (1959 [1915]) argued that, for a variety of psychological and organizational reasons, parties would become oligarchies where leadership elites would be able to dominate lower party strata at the expense of internal democracy. McKenzie (1963) found that such leadership dominance existed in his seminal study of power in British political parties.

These ideas continue to be influential. They are however based on the idea that the relationship between party leaderships and the broader party are necessarily conflictual, often because party activists are more radical than the more moderate and electorally oriented leadership (May, 1973). While not denying the potential for internal party conflict, recent perspectives have instead emphasized the 'stratarchical' nature of parties. This underlines the importance of internal consensus. It highlights the fact that parties have a number of fairly autonomous elites at different levels – local, regional, professional etc. – throughout their organizations. From this perspective, the party leadership's position, and ultimately the success or failure of the party, is conditional on their support. Compromise between different elements of the party is crucial to avoid a breakdown of this system (Katz and Mair, 1995; Carty, 2004). How do the mainstream British parties' organizational structures fit with these two contrasting perspectives?

The Conservative Party

1998 is a key dividing line for assessing organizational developments in the Conservative Party. Prior to 1998, the Conservative Party did not have a unified structure. In addition to the leadership, the party consisted of three essentially autonomous elements. First, constituency associations were essentially independent bodies, and had considerably more freedom of action than local organizations in other parties. These constituency associations were represented by the National Union of Conservative and Unionist Associations. The National Union was also responsible for organizing various party conferences. The second element was the parliamentary party. The leader could appoint MPs to the cabinet or party's 'shadow' cabinets, thereby assuring a degree of loyalty. The remaining MPs were members of the influential '1922 Committee' of backbench Conservative MPs. While this had informal, advisory powers vis-à-vis the leadership, the 1922 Committee was largely used as a 'means of managing dissent' (Fisher, 1996, p. 37). The third element was Conservative Central Office (CCO) which was responsible directly to the party leader and was home to the professional wing of the party. Policy-making was leadership dominated, with the party conference widely perceived to have no formal role in making policy, being instead seen as a stage-managed event designed to get good media coverage. Kelly (1989) however challenged this view, arguing that since the party ran a series of conferences at different levels, informal feedback from this 'hidden system' of conferences fed into many policy announcements made at Annual Conference. This notwithstanding, the party was seen as leadership dominated.

In the aftermath of the 1997 election, the new Conservative leader William Hague embarked upon extensive organizational reform, hoping to make the party more electable. The subsequent *Fresh Future* reforms had a number of elements. First, the three autonomous wings of the party – constituency, parliamentary and professional – were merged into a single structure under a unified constitution in 1998. Second, a party Board was established with responsibility for matters such as fundraising, membership and party management. Comprised of 19 members, the Board has representation from each of the formerly autonomous wings of the party on it. Third, a Conservative Policy Forum (CPF) was set up in an attempt to engage party members in policy-making. Under this system, 'outline' policy documents would be commissioned and sent from the Policy Forum's co-ordinating body, the CPF General Council, to constituency associations. Constituency parties would discuss these documents, reporting back to the General Council and from there to the Shadow Cabinet who may, or may not, incorporate the reports of local parties into their speeches at Conference (Kelly, 2001). Finally, members were to have a one-member-one-vote (OMOV) ballot in relation to party leadership elections and on matters relating to policy and organization.

The problem with the *Fresh Future* reforms was that they not only failed to help the party progress electorally at the 2001 general election, they were also justified in the somewhat contradictory language of both intra-party democracy and efficiency. While appearing to extend powers to party members and constituency associations, by definition creating a unified structure from the three separate wings removed the formal autonomy of constituency associations. Under the subsequent leadership of both Duncan Smith and Howard, the Policy Forum process and the Board were largely marginalized (Kelly, 2004). Moreover, participation in OMOV ballots on policy was seldom very high (Kelly, 2002). A subsequent consultation paper on organization issued under Howard's leadership, *A 21ˢᵗ Century Party* (Conservative Party, 2005), emphasized the need for a rationalization of the party's constituency associations, seeing them as holding 'franchises' awarded by party HQ. It argued for merging weaker associations and directing resources towards targeting marginal seats. These ideas were driven by the need for electoral efficiency, with little mention of internal democracy. Despite setting up six policy review groups, organizational developments have not been central to David Cameron's repositioning of the party. Nevertheless, the professional wing of the party has been strengthened and the policy process is again dominated by the leadership (Bale, 2008). Despite Hague's reforms, the leadership therefore continues to be the key element in understanding Conservative Party organization.

The Labour Party

Historically Labour has been a federal organization with three constituent parts: the trade unions; socialist societies (such as the Fabians); and Constituency Labour Parties (CLPs). Each of these elements were part of the Electoral College that elected the party leader, and were represented at Annual Conference and on the party's regional councils. Conference was formally the party's sovereign decision-making body, while between conferences the National Executive Committee (NEC), ultimately responsible to conference, would be in charge of day-to-day policy and organizational matters. The parliamentary party (PLP) had no formal policy-making power. The party was regularly portrayed as oligarchic and leadership dominated. Despite the supposedly democratic role of conference, the trade unions controlled up to 90 per cent of conference votes with their 'block vote'. Since the unions regularly supported the wishes of the leadership, this essentially meant that the leadership could, with some notable exceptions (Minkin, 1978), usually get its way at conference. A key contradiction of Labour organization was the tension between internal party democracy and democracy within the broader society. The PLP was essentially dependent upon, controlled by and had to represent decisions taken by the extra-parliamentary Annual Conference. Conference delegates were however selected by intra-party procedures and did not have the legitimacy of being externally elected like the party's MPs (McKenzie, 1982; Russell, 2005; Webb, 1992).

Organizational reforms during the 1980s–90s were widely perceived to have been necessary because the unions and constituency delegates at conference were thought to be more radical than the leadership. Having conference as the main decision-making forum therefore risked high-profile conflict over policy between radical activists and the party leadership. At the same time, some members were also keen to have more input to the party's policy process. Initial changes came under Neil Kinnock's leadership. Kinnock's Policy Review circulated policy documents for local parties' consideration. Even if not wholly successful, this was an early example of widening policy debate within the party (Russell, 2005, p. 132). Conference subsequently set up a National Policy Forum (NPF) which eventually came into being in 1993. This was based on a two-year cycle of policy discussion where constituencies and affiliated organizations could submit amendments to policy documents circulated in advance. Although the NPF had no formal power, it had the potential to undermine the influence of both the NEC and conference in policy-making. Reduction in the union block vote to 70 per cent was also proposed, and eventually agreed at the 1992 conference. This was reduced further during the 1990s with unions being required to ballot their members and split their vote accordingly between the competing policy options being voted for.

Tony Blair extended these reforms, often under the rubric of 'democratizing' the party for the ordinary member. Members were given OMOV ballots, already in use for candidate and leadership selections, on policy proposals. Although not used since, this tactic was used in Blair's successful 1994 attempt to reword Clause IV of the party's constitution and also to legitimate the 1996 draft manifesto. The key organizational reform to policy-making came with the introduction of *Partnership in Power* in 1997. This was justified as an attempt to build a constructive policy process between the party leadership, now in government, and the broader party. This was based on the NPF, running on a two-year cycle of policy debate. A number of policy commissions circulate documents for comment in the first year to members, CLPs, regional policy forums and affiliated organizations. During the second year, formal policy proposals are drawn up and presented to conference. This presentation may include majority and minority positions and conference decides whether to adopt these proposals as policy.

These reforms have opened up participation in the party's policy-making process beyond those delegates that would traditionally attend conference. Nevertheless, they have been widely criticized. First, there was a clear desire in *Partnership in Power* to minimize the potential for damaging splits at conference (Seyd, 1999, p. 393). This reduces conference to essentially having only a Yes/No vote on policy. Second, the format and leadership of policy forum discussions are likely to be dominated by middle-class professionals thereby excluding certain elements of the party. Consequently, the consultation process gives the leadership ample time to dilute or address criticism (Seyd, 1999; Webb, 2000, pp. 204–5). While Russell (2005, p. 168) suggests leadership-party relations under this system 'remain fluid', each of these criticisms nevertheless points to a process where the leadership remains potentially the most influential element in understanding power in the Labour Party. However, the increasingly rebellious nature of the PLP under Blair and Brown did to some degree act as a brake on the leadership's policy ambitions particularly towards the end of Labour's term of government (Cowley, 2005). Moreover, as evidenced by the 2004 Warwick Agreement, the trade unions have been able to use Labour's reliance on them for funds to regain some influence in policy-making (Quinn, 2010), although since becoming leader Ed Miliband has sought to downplay the party's union links after their votes contributed to his leadership victory in 2010. In early 2011, Miliband also embarked upon a further examination of the party's organization, entitled 'Refounding Labour', to assess how it could be improved and made more effective (Labour Party, 2011).

The Liberal Democrats

The organization of the Liberal Democrats is both Federal and aims to be participative. These aspects can be traced to the party's ideological concern with 'community politics'. The base level of Liberal Democrat organization consists of local parties across Britain. Depending on their membership size, these constituency parties are entitled to send a number of delegates to the party's Annual Conference. Party policy is decided upon democratically by votes at Annual Conference, which is the party's supreme policy-making body. The party's Federal Policy Committee (FPC), on which the party leader sits, has formal responsibility for reacting to policy between conferences and for developing the party's general election manifesto. Any policy made by the FPC must then be formally approved by conference. The party's Federal Executive Committee (FEC), chaired by the party President, is responsible for managing the party, and has Finance and Administration and Campaigning sub-committees responsible for running the party's finances and campaign efforts. The parliamentary party has no formal constitutional input into policy-making, although it is represented at conference. The party leader is elected by an OMOV ballot of party members. In the terminology of Liberal Democrat organization, 'Federal Party' essentially means the party at British level. Scotland and Wales have autonomous Liberal

Democrat organizations, referred to as 'state parties', both essentially replicating the party's Federal structure, with their own leaders, executives and Annual Conferences with policy-making powers. This means that the Scottish and Welsh parties are free to make policy which may differ from that of the party at national level.

Accounts of Liberal Democrat organization appear reluctant to identify where power lies (Ingle, 1996; Russell and Fieldhouse, 2005, ch. 3). A number of tensions can be identified as a result of the party's structure. The first is between the role of the FPC and conference in policy-making. A potential downside of having conference make policy is that this can be slow to react, ineffective and lead to not always electorally attractive policy. This notwithstanding, conference guards its power jealously. While many FPC policy motions are passed at conference, these can often be amended to bear little resemblance to the policy carefully worked out and proposed by the FPC (Bentham, 2007, p. 65). Secondly, Russell and Fieldhouse (2005, ch. 4) highlight a potential tension between leadership elites and the grassroots party. Local parties and activists may not always be willing to accept the party leadership line on policy and would point out that despite the party's increasingly professionalized campaign operation, it has been the 'community politics' approach of the party on the ground that gets the party elected. Finally, there is also a tension between the party leader and the broader party. Brack (2007b) argues that the leader must have communication skills, party management skills, and also something to say. When one or more of these elements is not present, the leadership is likely to be less successful. Indeed, Brack argues that Charles Kennedy's lack of party management skills and policy agenda contributed to him being replaced as party leader.

Where then does power lie in Liberal Democrat organization? An increase in size has given the parliamentary party a level of influence not foreseen in the party constitution. Indeed, recently it has often seemed that the parliamentary party has driven both policy and the party's leadership decisions. Russell et al. (2007a) highlight the parliamentary party's *de facto* veto on developments within the party. Cole (2009) indicates that the parliamentary party has been relatively disciplined in recent years. Providing Brack's criteria are met and the parliamentary party remains disciplined, it is not unreasonable to suggest that the party leader can have significant influence over the party. Indeed, the leadership's position was arguably cemented by two developments under Clegg: an internal review of party structures taking powers from the elected Federal Executive and giving them to a leadership-appointed group of senior figures (Evans and

Sanderson-Nash, 2011); and a reluctance to defeat the party leadership at conference after having lost two leaders in quick succession (Grayson, 2010). Nevertheless, party members and conference have traditionally not been afraid to embarrass the leadership, or the FPC, and so both must bring the broader party with them. That the party's spring 2011 conference defeated the leadership on a motion defending Conservative-inspired reforms to the NHS demonstrated that delegates had begun to find their voice again in the aftermath of the 2010 election, with the party's poor performance in the 2011 local and devolved elections likely to make them more inclined to speak out. The broad balance of power between these different party levels suggests that the Liberal Democrats are the party that most closely fits the 'stratarchic' model of organization.

Other Parties

These organizational perspectives can also be utilized when assessing other parties. To take one example, SNP organization has also approximated the 'stratarchic' model. The primary unit of SNP organization is the branch. These have traditionally been responsible for membership, fundraising and sending delegates to national bodies within the party. Constituency associations are formed from two or more branches, are responsible for both co-ordinating and expanding activity in the constituency, and contesting elections. Annual Conference is the party's main policy-making forum and delegates are sent as representatives of their branch or constituency association. Between conferences, the party holds quarterly National Council meetings. These have the authority to make policy and are also attended by local delegates. National Council members are also elected by conference delegates. The party's locally-based structure has historically been difficult to manage (Bennie et al., 1997). The SNP amended its constitution in 2004 in an attempt to make the party more manageable. It introduced changes to candidate selection procedures, expanded the number of local branches needed to initiate a leadership challenge, and introduced measures to ensure more women were selected as candidates. This was portrayed as an attempt to move the party's culture away from radical activists to give power to ordinary rank-and-file members, and was perceived by some as a leadership incursion into branches' traditional powers. Alex Salmond's resumption of the SNP leadership in 2004 has seen the leadership reassert its authority on the back of growing success while, since forming the Scottish government in 2007, the party's ministers and parliamentary group are also influential elements of party organization.

Smaller parties can sometimes seem to take organizational structures to the extremes. The BNP and Greens are good examples. The BNP's ideological heritage privileges strong leadership. The BNP leader is elected by a secret ballot of the party's membership. Once elected, the leader controls party administration, strategy, finances, and policy development. An advisory council, consisting of regional organizers, members of the party's national staff and leadership appointees, advises the leader and can meet up to three times per year. Below this level, the BNP also has a regional structure based on eight regions. Nevertheless, and despite the party's fractious nature, leadership domination is the party's key organizational principle (BNP, 2007; Copsey, 2008). By contrast, the Greens have a highly participative structure also derived from their ideological approach to politics. Until late 2008, the Greens did not have a leader, preferring instead to have two 'principal speakers', one male and the other female. Policy is made by votes at twice yearly conferences. An Executive responsible for the day-to-day running of the party is elected annually at conference, and the party has a number of internal committees responsible for various aspects of party development, such as policy, regional organization, campaigns and fundraising. While this represents a degree of specialization at elite level, the Greens nevertheless prioritize internal democracy over the tendency for hierarchical leadership found in other parties.

Grassroots Organization and Membership

Classic definitions of political parties suggest that having active, visible and essentially permanent organization at the grassroots level is a key indicator of the health of modern political parties. LaPalombara and Weiner (1966, p. 6) argue that parties must have continuity in organization – i.e. organization not dependent on the life span of current party leaders – and manifest permanent organization at the local level. Similarly, Sartori (2005, p. 10) highlights the importance of party organizational networks to parties seeking to expand their influence in the longer term.

A good indicator of the strength and durability of party organization is the size of membership that parties have in the constituencies. Table 9.1 estimates the average constituency party membership size for the Conservatives, Labour and the Liberal Democrats from 1992 to 2010. The national decline in party membership highlighted in Chapter 2 is further underlined in Table 9.1. The average constituency membership

Table 9.1   Estimated average constituency party membership, 1992–2010

	1992	1997	2001	2005	2010
Conservative	1542	729	650	892	402
Labour	444	592	476	349	272
Liberal Democrats	167	162	130	157	116
All	2153	1483	1256	1398	790

Source: Data from British Constituency Campaigning Surveys.

when all three parties are taken together was just over 2,100 in 1992. By 2001, this had fallen to just over 1,200. While the figure in 2005 appeared to have risen, it is necessary to treat this with some caution since the average figure for Conservative associations is not necessarily representative of the broader party and likely to over-represent Conservative strength (Fisher, 2008a, p. 266). The 2010 average makes the overall downward trend much clearer. Indeed, it demonstrates a sharp, downward trend, with total constituency membership for the three main parties only around a third of what it was in 1992.

Surveys of constituency parties also demonstrate a downward trend in Plaid Cymru's constituency parties from 226 in 1992 to 145 in 2010, while the SNP's average constituency membership has fluctuated, rising from 166 in 1992 to 204 in 2001, falling back to 130 in 2005, only to rise again to 186 in 2007 and 208 in 2010. Smaller parties do not have comparable levels of constituency organization. However, as Chapter 6 shows, some have bucked the trend of membership decline with the Greens, UKIP and BNP all showing a rise in membership between 2002 and 2009.

Table 9.1 highlights different patterns of constituency membership development within the main parties. Until 2005, membership developments appeared often closely related to electoral success and whether or not the party was in government. The Conservative Party had consistently the largest constituency memberships of all three main parties from 1992 onwards. Nevertheless, the party's constituency memberships declined by around 60 per cent between 1992 and 2001, with most of this decline occurring between 1992 and 1997, years associated with John Major's turbulent premiership and the party's defeat by New Labour. Labour showed an increase in average constituency party membership between 1992 and 1997 from 444 to 592. Indeed, success under Blair was closely associated with building up the party's grassroots membership.

From winning the 1997 election and taking office, however, Labour's constituency membership declined, falling to around 349 in 2005. Liberal Democrat constituency membership was more constant at around 160, despite a fall to 130 in 2001. This increased again to 157 in 2005, an election which saw the party win 62 seats. Similarly, SNP membership peaked in the years either side of devolution before declining somewhat. Moreover, the party's initial 2007 Scottish election success happened at a time when the SNP had been successful in rebuilding its local organization (Clark, 2008).

In 2010, a different trend is evident, breaking the pattern of local memberships rising in opposition. Indeed, both Conservative and Liberal Democrat organizations show a sharp decline, their electoral popularity not equating to any growth in their organizational network in 2010. With the continued exception of the SNP, all mainstream parties have therefore suffered a clear and sharp decline in their local party organizations.

Average figures hide considerable variations in party strength. Such variations are partly a function of the social composition of the constituency. However, membership size is often accounted for by the electoral context. Constituency memberships are likely to be higher where parties either hold the constituency, or in marginal or target seats which the party thinks it can win. The corollary is that local memberships are likely to be lower where the party does not hold the seat and is not targeting it as winnable. Evidence comes from Fisher et al.'s (2006a) study of the relative impact of members in constituency campaigning, presented in Figure 9.1. Across all three parties, membership size tends to

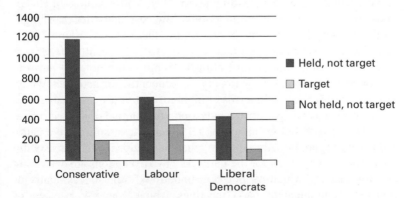

Figure 9.1   Average constituency membership by constituency type

Source: Data from Fisher et al., 2006a, p. 671.

be considerably higher in seats which parties either hold or are targeting. Memberships are lowest where parties do not hold the seat and are not targeting it.

Why are grassroots party members important? Whiteley et al. (1994, pp. 1–8) argue that members provide parties with a number of benefits. They provide income through subscriptions and donations. Members act as representative figureheads, or 'ambassadors' (Scarrow, 1996), in their community, providing feedback to party elites on local political views, while at the same time communicating the party's message to voters. Members can also be a source of ideas for the party, and help to select party elites. Finally, members provide a source of voluntary labour for the party which is especially useful during election campaigns.

Not all members are equally active. Whiteley et al. (1994, p. 73) suggest that activities should be thought of in terms of the potential cost – in time and effort as well as money – to the party member. The expectation is that more members will undertake 'low-cost' activities, such as signing a petition for the party, than will take part in potentially 'high-cost' and time-intensive activities such as standing for election. One difficulty in providing an up-to-date assessment is that studies of party membership are only occasionally carried out in the UK. The most in-depth surveys of Conservative, Labour and Liberal Democrat memberships are now all more than a decade old (Seyd and Whiteley, 1992, 2002a; Whiteley et al., 1994; Whiteley et al., 2006). It is nevertheless possible to get a snapshot of what members do, and whether their activities can be structured in such a manner.

Table 9.2 reports the types of activities undertaken by Labour party members in the five years leading up to 1997. With a couple of exceptions, more Labour members undertook 'low-cost' activities than 'high-cost' activities, thereby broadly confirming these ideas. Around 78 per cent displayed a party poster either occasionally or frequently, 70 per cent regularly donated money and almost 65 per cent signed a petition supported by the party occasionally or frequently, all activities which take little time or effort. In terms of high-cost activities, less than 15 per cent either occasionally or frequently stood for internal or elected office, helped at a street stall or undertook telephone canvassing for the party. Similarly, only around a third of party members helped to fundraise or did door-to-door canvassing for the party. The two exceptions are delivering election leaflets, which 59 per cent undertook either occasionally or frequently, and attending party meetings, which around 45 per cent of members reported doing at least occasionally. Nevertheless, neither requires the same amount of effort as standing for office and the main cost

Table 9.2   Labour Party members' activity, 1997 (percentages)

Activity	Not at all	Rarely	Occasionally	Frequently
Displayed poster	16.6	5.1	23.4	54.9
Signed petition	23.5	11.7	37.0	27.8
Donated money	16.9	12.8	38.8	31.5
Helped fundraise	51.3	13.5	20.3	14.9
Helped at street stall	83.1	5.4	6.4	5.1
Delivered election leaflets	35.4	5.6	18.9	40.1
Attended party meeting	39.0	15.5	19.8	25.8
Door-to-door canvassing	62.0	6.6	12.7	18.8
Telephone canvassing	86.0	4.1	4.8	5.2
Stood for internal office	82.9	3.0	6.7	7.4
Stood for elected office	89.3	1.9	3.2	5.5

Source: Data from Seyd and Whiteley, 2002b.

to members with both activities is one of spending a short period of time occasionally attending a meeting or delivering leaflets. Broadly similar patterns were found among Conservative and Liberal Democrat party members (Whiteley et al., 1994, 2006).

Party members do not necessarily spend a lot of time on party activities. Seyd and Whiteley (2004) found that around two-thirds of Labour members spent no time in the average month on party activities. The proportion was closer to three-quarters for Conservative members, although much smaller at just over half for the Liberal Democrats. Liberal Democrat members seem to spend more time on party activities than Labour or Conservative members. The proportion of Liberal Democrat members spending between 5 and 10 hours on party work per month in 1999 was around 36 per cent. This compared with around 30 per cent for Labour party members, also surveyed in 1999, and around 20 per cent for Conservative members.

Seyd and Whiteley (2004, p. 359) also point to a greater proportion of members in all three parties reporting they are becoming less rather than more active. It may be that the nature of party activism has evolved, moving away from these more traditional party activities. Scarrow (1996) suggests that members act more generally as 'ambassadors in the community' for parties, and there is some evidence to support this proposition; 86 per cent of Labour Party members talk about politics with people who are not members (Seyd and Whiteley, 2004, p. 362). Moreover, most parties now also rely on a broader group of 'supporters'. These are people who are not paid-up members of the party, but who may be broadly supportive of its aims and therefore prepared to help out when necessary, particularly during elections.

If members are not particularly active, why do they join political parties in the first place? This is an important question, since most people do not join parties and 'free ride' on any benefits that parties bring to society. Membership studies suggest that individuals are motivated by a range of incentives to join. The idea is that individuals weigh up the potential costs and benefits of membership before deciding to join a party, with the benefits outweighing the costs. This 'general incentives' theory revolves around *selective*, *collective* and *individual incentives*. *Selective* incentives are those benefits which individuals get only from being a party member. They can be grouped into three types. First, process incentives relate to the experience of participating within a political party. Second, outcome incentives relate to the private benefits which members can achieve through party membership, such as the opportunity to stand for office or make contacts not available to non-members. Third, ideological incentives relate to members being able to meet and express their political ideology with others of a similar outlook.

Collective incentives refer to the policy aims of political parties. These can be of two types. Positive collective incentives can be gained by helping the party achieve its policy goals, while negative collective incentives can be achieved by attempting to prevent other parties from implementing their policies. In addition, *individual* incentives relate to the extent to which party membership is a sense of duty or altruism, an expression of emotional attachment to the party, or the product of a social norm or expectation of people the party member knows.

Various studies have found evidence for these ideas (Seyd and Whiteley, 1992; 2002a; Whiteley et al., 1994; Whiteley et al., 2006). However, there are different patterns amongst the parties. The three most important incentives for Conservative members were expressive attachments to the party and its principles, collective positive incentives in promoting party policy, and negative collective incentives which aim to oppose other parties' policies. Process incentives and social norms were also important, although less often cited as a reason for joining. With Labour altruistic concerns, for instance a desire for social justice, outweighed all other incentives, with political process and negative collective incentives coming a distant second and third place in motivating people to join. With Liberal Democrat members, expressive attachments appeared to be most important and in particular a positive attitude towards party principles. These attitudes extended to party policies, meaning that the second most important incentive explaining Liberal

Democrat members joining the party fell under the heading of collective positive incentives.

There are more ex-party members than party members in Britain today (Whiteley, 2009a, p. 248). There are a number of explanations. Parties failing to provide specific incentives may lead to members deciding to leave the party. Indeed, disillusion with Labour policies in office has been used as an explanation to explain the party's declining leadership. Some members join but are not strongly committed to the party and fail to renew their membership. Such a dynamic is widely held to explain the drop in Labour Party membership in the aftermath of the 1997 election. Finally, there can also be mundane reasons for members leaving the party. The member may move and not receive party mail or the local party may not be particularly active in following up former members.

Far from extending parties' reach in society, party organizational networks appear to be in decline, as do levels of activism. This makes it more difficult for parties to carry out many of their functions. It also means that parties find it increasingly hard to raise funds from subscriptions and donations from an ever-declining membership base. It is to party funding that the next section turns.

The Funding of Political Parties in the UK

Party Income and Expenditure

Representative democracy is expensive. Many countries recognize the importance of political parties to their democracy and have advanced extensive state subsidies to help finance parties. Political parties in the UK have not had such comprehensive state support available to them. British parties have essentially been funded by voluntary means and, consequently, are underfunded. Sources of funding fall into seven broad categories, which can be applied to both mainstream and smaller parties. First, parties receive funding from membership *subscriptions*. Second, parties can be the recipients of *donations* from individuals. These donations can range from the relatively small to large donations of millions of pounds, and include money from party fundraising drives. Third, parties can also receive *institutional or corporate donations* from, for instance, pressure groups or companies. Fourth, parties can receive *affiliation fees* from associated organizations. The primary examples of these in the UK are the financial subventions given to the Labour Party by the trade unions. Fifth, parties can benefit from some limited *government grants and subsidies*, and from *institutional allowances* paid to elected representatives. Sixth, parties can also obtain some of their funding from *loans*. Finally, parties can also earn money from *commercial transactions and investments*. For example, the Conservative Party sold its former party HQ in London for around £30 million in 2007 in an attempt to clear the party's outstanding debts.

Table 9.3 sets out the sources of funding for both the Conservative and Labour parties for every second year between 2003–09. From this, a broad pattern is evident. Conservative Party income has steadily increased through this period to around £42 million, while Labour Party income peaked at just over £35 million in 2005, before fluctuating in the next four years. Membership income rose in both parties until 2007, but has started to decline with the Conservatives and has fluctuated with Labour since then. These figures also highlight the importance of donations to both parties; donations and fundraising contribute by far the largest proportion of party income. This peaked for the Conservatives in

Table 9.3　　Conservative and Labour Party funding, 2003–2009 (£000s)

	Type of income	2003	2005	2007	2009
Conservative	Membership fees	814	843	1,214	1,085
	Donations and fundraising	7,647	14,279	19,266	26,129
	Commercial	96	2,476	1,427	1,418
	State subsidies/ grants	4,144	4,586	5,104	5,183
	Other income	918	1,804	5,935	8,169
	Total	13,619	24,227	33,509	41,984
Labour	Membership fees	3,452	3,685	4,447	4,497
	Donations and fundraising	10,487	14,980	13,133	6,410
	Commercial	3,201	3,659	3,355	3,743
	Affiliation fees	6,762	8,009	7,915	7,969
	State subsidies/ grants	439	440	368	995
	Other income	2,599	4,531	3,140	3,184
	Total	26,940	35,304	32,358	26,798

Source: Data from party accounts registered with the Electoral Commission, http://www.electoralcommission.org.uk/party-finance.

the European election year of 2009. Donation and fundraising income peaked for Labour in 2005 at just under £15 million, before fluctuating thereafter with the party raising just under £6.5 million in donations and fundraising in 2009.

Although Britain does not have a comprehensive system of state subsidies, some limited subventions are available to parties. So-called 'Short Money' is paid to opposition parties to help them execute their parliamentary duties and depends on the number of seats and vote share achieved at the last election. A Policy Development Fund (PDF) was also introduced for parties as part of the Political Parties, Elections and Referendums (PPERA) 2000 Act (see below). Both parties benefited from these subsidies, with the Conservatives receiving considerably more, just over £5 million in 2007–09, because of their entitlement to 'Short Money'. This also helps fund the Office of the Leader of the Opposition and was therefore of considerable benefit to the Conservatives in opposition in the House of Commons. The Liberal Democrats survive with much less income and this appears much more reliant on the election cycle. Party accounts show that Liberal Democrat Federal Party income rose from just over £4 million in 2003 to more than £8.5 million in 2005, before falling back to around £6.5 million in 2009. Like the other parties, the Liberal Democrats are heavily dependent on donations and fundraising. They have also been relatively more heavily reliant on Short Money, the loss of which, since becoming part of the coalition government from 2010, led to a number of redundancies and financial difficulties at Liberal Democrat HQ (Evans and Sanderson-Nash, 2011).

Of the other parties, four broke through the £1 million income barrier between 2002–09. SNP income has been consistently over £1 million since 2003, peaking at £2.56 million in 2007, the year of the party's first success in Scottish parliament elections. UKIP raised £1.7 million in 2004 and £1.2 million in 2009, while the BNP raised around £1.9 million in 2009. In Northern Ireland, Sinn Fein has consistently raised over £1 million from 2007 onwards. Plaid Cymru, the other Northern Irish parties and minor parties in Great Britain survive with far less money, with, for example, averages across the 2002–09 period of £691,000 for Plaid Cymru, £306,000 for the DUP and £467,000 for the Greens.

Party expenditure often outstrips total income, particularly in general election years. Figure 9.2 provides a snapshot of this relationship for each of the three major parties. Where a party's figure is above 0, the party has had more income than expenditure that year. If a party's figure extends below 0, the party's expenditure exceeded its income in that year. In three

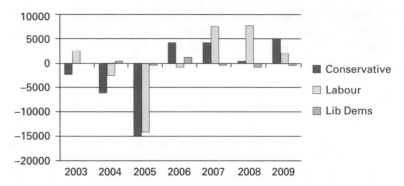

Figure 9.2   Party income and expenditure, 2003–2009 (£000)

Source: Data from party accounts registered with the Electoral Commission, http://www.electoralcommission.org.uk/party-finance.

of the seven years assessed, both Conservative and Labour Party income has fallen short of the party's expenditure. This is particularly evident in the general election year of 2005, when both the Conservative and Labour parties had deficits of close to £15 million and the Liberal Democrats had a deficit of around £200,000. Even where a party shows a surplus, this is rarely very high, with only Labour demonstrating a surplus of more than £5m in 2007–08. Other parties show a similar pattern. Indeed, of the Scottish and Welsh nationalists, the Northern Irish parties and the smaller British parties, most were in deficit for three or more years in the 2002–09 period. By contrast, UKIP only posted one deficit in 2003, while Plaid Cymru recorded deficits on only two occasions, equating to Welsh Assembly elections, in 2003 and 2007.

It is important to note that Figure 9.2 is based only on parties' total income and expenditure figures. Neither Figure 9.2 nor Table 9.3 take account of any assets, or loans and liabilities that the parties may have. Crucially, if the parties had to rely solely on membership subscriptions and donations for their income, all three parties would have sizeable gaps between what they spend and the money they raise. For instance, the amount raised by Conservative membership fees and donations in 2009 falls more than £11 million short of the party's total expenditure. Such income can be highly variable, peaking in the run up to election years, even if parties must continue to meet their costs throughout the whole of the electoral cycle. Fisher (2002, p. 396) therefore observes that 'voluntary funding simply does not generate sufficient income for modern political parties'. When loans and other liabilities are taken into account, this variability in income means that parties can often appear in an extremely perilous financial state. For example, such a situation meant that the Labour Party was reported as being close to bankruptcy in the summer of 2008.

The Regulatory Framework

Until recently, British party finance was relatively unregulated by comparison with many other countries. While the Houghton Committee (1976) recommended state subsidies for parties to allow them to carry out their functions effectively, this was never acted upon. Party funding reform has however now been at the centre of debate for more than a decade with a number of extensive reviews of the issue, and key pieces of legislation being implemented to regulate political parties and their finance.

Having come to power partly through exploiting the Conservative Party's vulnerability to 'sleaze', the catalyst for debates on party funding was the perception that the Labour Party had changed its policy after taking a £1 million donation from Formula One boss, Bernie Ecclestone. Labour consequently commissioned a review of party finance under the auspices of the Committee on Standards in Public Life (CSPL) (1998). This made a range of wide-ranging proposals. These were accepted by the Labour government, which passed legislation regulating party finance in the Political Parties, Elections and Referendums Act (PPERA) in 2000.

Fisher (2002, p .392) describes PPERA as 'the most comprehensive and radical overhaul of British party finance for over 100 years'. PPERA regulated in a number of key areas (Fisher, 2001, 2002; PPERA, 2000). First, an Electoral Commission was created to regulate and oversee the implementation of laws relating to party finance. Parties are now required to submit annual audited accounts to the Commission and these are made publicly available for scrutiny. Parties were also obliged to make regular declarations about the source of donations. The Commission is responsible for monitoring and publishing details on election spending both by parties at national level, and also for candidates at constituency level. It was also given responsibility for registering political parties, and overseeing the implementation of election regulations in the UK. Since its establishment, the role played by the Electoral Commission has led to a considerable degree of transparency in British party finance. This transparency can also extend to the local level (Johnston and Pattie, 2007).

The second major area addressed by PPERA was the regulation of donations to parties. Donations of £5,000 and over, and £1,000 at constituency level, were to be declared publicly. This also included gifts 'in kind'. Anonymous donations of more than £200 were banned, as were foreign donations and those made through so-called 'blind trusts' which aim to hide the donor's identity. Companies wishing to donate were now also required to ballot their shareholders. Donations were to be declared quarterly between election periods, and weekly during general election campaigns. These laws on donations meant that the two broad categories of potential donors to parties were those individuals entitled to register as voters in the UK, and a range of different company and corporate organizations also registered and conducting most of their business in the UK.

Third, PPERA legislated for an increase in 'Short Money' to opposition parties to help them meet their parliamentary functions. It also legislated to allow for a Policy Development Grant, administered by the Electoral Commission, to allow eligible parties to develop policies more effectively. While this represented an increase in state subsidies to political parties, PPERA did not legislate for the sort of extensive system of state financing found in many European countries.

Most importantly, PPERA legislated to introduce limits to party spending in election campaigns in Westminster, devolved and European elections. The relationship between election spending and positive electoral outcomes is well documented, not least at constituency level (Johnston and Pattie, 1995). The idea of such 'caps' to spending is to prevent a so-called 'arms race' developing where parties attempt to outspend each other in elections, thereby potentially increasing their financial difficulties. The limits outlined in PPERA were:

- UK general elections – £30,000 per constituency contested.
- Scottish Parliament – £12,000 per constituency, and £80,000 per region contested.
- Welsh Assembly – £10,000 per constituency, and £40,000 per region contested.
- Northern Ireland Assembly – £17,000 per constituency contested. (PPERA, 2000, Schedule 9)

These limits applied to the 365 days before a Westminster election, and to the four months before elections to the devolved institutions. A party spending to the maximum in a Westminster election could spend up to £30,000 for each constituency they contested. With 632 constituencies in mainland Britain (as at 2011), this means that the mainstream parties can spend up to around £18.9 million on a general election campaign, while the Northern Irish parties can spend up to £540,000. The effective limits for the devolved institutions are approximately £1.5 million for the Scottish Parliament, £600,000 for the National Assembly of Wales, and just over £300,000 for the Northern Ireland Assembly.

Recent Developments

Despite the introduction of PPERA, concerns about party funding remain. Indeed, greater transparency has led to more stories about party finance. Parties have infringed the rules in a number of ways. In part, this stems from party organizations, not least at the local level, not always having the expertise to maintain complex financial records (Fisher, 2000). However, parties have also attempted to exploit loopholes in the legislation. The 2006 'cash for honours' case suggested that Labour had received sizeable loans from individuals who were subsequently nominated for peerages in the House of Lords. While a police investigation did not press charges, and the peerage nominations were rejected by a House of Lords committee, Labour were not the only party that had been using loans as a method of funding (Fisher, 2009). The Electoral Administration Act (2006) closed this loophole by legislating to ensure that parties must now report all loans of more than £5,000 to central party organizations, and £1,000 to party accounting units, such as constituency parties. All loans must be declared in the quarter in which they are entered into.

In the aftermath of 'cash for honours', a review into party funding was set up under Sir Hayden Phillips. This was in addition to a House of Commons Constitutional Affairs Committee investigation which was already looking into party funding (2006). The important difference was that the Phillips review was independent and led by a former senior civil servant. It was extensive and looked at donations, limiting spending, the public funding of parties and the regulation of public funding. The Phillips review (2007) made eight recommendations. First, it argued that the present funding situation was unsustainable and that donations to parties should be limited further. Second, restrictions on donations required better measures to prevent breaches of the regulations. Third, expenditure on general election campaigns has grown and should be reduced. Fourth, controls on expenditure on all third parties should be strengthened. Fifth, the price of a more sustainable, fairer system of party politics may be an extension of state funding. Sixth, any extension of public funding should be linked to a recognized measure, or measures, of public support and should encourage greater democratic engagement. Seventh, the public should have access to better and clearer information on the sources of party finance. Finally, the Electoral Commission should be given the powers, capacity and experience needed to fulfil its new role (Phillips, 2007).

Phillips (2007) argued that reform had to be based on consensus between the parties, that a solution should serve the long-term interests of the parliamentary system and that 'nothing should be agreed until everything is agreed'. However, two issues were problematic and led to deadlock. These were setting a limit to donations, and setting controls to party spending. For the Conservatives, the issue related to controls on spending. In the last two general elections, Lord Ashcroft funded a number of Conservative constituency organizations in marginal constituencies over a longer period of time than the year before an election. Proposals to restrict constituency spending for a period of at least one year were therefore opposed by the Conservatives. In advance of the Phillips review, the Conservatives suggested a £50,000 cap on individual donations. Proposals to also cap corporate donations caused problems for Labour. The proposals put the issue of contributions by affiliated organizations in the spotlight, not least because they posed a threat to the collective nature of trade union funding of the Labour Party. This was problematic for a number of reasons, but given the long and increasingly important relationship between Labour and the unions (Quinn, 2010), was always unlikely to be accepted by the party. In essence, both the Conservatives and Labour sought partisan advantage and the Phillips talks on party funding broke down (Fisher, 2008b).

The Labour government's response was a White Paper from the Ministry of Justice (2008), the third comprehensive report into party funding in the UK since 2006. This made further suggestions. These included the idea that a cap on donations at £50,000 was actually too high and could be reduced, a re-examination of qualifying expenses for elections and the date from which campaign, and candidate, expenditure is assessed. It also included proposals to increase transparency and to provide the Electoral Commission with more powers. The issue of state funding was avoided, merely stating that the government was considering the issue carefully. Finally, the White Paper appeared sympathetic to the issue of a limit to campaign spending of around £15 million (Fisher, 2009; Ministry of Justice, 2008).

Subsequently, the Political Parties and Elections Act (PPEA) 2009 introduced further legislation on party financing. It gave the Electoral Commission new enforcement powers. It also raised the permissibility and reporting thresholds for loans and donations, from £200 to £500, while requiring loans and donations over £7,500 to be accompanied by a declaration of the source of the donations and the donor's tax status. It also introduced limits to pre-election candidate spending where parliament is dissolved after 56 months in an attempt to regulate constituency spending of the type deployed by Lord Ashcroft and the Conservatives in 2005 and 2010 (Wilks-Heeg and Crone, 2010).

Debates on party funding in the UK have focused on issues important to the Conservative and Labour parties, and other parties' concerns have essentially not been central to this debate. Developments remained stalled over the issues of limits to donations and controlling party spending. A further inquiry into party funding by CSPL took place in late 2010 and was due to report in late 2011. The key issue facing the parties and policy-makers remains how to finance parties so that they can effectively execute their democratic functions when the current system of voluntary income falls short. As debates over the last decade and a half demonstrate, further reform is likely to be incremental and have to take place over the longer term, with the likelihood of a gradual increase in state funding for parties being a potential outcome (Wilks-Heeg and Crone, 2010).

Conclusion

British parties maintain complex organizational structures. Although they may differ in form from party to party, these structures are necessary to manage parties' internal affairs and develop, make and agree on policy. At the same time, party organizations on the ground appear to be in decline with constituency memberships demonstrating a downward trend and members appearing less active than they were. Such features – complex organizational structures yet declining memberships – are reminiscent of the models of party organization found elsewhere (Koole, 1994). Unlike parties elsewhere however, political parties in the UK cannot rely on large state subsidies to finance their operations. In terms of organization and membership there are two key challenges for parties. The first is the challenge of maintaining organizational networks, while also ensuring that the incentives to membership are sufficient to recruit and keep members within the party fold. Failure to do so means that membership and activity levels are likely to continue to fall. Consequently, parties will find it increasingly difficult to communicate with voters at local levels unless they look to alternative strategies to do so. The second challenge is the need to secure sustainable funding. Voluntary income alone is clearly insufficient for parties in the UK. All mainstream parties have been affected by party funding 'episodes' (Fisher, 2008b), although evidence of corrupt activity is weak in the UK. Arguments for and against extending state subsidies are finely balanced, but in the aftermath of the parliamentary expenses scandal are unlikely to be popular with voters. Without adequate funding, the dominant approach has been to set limits to party election spending. While perhaps appropriate from the party funding perspective, this can be argued to be potentially counter-productive when viewed from the voters' viewpoint. If voters are meant to judge parties on the basis of their communications during election campaigns, restricting election expenses has the potential to limit parties' ability to communicate and campaign effectively across the country. It is to the question of elections and campaigns that the next chapter now turns.

10

Party Campaigns and Elections

In most attempts to define political parties, the key thing that sets them apart from other political organizations is that they contest elections. Britain is well served by commentary on the conduct of elections and campaigns (for instance: Allen and Bartle, 2011; Geddes and Tonge, 2010; Kavanagh and Cowley, 2010). In recent decades, the process of party campaigning has undergone radical change. In addition to the era of 'permanent campaigning', analysts have identified a shift to so-called 'post-modern' campaigns (Farrell and Webb, 2000; Norris, 2000). This chapter therefore examines the development of election campaigning in Britain. Discussion proceeds in three main sections. Key to electioneering is an understanding of the electorate. The first part therefore briefly introduces the main models of voting behaviour and briefly outlines the socio-economic structure of the vote in the UK. The second section introduces and assesses the increasingly targeted and marketed nature of electoral competition in British political parties, tracked through developments in the main parties. Far from seeing local campaigns as unimportant, a 'revisionist' school of party research has shown that stronger local campaigns can make a difference to electoral outcomes in constituency contests in Britain. The third section therefore assesses the importance of constituency campaigns in Britain. The chapter ends by assessing 'post-modern models' of campaigning in light of these British developments.

Voting Behaviour in the UK

If parties are to campaign effectively, they need to know both who their voters are, and why they vote the way they do. A range of theories have been forwarded to explain how people vote. These explanations are covered elsewhere at length (Denver, 2007). For the purposes of this chapter it is however useful to have a brief overview of these explanations.

The first explanation revolves around the social structure of the vote.

Famously, Pulzer suggested that 'class is the basis of British party politics; all else is embellishment and detail' (1967, p. 98), while, according to Harrop and Miller (1987, p. 173), 'a cross on the ballot is an implicit statement of social identity'. As noted in the introduction to this book, such explanations have become less important as changing socio-economic conditions have weakened group and party loyalties (Clarke et al., 2004), although some have tried to accommodate changing socio-economic structures by proposing classifications more appropriate to new circumstances (Dunleavy, 1980; Heath et al., 1985; Sarlvik and Crewe, 1983). The social-economic structure of the vote is nevertheless an important starting point for any assessment of voting behaviour in the UK. Table 10.1 sets this out for the 2010 general election.

Differences in voting patterns between men and women have historically been noted with a 'gender gap' between women who tended to be more Conservative-minded than men in the 1960s. Residual traces of this could be found in the 2005 election (Denver, 2007, pp. 55–6 and pp. 182–3). In 2010, it appears that the gap between women and men had closed somewhat. Any gender gaps are not large however, at most 3.5 percentage points for the Liberal Democrats. Age effects have also been observed with older age groups tending to be more Conservative than younger age groups. This effect remained in 2010, with Conservative voters having a considerably older profile than Labour or Liberal Democrat voters, whose support, particularly with the Liberal Democrats, appeared concentrated around younger age groups.

Labour and Conservative parties draw on voters in distinct types and sectors of employment. Residual traces of the manual/non-manual class divide are evident with Labour support in 2010 highest amongst supervisory, skilled and semi- or unskilled workers. Labour also has a greater proportion of public-sector workers voting for it, than private-sector workers. By contrast, the Conservatives draw their support from the managerial, professional and white-collar classes, in addition to the almost half of small business voters who voted for the party. In an early assessment of how the Conservatives could win in 2010, Sanders (2006) indicated that the party needed to attract a greater proportion of public sector workers who may be put off by the party's claims to want to reduce the size of the state sector. However, more Conservative support is drawn from voters employed in the private, not public, sector. Liberal Democrat voters share a similar profile to Conservative voters – managerial, professional and white-collar – except that their support is drawn more from public-sector workers than those employed in the private sector.

Geography also impacts upon electoral support. Labour traditionally

Table 10.1   Structure of the vote at the 2010 General Election (%)

	Labour	Conservative	Lib Dems	Nationalists
Share of the vote	29.0	36.1	23.0	2.2
Seats	258	307	57	9
Gender				
Male	31.4	36.1	20.1	6.4
Female	32.6	35.4	23.6	4.4
Age				
18–24	29.5	25.3	34.7	2.1
25–34	37.7	29.0	23.8	5.6
35–44	33.0	32.2	25.4	5.6
45–54	31.5	32.0	26.3	4.8
55–64	30.0	37.4	21.2	6.2
65+	31.6	42.7	15.7	5.4
Employment				
Professional/Higher technical	27.5	38.1	24.7	6.5
Manager/Senior administrator	23.1	43.8	27.2	2.4
Clerical	27.5	40.5	24.4	2.4
Sales/Services	30.9	36.1	23.6	2.6
Small business owner	19.0	46.8	18.3	7.9
Foreman/Supervisor	45.1	23.5	13.7	9.8
Skilled manual	40.4	31.5	16.2	6.2
Semi-skilled/Unskilled manual work	49.7	19.7	16.8	8.1
Sector				
Private	30.4	39.2	19.2	5.3
Public	34.5	31.5	25.2	5.7
Region				
North East	49.5	23.1	23.1	–
North West	42.7	35.3	17.4	–
Yorkshire	30.2	39.0	27.0	–
East Midlands	33.3	43.5	18.1	–
West Midlands	29.0	40.9	19.9	–
Eastern	16.0	51.5	29.0	–
London	40.0	37.4	16.8	–
South East	17.4	51.7	23.3	–
South West	18.1	40.4	38.3	–
Scotland	42.1	17.1	15.1	22.7
Wales	36.0	27.5	23.0	8.4

Source: Data from the British Election Study 2010, http://www.bes2009-10.org/, 24 January 2011.

has drawn its support from urban and formerly industrial areas of Britain. By contrast, Conservative voters have been based in more prosperous rural and suburban areas of Britain. Labour voters are concentrated in cities and regions dominated by their previous industrial role, such as the North West and North East of England which include the cities of Liverpool, Manchester and Newcastle-upon-Tyne. Labour also has the greatest proportion of London-based voters and was the dominant party in Scotland and Wales in 2010, although, as the dramatic SNP victory in the 2011 Scottish elections demonstrates, voting patterns can differ considerably for the devolved elections. Conservative support is drawn from the South East, South West and Midlands, steadily weakening the further north analysts go. Less than a quarter of voters in the North East voted Conservative, and less than a fifth in Scotland. Liberal Democrat support is more diffuse than for the other two main parties and is highest in the South West, East England and Yorkshire.

Scottish and Welsh nationalists, treated together in Table 10.1, draw support largely from similar groups to Labour – supervisory, skilled and semi- or unskilled workers, in Scotland and Wales. Although less is known about Welsh voting behaviour, these findings have been echoed in SNP support in devolved elections for the Scottish parliament (Paterson et al., 2001). However, nationalist support has tended to have a more rural feel to it; Plaid Cymru has struggled to get a consistent foothold in Labour's post-industrial strongholds, and the same could be said about the SNP until the 2011 Scottish election.

A second set of explanations for voting behaviour can be grouped under the general heading of 'rational choice' voting. First, voters can vote on the basis of their proximity to the issues offered by parties and candidates standing for election (Butler and Stokes, 1969, ch. 8). Second, they can choose how to vote on 'valence' issues. These are issues on which there is broad agreement upon, such as, for instance, the economy. Electors choose between candidates and parties on the basis of their performance and competence in handling these key issues (Butler and Stokes, 1969; Clarke et al., 2009). Third, egocentric 'economic voting' is where voters choose through a consideration of how economic policies are likely to affect them. There is considerable technical debate about many of these explanations (see Denver 2007). However, the ideas behind them – issues, competence, economic voting – all impact upon how parties campaign, and the explanations themselves are clearly inter-linked. As Clarke et al. (2009, p. 55) note, the issues that voters think most pressing are crucial elements in their judgements over how compe-tent parties are.

The issue agenda has changed in recent elections. Traditionally, issues such as the health service, education and the economy have been amongst voters' highest priorities. This changed after 2001 when international events and security related issues, such as the Iraq war, terrorism and immigration rose sharply up the agenda so that the 2005 election was fought on a mixture of concern about traditional public service and economic issues, and worry about new 'security' issues (Clarke et al., 2009, ch. 3). Voters prefer different parties for different issues, leading to the idea that parties 'own' particular policy areas. Thus, Labour has tended to be preferred on issues such as health, education and unemployment, while the Conservatives tend to be preferred on law and order, taxation and asylum/immigration policy (Denver, 2007, p. 101).

In 2010, the economic crisis ensured that the issue agenda had changed again, with public services seemingly less important to voters. Polling company Ipsos MORI indicated that 55 per cent saw the economy as the most important issue facing Britain in April 2010 just prior to the election. Race relations and immigration were the second most important issue (29 per cent), followed by crime/law and order (24 per cent), unemployment and the NHS (24 per cent each), and education and schools (21 per cent). Foreign affairs and terrorism merited only 11 per cent, while morality and individual behaviour was cited by only eight per cent (Ipsos MORI, 2010).

Respondents to the 2010 British Election Study were asked in advance of the election how they thought Labour and the Conservatives handle a range of nine policy issues. Table 10.2 reports the combined proportions of respondents who thought the parties were handling the issue either very or fairly well. This shows that Labour led the Conservatives on only two issues in the run up to the 2010 election, the NHS and terrorism. The Conservatives maintained sizeable leads on immigration, crime and the economy generally. They were also preferred on the current financial crisis, and had eased ahead on education, previously an issue 'owned' by Labour. In short, the Conservatives were preferred by most voters on most issues in the run up to the 2010 election. Most importantly, they were preferred over Labour on the issue deemed most important by voters, the economy.

A key element of judging party performance is how competent party leaders are perceived to be. In 2005, Tony Blair was rated as more competent than either Michael Howard for the Conservatives or Charles Kennedy for the Liberal Democrats, although Kennedy tended to have more 'likeability' than either of the other leaders (Clarke et al., 2009, ch. 5). Leadership factors were likely to be equally, if not more, important in

Table 10.2   Perceptions of parties' issue competence at the 2010
General Election (%)

	Conservatives	Labour
Crime	40.3	30.6
Education	41.2	40.7
Immigration	37.1	12.8
NHS	36.3	48.5
Terrorism	44.0	53.5
Economy generally	34.5	24.5
Taxation	26.2	25.1
War in Afghanistan	24.4	13.6
Current financial crisis	30.4	27.3
(N)	(1,935)	(1,935)

Source: Data from the British Election Study 2010, http://www.bes2009-10.org/
24 January 2011.

2010 because all three main parties went into the election with new leaders, only Gordon Brown having had a major public profile prior to
becoming party leader (and prime minister) in 2007. Table 10.3 reports
the average scores from 0–10 scales asking how respondents to the
British Election Study viewed the competence, trust and likeability of the
three main party leaders. The higher the score, the more competent, trustworthy and likeable the leader was viewed in advance of the election. On
all three indicators the Conservative Party leader, David Cameron, came
out ahead. Gordon Brown came third on all three indicators, seen as less
competent, trustworthy and likeable than both his Liberal Democrat and
Conservative competitors.

So-called 'valence' models of voting behaviour focus crucially on the
party that voters judge best able to deliver competently on issues where
there is otherwise broad agreement. As Clarke et al. (2004, p. 326) put it,
in Britain 'electoral politics is largely valence politics, and public debate
and inter-party competition focus on which party and which leader are
best able to deliver'. Such explanations have been used to account for
how voters cast their vote in both the 2001 and the 2005 general elections
(Clarke et al., 2004, 2009). They have also become important in non-
Westminster settings. Research on Scottish parliament elections suggests
that 'valence' judgements were also an important factor in the SNP's
narrow victory over Labour in 2007 (Johns et al., 2009). The initial
evidence presented above suggests that such judgements also play an

Table 10.3   Average leadership ratings during the 2010 General Election

	Brown	*Cameron*	*Clegg*
Competence	4.56	5.53	4.67
Trust	4.23	4.68	4.51
Likeability	4.34	5.09	4.56

Source: Data from the British Election Study 2010, http://www.bes2009-10.org/, 24 January 2011.

important part in explaining the outcome of 2010; the Conservatives emerged as the largest party because voters preferred them on most issues and their leader, David Cameron, was thought competent and able to deliver. In addition to understanding the demographic characteristics of voters, the importance of leadership, issues and competence ensure that they play a key part of the modern election campaign.

Election Campaigning

Election campaigning has changed radically in recent decades. This has been driven by technology with the rise of television, opinion polling and advertising necessitating changes to how parties conducted their campaigns. Typically, party campaigns became increasingly professionalized and targeted towards specific sectors of the electorate, leading some to herald an era of 'designer politics' (Kavanagh, 1995; Scammell, 1995) and others to highlight the 'electoral-professional' model of party organization (Panebianco, 1988). Both Norris (2000) and Farrell and Webb (2000) provide similar frameworks to understand the development of campaigning. Both highlight three stages in the development of party campaigns. Norris (2000, ch. 7) labels these as the '*pre-modern*', '*modern*' and '*post-modern*' stages of campaigning. *Pre-modern* campaigns pre-date the rise of television and focus on activity at local level. Campaigning was based on direct communication between candidates, their volunteer organizations, often supported by a partisan press, and voters. Planning was ad-hoc and focused around the immediate period between dissolution of parliament and polling day, commonly referred to as the short campaign. *Modern* campaigns date from the rise of television in the 1950s through to the late 1980s. These involved more central co-ordination, and an increasing nationalization and professionalization with party leaders advised by a range of pollsters, advertising and marketing specialists. Leadership itself became an important theme, and the campaign evolved over the year or so before the election, commonly known as the long campaign. The focus was largely on selling the party's message to voters, who were essentially spectators in the process.

Post-modern campaigns have evolved in reaction to the fragmentation of television outlets, the rise of rolling news coverage, and opportunities for direct interaction with voters on the Internet. Campaigns remain professionalized, but have become essentially permanent with continual focus groups and polling informing parties' messages. This constant research means that messages can be increasingly targeted to groups of voters to fit with their opinions, suggesting that in this model campaigning 'is overwhelmingly preference-accommodating rather than preference-shaping' (Farrell and Webb, 2000, p. 106). This model also accommodates activity at the local level, which is also targeted in order to maximize the party's vote. Post-modern campaigning is, therefore, a mixture of pre-modern and modern campaigns, which is increasingly targeted towards voters at both national and local levels.

Parties' campaigns have certainly become more centralized and professionalized. British parties have seen increasing numbers of staff employed at central level, and a corresponding sharp decrease of the numbers of staff employed at the sub-national level from the 1960s onwards (Webb, 1994; Farrell and Webb, 2000, p. 117). Not all staff employed by parties can be classed as professionals however and it is important to make a distinction between those who are employed directly by parties to work on campaigns, and outside expertise which is drafted in to help parties design their election message. It tends to be in this latter sense that campaign professionalization has been discussed (Webb and Fisher, 2003). Such outside expertise typically reports to a small group of campaign managers and leaders within the party they are working for.

A number of examples highlight these trends. Although the Conservatives first worked with an advertising agency as early as 1929, in the late 1960s the party essentially relied on volunteers from outside the party for advice on campaign communications (Kavanagh, 1995, ch. 3; Webb, 1994, p. 126). In the run up to 1979, the Conservative Party formally appointed the advertising agency Saatchi & Saatchi to advise and design its marketing and advertising. The party used Saatchis in this role throughout the 1980s, although the relationship was less close in 1987 than in the previous two campaigns. Market research by the agency in 1978–79 led to the Conservatives running a campaign focused on criticizing Labour's performance in government, producing some memorable campaign advertisements. One of these, 'Labour Isn't Working', showed a line of unemployment claimants, fed into concerns about Labour's management of the economy, and is still regarded as a classic political advertisement. Reappointed for the 1992 election, Saatchis were given a greater role, involved in broadcasts, press conferences and advertisements. Research demonstrated that the Conservatives were less trusted than Labour on social policy issues, and that the issues the party was weak on tended to have high salience among voters, such as health. However, the party was preferred on the economy, taxation and law and order. These were the key themes of the Conservative campaign, again producing memorable advertisements on taxation such as 'Labour's Tax Bombshell', and 'Labour's Double Whammy' which referred to rising prices and taxes (Kavanagh, 1995, ch. 3; Scammell, 1995).

Under Neil Kinnock, Labour utilized a group of advertising and media professionals in the party's Shadow Communications Agency (SCA). While former TV producer Peter Mandelson had been appointed Director of Communications for the party in 1985 to strengthen its campaign message, the SCA worked for the party largely on a voluntary basis. Initially consisting of pollsters Philip Gould and Deborah Mattinson, by 1987 it is estimated that around 200 volunteers were working for Labour on its campaign (Webb, 1994, p. 125). The SCA was associated with a number of initiatives, including, for instance, the rebranding of the party logo as a red rose in 1986. The SCA's continual programme of focus group and public opinion research also fed into the party's 1989 policy review (Gould, 1998a).

It is with the rise of Tony Blair and the landslide election victory of 1997 that permanent, voter-oriented campaign activity is most associated. Gould (1998a, 1998b) shows how his constant public opinion research led to the rebranding of the party as 'New' Labour and to Clause IV of the party's constitution being changed. This also led to ten campaigning principles being adopted. These were to: concede issues the party had lost the argument on and move on; establish new dividing lines between the parties; take the Conservative Party's ground; balance the positive with the negative; work with the news rather than against it; never compromise on trust with voters; put substance before style; remorselessly focus on 1992 Conservative voters; neutralize tax as an issue; and make only small, concrete promises (Gould, 1998b, pp. 6–7). Campaign activity was therefore driven by voter research, and had an impact on party strategy, party message and even party policy in the way that 'post-modern' campaign theories suggest. This was complemented organizationally by the party setting up a campaigning 'war room' at

Millbank in London, where all the party's campaign staff were situated. Constant market research activity also had an impact on government policy and Labour's leadership emphasis; noting polling in 2000 that suggested Labour was losing touch on some issues, Blair wrote that the government needed to launch 'three or four eye-catching initiatives … I personally should be associated with it' (cited in Rawnsley, 2001, pp. 390–1).

Appointing campaign professionals does not necessarily lead to electoral success however. Three main things can constrain their ability to win elections. First, if the party is perceived as out of touch with the electorate, no amount of campaign expertise can help it win although it may help stem any losses the party has. Thus, for the 2005 election the Conservatives appointed a strategist, Lynton Crosby, who had conducted successful campaigns in Australia. Despite designing controversial messages designed to subtly appeal to Conservative supporters on issues such as immigration and Europe, the party was still considered out of tune with voters (Ashcroft, 2005; Bale and Webb, 2011). Second, campaign expertise is expensive. The SCA's volunteer services in 1992 are estimated to have saved Labour around £500,000, while five years later around £2m was spent on equipment for the party's Millbank campaign operation (Fielding, 1997, p. 28; Webb, 1994, p. 125). Money therefore acts as a potential constraint. Neither the Conservatives in 1997 nor Labour in 2010 commissioned many opinion polls largely because they did not have enough money to do so (Kavanagh and Cowley, 2010; Norris, 2000, p. 149). The Liberal Democrats' relative lack of funding is one reason that they have not experienced the same level of campaign professionalization and centralization as the other two main parties. Finally, as Farrell and Webb (2000, p. 109) observe, such a process is easier in parties with low levels of ideological baggage. Many in Labour, for instance, resisted the influence of the SCA and campaign professionals under Kinnock because they felt this went against the party's principles and watered down the party's policy positions (Gould, 1998a).

To assess the impact of developments in campaigning, Table 10.4 outlines spending trends in recent general elections for the three main British parties. A number of patterns are evident. First, between 2001–2010 the Conservative Party generally spent more in total than Labour, while Liberal Democrats never spent more than £5m and only just spent more than £1m in 2001. Second, the major element of spending for all three parties in each election has been advertising, the Conservatives comfortably outspending Labour and Liberal Democrats combined in 2005 and 2010. Third, market research and canvassing has

Table 10.4 Parties' expenditure on General Elections, 2001–2010 (£000)

	Con			Lab			Lib Dem		
	2001	*2005*	*2010*	*2001*	*2005*	*2010*	*2001*	*2005*	*2010*
Party Political Broadcasts	567	293	699	273	470	430	55	125	153
Advertising	4,409	8,175	7,533	5,024	5,287	786	197	1,583	230
Unsolicited material to electors	1,217	4,493	4,779	1,452	2,698	4,155	54	1,235	3,052
Market research and canvassing	1,717	1,292	702	869	1,577	478	66	165	497
Media	357	448	439	750	375	166	231	106	147
% of total expenditure	64.8	82.3	84.8	76.5	58.0	75.1	44.3	74.3	85.2
Total expenditure	12,752	17,852	16,682	10,945	17,940	8,009	1,361	4,325	4,788

Notes: Expenditure categories not included are: Manifesto/Party political documents; Transport; Rallies and other events; and Overheads and general administration.
Source: Data from Electoral Commission, Register of Campaign Expenditure, http://www.electoralcommission.org.uk, 26 January 2011.

varied by party, with the Conservatives spending decreasing amounts across the three elections, Labour spending most in 2005 and least in 2010, and the Liberal Democrats steadily increasing to actually outspend Labour in 2010. Fourth, lesser amounts have been spent on Party Political Broadcasts (PPBs) and assorted media, although the sharp increase in Conservative spending on PPBs in 2010 is particularly notable. Finally, one way in which the targeting of strategists impacts upon voters is in the increasing amounts of direct mail sent by the parties. Addressed to individual voters, who are identified through a combination of canvassing activity and increasingly accurate market research software, this mail addresses issues parties perceive to be of interest to those voters. Kavanagh and Cowley (2010) have suggested that 2010 was the 'direct mail' election. This is borne out by these figures. The amount spent on unsolicited material to voters increased across all three parties, with sizeable increases for Labour and the Liberal Democrats.

A key aim of campaigning is to seize the initiative from the other parties. The objective is to both put opponents under pressure, through so-called negative campaigning, while at the same time highlighting polices that can be presented positively to benefit your party. Campaigns are therefore carefully planned and stage managed. Labour has famously had a campaign 'war book' in recent elections, which carefully set out each day's events, visits and announcements. Sometimes campaign planning goes well; the Conservatives successfully seized the initiative against Labour's national insurance 'jobs tax' in the first week of the 2010 election. However events can conspire against careful planning. Labour's manifesto launch in 2001 was overshadowed by deputy leader John Prescott punching a protestor and Tony Blair being severely criticized over health policy by a voter. Until 2010, the typical campaign day has comprised of early morning press conferences to launch the theme of the day, followed by leaders and senior party members touring the country visiting target seats, attending set piece events and launching campaign posters (Butler and Kavanagh, 2002, ch. 6). In 2010, this routine was upset by the introduction of the televised Leaders Debates. Fewer press conferences were held, and, while leaders and party elites still toured the country, preparation for the debates, their anticipation and reaction to them became a key organizing factor of campaign activity in 2010 (Allen et al., 2011; Kavanagh and Cowley, 2010).

Much of the preceding discussion deals with the organizational aspects of campaigning. An important question remains however. How do parties actually decide which aspects to highlight and emphasize in their campaigns? Rohrschneider (2002) has specified five trade-offs that party strategists face when designing a campaign. The first is a choice over whether to maximize votes or emphasize policies. Second, should the party aim to mobilize its core vote or unaligned voters? The third choice is over whether to emphasize ideology or modern technologies in designing an election campaign. Fourth, to what extent does the party emphasize leadership or the party's core constituencies? Finally, to what degree can intra-party democracy and organization be used as a symbolic campaign component or merely a mechanical instrument to reach voters?

Rohrschneider uses these five trade-offs to propose what he calls the mobilizing–chasing continuum of party campaigning. At one end of this, parties concentrate on mobilizing their core vote, while at the other end, parties are actively seeking to convert both undecided and other parties' voters. A *mobilizing* strategy is motivated primarily by policies, focuses on a party's core voters and ideological heritage, emphasizes its core constituencies, and views organization as an instrument to contact voters and get the vote out. A *chasing* strategy aims to maximise vote share mainly by attracting unaligned voters, uses modern technology, not ideology, to help design its election appeal, emphasizes leadership and uses organizational innovation as part of the campaign theme to make the party more attractive. The argument is that, even if parties may not fully meet each of these conditions, they will nevertheless be able to be placed on Rohrschneider's mobilizing–chasing continuum thereby giving an indication of the type of campaign run by the party.

How might this model be applied to British general elections? On the face of it, Labour in 1997 appears to have run a classic chasing campaign. As Gould's (1998b) campaign principles show, the party was acutely aware of the need to target both undecided and Conservative voters to maximize its vote. Consequently, it achieved what Fielding (1997, p. 34) called 'the biggest shift of support from one party to another this century'. This success was in large part attributed to the use of modern technologies in public opinion research and polling to help design the party's message, leading to the party downplaying ideology and its core constituencies. For instance, in addition to Clause IV of the party's constitution being changed to remove the commitment to common ownership, the party sought to downplay its past reputation for higher taxes, indicating it would stick to Conservative spending plans for the first two years in office. It also downplayed its links with the trade unions and other groups which had become associated with the party during the 1970s and 1980s. It emphasized Tony Blair's leadership and used organizational change, such as the extension of OMOV to party members and the rise in party membership under Blair, as themes symbolic of how the party had changed (Mandelson and Liddle, 1996).

It is important to recognize that this represents only a partial picture. Even if parties chase undecided voters, they still also need to mobilize party loyalists to go out to vote. Hence, Labour did not completely ignore its past traditions, emphasizing issues such as the public services, albeit by making small and concrete promises. While organization may have been a symbolic campaign theme, it was also used as an instrument to get out the vote (Whiteley and Seyd, 2003), with many of the local activists having been involved in doing so sceptical about the modernization process in the first place. Chasing undecided voters therefore has to build upon mobilizing core voters if a party wishes to maximize its vote.

The Conservatives in 2001 provide a good example of a failed attempt at a chasing strategy which turned into a mobilizing campaign. Initially, under William Hague's leadership the party tried to downplay its ideological heritage. Prominent figures tried to recast the party as 'Compassionate Conservatives' with, for instance, then Deputy Leader Peter Lilley making a controversial speech in 1999 emphasizing the Conservatives' commitment to improving public services. They also sought to emphasize William Hague's leadership while some have also seen Hague's organizational reforms as a symbolic attempt to market and position the party for the 2001 general election (Lees-Marshment and Quayle, 2001).

This provides a good example of how ideology can prove a brake on a party's campaign development. Lilley's speech was reported as being a repudiation of Thatcherism, and was met by an outcry of criticism within the party and the traditional conservative press. This prevented further attempts to downplay the party's ideological and policy heritage, largely because the Conservative Party remained convinced by these ideas and would not accept the need to moderate their approach (Bale, 2010, pp. 88–96). Organizational change was undermined as a campaign theme both by the fact that only a third of all Conservative members bothered to vote in the membership ballot to approve the reforms, and that the reforms were also weaker on democratizing the party than was claimed (Bale, 2010, pp. 74–5). The Conservatives were therefore forced back onto a mobilizing strategy, where the party stressed traditional policies such as cutting taxes and spending, law and order and immigration. They also focused heavily on Eurosceptic issues, famously claiming that there were only 24 hours left to save the pound from being replaced by the Euro. Organizationally, while the party ran its strongest constituency campaigns in target seats, in classic mobilizing style it also ran the strongest campaigns of all three main parties in seats that it already held (Denver et al., 2002a, p. 83). Moreover, the party largely ignored polling evidence, convinced that its ideological and policy positions were attractive to voters. A similar process was evident under both Duncan Smith and Howard's leadership; initial moderation, followed by a populist campaign, which, despite the appointment in 2005 of a controversial strategist, Lynton Crosby, did little to improve the long-term image of the party.

It is more difficult to classify the parties' 2010 campaigns. Cameron's initial efforts to moderate the Conservative image clearly took note of opinion research on the party such as that carried out by Lord Ashcroft (Ashcroft, 2005). Thus, the initial long-term strategy was to 'decontaminate' the Conservative Party by emphasizing policy areas the party did not have a lead on. These included the environment, and public services such as the NHS. At the same time, traditional Conservative policy areas – Europe, emphasizing private provision in health and education for instance – were downplayed. In addition to 'decontaminating' the party, the aim was to maximize the vote, appealing to undecided voters, those who had voted for other parties, including the Liberal Democrats, and to those who worked in the public sector that might also prove crucial to victory (Sanders, 2006). Organizationally, much was made of Cameron's leadership both for its decisiveness and as a symbol of how the party had changed. This process stalled from around late 2007 onwards, partly because of resistance from some within the party, partly because Brown's decision not to hold a snap election had eased the urgency, but also because the financial crisis eventually allowed the party to emphasize traditional themes such as cutting the state and public spending (Bale and Webb, 2011; Osborne, 2009b). Moreover, in the aftermath of the election the leadership was criticized by the ConservativeHome activist website for not focus-group testing major policy announcements such as the 'big society' to ensure it went down well with voters (ConservativeHome, 2010d). The Conservative's 2010 campaign therefore fell somewhere between a mobilizing and a chasing campaign.

It is difficult to classify Labour's campaign in 2010 for a different reason. Despite having advice from key pollsters like Philip Gould, Kavanagh and Cowley (2010, ch. 3) observe that it had confused lines of accountability, had an unclear message and was organizationally and financially weak having been in office for so long. The party did not perform as badly as it had feared, thereby suggesting that its core electorate had voted for Labour and that ultimately, with an unpopular leader and policies, its campaign could not have been much more than a mobilizing campaign.

Constituency Campaigning

Since most campaign coverage focuses at the national level, it is easy to forget that general elections are actually fought and won in over 600 (650 in 2010) local constituencies across the UK. What happens in these constituencies determines both the make-up of the House of Commons, and whether or not a party has enough seats to form a government. Constituency outcomes are therefore important. However, much of the period Norris (2000) suggests can be classified as the modern campaign, constituency campaigns were typically argued to be largely irrelevant to the national outcome. Kavanagh's (1970) survey of constituency campaigns argued that they were essentially ritualistic, conducted as much for the camaraderie amongst activists as for any expectation that they would influence the election outcome at the national level. Similar sentiments could be found in the influential Nuffield studies of British general elections (Butler and Kavanagh, 1980, 1988). From the 1987 and 1992 general elections onwards, this argument was challenged by a 'revisionist school' of constituency campaign analysts (Denver and Hands, 1997; Fisher, 2000; Johnston and Pattie, 1995; Pattie et al., 1994; Whiteley and Seyd, 1994). While these scholars all measured constituency campaigning in different ways, the basic argument has consistently been that campaigning at the constituency level can improve a party's electoral performance and impact upon the outcome of the election. Consequently, scholars and party politicians both now accept that the constituency level is an important arena where local activity can make a difference between winning and losing. Pattie and Johnston (2003a, p. 306) go further and indicate that this argument has become a 'new orthodoxy' in campaigning studies. In similar vein to Rohrschneider's (2002) mobilizing–chasing model, constituency campaigns can also be directed in varying degrees to either mobilizing voters, or towards educating and converting undecided voters (Denver and Hands, 1997).

It is apparent during elections that the campaign in some constituencies is much more intense than in others. What determines levels of constituency campaigning in British elections? Since local party organizations are more likely to put effort into seats that they can win, the first determinant is electoral geography. Local organizations are more likely to put considerable effort into winning marginal seats which may be held by only a small majority. By contrast, if a party holds a seat by a large majority, or is a long way from winning the seat, it is unlikely that the local organization will expend much time, effort or resources in campaigning for the seat. Related but contrary to the marginality argument, having an incumbent MP in the constituency can also lead to the local organization running a strong campaign. For instance, in the 1992 and 1997 elections, Conservative associations ran their strongest campaigns in seats that they held safely (Denver and Hands, 1993, Denver et al.,1998). The strength of the local party is also important; where the constituency party has more members, it is also more likely to run stronger constituency campaigns (Denver and Hands, 1997). Finally, money also plays a role. Constituency candidate spending has been successfully shown to be an effective proxy measure for local campaign strength in a number of studies (Denver and Hands, 1993; Pattie et al., 1994). The more that a candidate spends relative to the limit set by legislation, the more likely they are to run a successful constituency campaign.

Traditional constituency campaigning involved the volunteer local organization, co-ordinated by a full-time election agent, undertaking various activities with or on behalf of their candidate. Thus, Denver and Hands (1997) highlight a range of activities typically undertaken by constituency organizations in their early study of the 1992 campaign. These included sending election addresses to voters, holding public meetings, delivering party leaflets, putting up posters, arranging postal votes, trying to get local media coverage, arranging doorstep visits by the candidate, and canvassing voters either by telephone or in person to identify their voting intentions and, as a consequence, establish in which areas of the constituency their party's support lies. According to Whiteley et al. (1994), individual party members are likely to participate in these activities in different ways, with the more active members canvassing for the party delivering leaflets and helping at party functions, and the less active perhaps displaying election posters and donating money to the local party's 'fighting fund'. On polling day itself, getting out the vote is crucial and constituency campaigns will deliver 'good morning' leaflets reminding people to vote, take numbers at polling stations, knock on voters' doors, drive some voters to the polls and use loudspeakers to highlight that it is election day.

The profile of constituency campaigning has changed over time. Fisher et al. (2006b) show how numbers of full-time election agents employed to run constituency campaigns have declined considerably, being replaced instead with volunteers whom parties have trained up so that they have sufficient expertise. Many of these volunteer agents are increasingly focused not just on maximizing the vote in the immediate election, but on building up support in the longer term through, for instance, contesting local government elections in the area. Similarly, Denver and Hands (1997) observe how the increasing number of computers and fax machines were helping local organizers complete routine tasks such as leaflet design and printing in the 1992 election. In 2010, computing technology was commonplace and developed to the point that constituency campaigns are now able to input the information they glean from voters directly into internet-based software and uploaded to a central party database. In conjunction with sophisticated market-research software, such data is then used to target voters directly. This is combined with increasing levels of telephone canvassing, often organized from party call centres outside the constituency. One consequence of these developments is that constituency campaigns have become less reliant on local volunteers since many of these tasks can be carried out by campaign professionals (Fisher and Denver, 2008).

A key development has been the increasing centralization of constituency campaigning by parties as they have become more aware of the potential benefits of strong campaigns in seats that can be won (Fisher and Denver, 2008). While there has been some debate about the effectiveness of such targeting (Denver and Hands, 2004; Whiteley and Seyd, 2003), there is little doubt that targeting of constituencies by party HQ is now central to most parties' campaign strategy. Considerable resources are then put into winning these constituencies. Leaders' tours visit them, they have greater levels of direct mail, telephone and doorstep contacting, activists from elsewhere are asked to help out in them, and parties ensure that their billboard posters are situated in these targets. In 1997, Labour targeted 91 seats, in a campaign strategy labelled 'Operation Victory', while in 2001 this had risen to 148, most of which the party were defending, having won them in the previous election (Denver et al., 2002b, 2004). In 2010, Labour initially had a target list of 146 constituencies as the party aimed to prevent a Conservative victory, with a further 20 being added later in the campaign to counter potential Liberal Democrat gains (Kavanagh and Cowley, 2010, p. 231).

Developments in the Conservative Party further highlight the importance of centralization and targeting as parties develop and implement their campaigns. In 2005, the Conservative peer Lord Ashcroft, with others, funded and ran a 'target seats' programme aimed at focusing resources on constituencies which had viable plans to defeat Labour incumbents. This was extended in 2010, and brought in house to be operated through Conservative Central Office. Johnston and Pattie (2011, p. 217) highlight three main tasks of the 2010 Ashcroft targeting programme. First, to identify possible Conservative voters in target seats and send them material promoting the party and its candidates. Second, providing financial grants to constituency parties with viable business plans to organize campaign activity promoting the party's candidate. Third, to redirect resources to key constituencies, even during the last weeks of campaigning.

These developments were controversial. The Ashcroft targeting programme was a long-term one. It targeted resources at constituencies over the long campaign where there was no restriction to constituency expenditure, leading to worries that sizeable grants to Conservative targets would put incumbents being challenged by Ashcroft-supported candidates at a considerable disadvantage. The exact list of target seats was kept secret. Kavanagh and Cowley (2010, p. 235) suggest that most Ashcroft resources went into 69 seats, 45 of which the Conservatives contested with Labour, 24 with the Liberal Democrats. These priorities changed during the election; resources were withdrawn from some of the Liberal Democrat contests and reallocated to 14 further Labour contests as a result of the Liberal Democrat surge in the polls.

Voters experience constituency campaigns through the level of contact that parties make with them. Table 10.5 reports levels of party contact experienced by respondents to the 2010 British election study, both overall and broken down by various different types of contact. The Conservative Party demonstrates the highest level of contact with voters, closely followed by Labour, both around 34–35 per cent. The Liberal Democrats had slightly lower reported levels of contact, falling just short of 30 per cent. The main method of contact was through

Table 10.5   Parties' methods of voter contact during the 2010 General Election (%)

	Labour	Conservative	Liberal Democrat
Contacted	34.2	35.4	29.6
Phone	1.8	1.3	1.2
Leaflet	31.6	32.7	28.0
Email/text	0.4	0.7	0.3
Home visit	5.4	5.5	3.5
Street	0.8	0.6	0.6
Internet (Facebook, Twitter, YouTube)	0.1	0.1	0.3
(N)	(3,512)	(3,512)	(3,512)

Source: Data from the British Election Study 2010, http://www.bes2009-10.org/, 24 January 2011.

leaflets or material delivered to voters, with up to 32.7 per cent indicating that leaflets had been delivered to them by the Conservative Party. While it is not possible to distinguish between direct mail and locally delivered leaflets from this figure, this underlines Kavanagh and Cowley's (2010, pp. 240–1) observation that 'the key activity of local activists of all three parties in the run-up to the election was delivering leaflets'. Voters were much less likely to be contacted by a doorstep visit, even if this was the second most regular mode of contact. Few voters reported telephone contact by parties, with at most 1.8 per cent indicating that Labour had contacted them by telephone. Finally, advocates of interactive and internet politics will find little solace in levels of party contact; barely any respondents indicate contact by email, text or various internet-based forms of communication. Such a pattern of activity in 2010 – extensive leafleting with much lesser levels of doorstep visits and telephone contact – has also been found in other studies (Kavanagh and Cowley, 2010, pp. 240–2).

To what extent does constituency electioneering make a difference? Research on the 2001 general election indicated that, depending on the strength of campaign a local party ran, their share of the electorate could be increased by up to 2.0 per cent for the Conservatives, 4.2 per cent for Labour and 6.8 per cent for the Liberal Democrats (Denver et al. 2002a, p. 88). In 2010, Kavanagh and Cowley (2010, ch. 11) suggest that the Conservative Party achieved an additional 1.6 per cent of the vote over their national average in their Labour-held targets, while Johnston and Pattie (2011, p. 230) indicate that of the 25 Conservative associations receiving Ashcroft money in 2008, well in advance of the 2010 election, the party won 22 of the seats. Such targeting was not successful everywhere, but clearly was beneficial to the party overall. Kavanagh and Cowley (2010, ch. 11) also argue that Labour's constituency efforts stopped the party from losing more seats than they did. Other research has shown that constituency campaigns lead to greater voter knowledge of local candidates and a greater likelihood of voting for a party's candidate (Pattie and Johnston, 2004). Voters who are contacted are also more likely to switch support than voters who are not contacted (Pattie and Johnston, 2003b). How a party contacts voters is also important. Evidence has shown that traditional face-to-face doorstep canvassing is more effective than telephone canvassing in encouraging voters to vote for a party (Pattie and Johnston, 2003a), although doing this extensively is difficult for party organizations with declining memberships. Finally, local activity can also have a beneficial impact upon election turnout. Denver et al.'s (2004) work found that, depending on the strength of campaign, constituency turnout could have increased by as much as 2.9 per cent in 1992, 4.4 per cent in party target seats in 1997, and 4.6 percentage points in 2001.

Discussion of local campaigning has primarily focused on developments with the main two parties and in Westminster elections. It has also proved effective in devolved elections (Clark, 2006) and has benefited other parties. Some parties have gained a reputation for local campaigning, albeit largely through necessity. Simply, they do not have sufficient resources to run effective campaigns everywhere, and must focus on a small number of constituencies and areas where they have some strength. The Liberal Democrats are a case in point, having become renowned for their 'community politics' approach to campaigning. This involved initially establishing a foothold on the local council by addressing community concerns, then using this as the springboard to build the party's credibility locally to eventually be able to challenge for the parliamentary constituency (Russell and Fieldhouse, 2005). Cutts (2006) examined Liberal Democrat campaigning in local elections in the South West, highlighting how greater local campaign intensity benefited the party electorally in those elections. However, the effectiveness of building from local council to parliamentary success has been questioned (Cutts and Shryane, 2006; Harrison, 2007). Winning a constituency seat has not always been the outcome, in part because the party's resources have been limited, but also because holding office in the local council can involve Liberal Democrats in unpopular decisions which do not always have an electoral pay-off. Similarly, the BNP also built their representation in local government on the basis of attending to community concerns (Clark et al., 2008; Copsey, 2008). While this appears to have reached a limit with the loss of many council seats and the failure to win a Westminster seat in 2010, the party's success in the 2009 European elections can nevertheless in part be attributed to the effectiveness of building up support through local campaigning.

Conclusion

The nature of voting behaviour and party campaigning has changed in recent decades. A decline in social structural explanations for voting behaviour has coincided with declining party loyalties and a concomitant increase in the numbers of voters who are undecided and have weak party loyalties. Under these circumstances, how parties campaign is increasingly important. Three sets of campaign developments have been highlighted. Pre-modern campaigns were based on ad hoc planning and traditional methods of local electioneering. Modern campaigns were associated with the rise of television, focused at the national level and involved parties taking professional marketing advice, but essentially aimed to sell the party's pre-existing range of policies. By contrast, post-modern campaigns involve increased levels of voter research, which feeds back into party announcements and policy positions. This enables much closer targeting of voters in terms of messages, and in terms of the contact they receive from parties. These changing campaign techniques have been tracked through major developments in the two main parties, and the various trade-offs they have had to make over the type of campaign that they will run. A key point is that, rather than the national and local campaigns being separate entities, campaign activity is now much more tightly integrated and targeted at both national and constituency levels than previously, particularly in party target seats. Technological developments are likely to ensure that campaign activity continues to evolve. The Leaders Debates in 2010 clearly impacted upon campaign planning and activity in 2010, and how these major set piece events will be accommodated in planning for the next general election remains to be seen. Campaigning then matters. It does so from a democratic perspective; the increasingly targeted nature of campaigns raises uncomfortable questions about how extensive parties' democratic engagement with the electorate actually is. It also matters because the need to compete for election impacts upon how parties behave and fulfil their functions more generally. Ultimately however it matters because the outcome of campaigning – the number and share of votes a party gets in the election – determines which party or parties will form the next government.

11

Conclusion: Political Parties
in the UK

This book has done a number of things in the preceding chapters. It has introduced the three main political parties in the UK, and discussed their ideologies, policies, leadership and performance in office. It has taken a thematic approach to a number of issues such as the rise of small parties, the importance of the UK's 'multi-level' party systems, the relationship between parties and the media, and how parties organize, finance themselves and campaign for election. More generally, it has also introduced broader debates about the nature of the UK party system and how parties may, or may not, fulfil their functions in Britain today. This concluding chapter returns to these more general concerns in order to reflect on some of the challenges facing the UK party system and political parties in the aftermath of the 2010 general election and the subsequent novelty of coalition government at Westminster. Discussion proceeds in four parts. The first section assesses the party system and asks whether the very notion of a British party system itself is coming under threat from political developments in the UK. The second part questions whether or not the UK's political parties are in decline or whether they have adapted to changing circumstances and continue to fulfil certain functions in British democracy. The third section identifies a range of direct challenges to parties both collectively and individually. The final section places the UK in comparative perspective. In other words, are these challenges unique to political parties in the UK, or are they part of a range of broader difficulties facing political parties in advanced industrial democracies more generally?

The UK Party System: A 'Dead Man Walking?'

Writing in advance of the 2010 general election, Lynch (2007, p. 344) suggested that the popular notion of the Westminster two-party system was the 'dead man walking' of British politics. In the run up to the 2010 general election, this was far from clear; certainly, the two main parties did not think that this was the case, with both seeing each other as the primary competitor for power. Nevertheless, other analysts made similar arguments in advance of the 2010 election (Dunleavy, 2005; Mair, 2009). Moreover, in the introduction to this book it was also claimed that the party system had already undergone a process of general change prior to 2010, even if the Conservative–Liberal Democrat coalition arrangements may yet prove to be a temporary phase in British politics. Given the supposed stability of the British party system, it is worth revisiting the question of what has changed since the two-party heyday of 1945–1970. Moreover, it is also worth assessing whether or not these circumstances are likely to be reversible. If not, political analysts need to develop new ways of conceptualizing the UK party system.

Mair (2009) suggests that the stability of party systems revolves around three main sets of variables. These are: the cleavage structure; the structure of party competition; and the stability of a country's institutional order. Cleavage structures are argued to have provided one of the key pillars of stable party voting. Across Britain, the decisive cleavage in explaining the two-party system traditionally revolved around class with 75 per cent and upwards of the middle and upper classes voting Conservative and more than 70 per cent of the working class voting Labour (Butler and Stokes, 1969). This class cleavage was also complemented by stable attitudes towards parties, primarily learned through socialization within the family, and leading to high levels of party identification during the 1950–60s. The classic British two-party system was thus supported both by stable social cleavages and by extensive party loyalties inculcated at an early age.

These circumstances no longer apply. Changes to the occupational structure have resulted in an increasingly affluent society where collective class ties have been replaced by much more atomized and individualistic economic experiences. While residual class-based effects are still evident, there has nevertheless been a sizeable decrease in class-based voting; absolute class voting had fallen from 63 to 41 per cent between 1964 and 2005, while by some measures levels of class voting have declined by around a half or more of what they were in 1964 (Denver, 2007, p. 69). In recent years, class has most obviously impacted upon turnout, with a close association between lower-class areas and lower levels of turnout (Denver, 2007, ch. 2). In terms of attitudes and loyalties towards parties, the proportions reporting a very strong party identification had fallen from 42 to 10 per cent in 2005. The cleavage and attitudinal pillars of the British party system have therefore eroded considerably.

Consequently, there has been a fragmentation of the vote across Britain. While the two main parties once commanded upwards of 90 per cent of the vote in the 1950s, this had fallen to 65 per cent in 2010. Taking turnout into account, the two main parties accounted for only 42 per cent of the UK electorate in 2010, with the largest party, the Conservatives, only achieving 23.5 per cent of the total electorate. By contrast, in 2010 the vote share for the Liberal Democrats continued to rise, as did the vote for various small party options and the Scottish and Welsh nationalists. The fragmentation of the vote manifests itself more obviously in contests for institutions such as the European parliament and devolved assemblies. In the European parliament, parties with no representation at Westminster, such as UKIP, can command a sizeable share of the vote, outperforming mainstream parties in the process. This combines with an increasing regionalization of the vote, with Scotland and Wales demonstrating different voting patterns to the rest of Britain, and in England a 'North–South' divide evident between a largely Labour-voting North and predominantly Conservative-voting South. This fragmentation also manifests itself in the numbers of people who actually vote in elections. While turnout recovered to 65 per cent in 2010 from the 59.4 per cent in 2001, 2010 remained the third poorest general election turnout in the post-war period.

Mair's (2009) second pillar of stability relates to the structure of party competition. The foregoing argument about the declining grip of the cleavage structure and subsequent fragmentation of the vote means that the structure of Westminster party competition is increasingly under pressure. Certainly in non-Westminster elections such as to local government, European and the devolved institutions, Chapter 7 has shown how these deviate from the pattern of competition at Westminster. At Westminster the two main parties have been sustained by two things: that they have, at least until 2010, been the only parties perceived to be in competition for office; and by the first-past-the-post electoral system which penalizes parties who have a broad popularity but little geographical concentration. These conditions still apply since the failure of the 2011 referendum on changing the voting system. Even if a coalition administration is necessary in the event of a hung parliament, the competition for leading the government is still dominated by Labour and the Conservatives.

There are a number of related issues. First, it is in the interests of both main parties to prevent competition between them being displaced by another party or area of political conflict (Mair, 2009, p. 295). The two mainstream parties can therefore act like a 'cartel', bolstering their own positions in political life in order to ensure they are not overtaken by some conflict which they are unable to control (Dunleavy, 2005; Katz and Mair, 1995; Mair, 2009). This need not be open collusion but can result from the centrist direction of electoral competition which means that some policy issues are addressed while others are essentially ignored.

This leads to a narrowness of political debate where 'safety first' is the order of the day for the parties. Thus, during the 2010 general election, the debate about public spending revolved around the relatively small amount of £6bn with neither main party willing to discuss how it would actually implement the much greater cuts in public expenditure deemed necessary. Other areas of discussion neither openly nor extensively considered were issues such as, for example, how increased and progressive income taxation may have helped resolve the perceived public spending crisis, and a defence of the public sector which had, after all, stepped in to prevent the British economy from collapsing after a case of vast market failure. Between 1945 and 1979, such debates may have been central to party competition. From the late 1980s, and particularly Labour's 1989 policy review, they have been less evident. In other words, the grounds of political debate and policy competition have moved rightwards from the 'Butskellite' social democratic consensus of the 1950s and 1960s, to a consensus around the desirability and efficiency of markets in delivering almost everything from scarce economic goods to many public services, including education, health, public utilities and even justice-related services such as prisons. Despite a necessary increase in state intervention by Labour during the financial crisis, neither main party has ultimately appeared willing to break with this consensus (Hay, 2007). This is not the same as saying the two parties are the same; the choice between the two main parties can certainly have important policy consequences. Nevertheless, even if Labour did invest more in public services from 1999, this was done quietly and with a clear orientation towards the perceived efficiencies of the market. One key criticism of Labour's time in office is that the party did little, despite large majorities, to explicitly challenge such narratives (Toynbee and Walker, 2010). Consequently, the main parties contest ever narrower territory which excludes a wide range of policy options.

The third pillar of stability refers to the institutional order (Mair, 2009). From being relatively stable in the post-war period, the British polity has undergone considerable constitutional and institutional change in recent years. Arguably the first fundamental change was under Heath when Britain acceded to the EEC, while the actions of subsequent governments, including those of Margaret Thatcher, have since extended the impact of European institutions. Institutional change accelerated considerably under Labour between 1997–2010 with the creation of a Scottish Parliament, Welsh Assembly, and the devolution of powers to Northern Ireland, London and also to a number of elected mayors across England. This was combined with a proliferation of electoral systems for these new institutions. European elections are now held under a closed-list proportional electoral system, the Scottish Parliament, Welsh Assembly and Greater London Assembly elect their representatives by the Mixed-Member Proportional (MMP, also known as the Additional Member System or AMS) system, directly elected mayors are chosen by the supplementary vote and the Northern Ireland Assembly is elected by the Single Transferable Vote (STV).

Taken together, these institutional changes have had the effect of opening political competition to party options representing a wide variety of viewpoints. Thus, UKIP represent a segment of the electorate who wish to withdraw from the EU, while the Greens equally represent those with more post-material values. Both parties have had success at the European level in a way that would have been unlikely at Westminster, even if the Greens have subsequently developed a local profile which has enabled the party to elect one MP in 2010. Similarly in Scotland and Wales, even the competition for government has opened up to include the two Nationalist parties, the SNP forming a minority administration in Edinburgh and Plaid Cymru forming part of a coalition government in Cardiff between 2007–11. Moreover, Northern Ireland's party system is unique in the UK featuring none of the mainstream British parties as serious competitors. Research has demonstrated that in these institutions voters cast their vote in relation to the local issues to hand in elections to the devolved bodies. As graphically demonstrated by the SNP's stunning victory in the 2011 Scottish elections, these issues are often substantially different from those to the fore in Westminster elections (Wyn Jones and Scully, 2006).

Where does this leave debates about the British party system? A number of points are pertinent. It remains true to say that Labour and the Conservatives continue to dominate party competition at Westminster. Notwithstanding this, none of the developments outlined above – the fragmentation of the vote and party competition; devolution – are likely to be reversed. While this means that the Westminster party system can, with the accession of the Liberal Democrats to power, be correctly classified as moderate pluralist, this fails to capture significant developments. As Mair (2009, p. 298) notes:

One of the main reasons why British politics continues to be about Labour versus Conservative is that it always has been believed to be about Labour versus Conservative. There has been no other alternative. Now that new party systems and electoral systems have developed beyond Westminster ... this familiarity and predictability is no longer so self-evident or constantly reinforced.

Citing a similar range of causes, Dunleavy (2005, p. 530) argues that this

reflects the exhaustion of previous main party and governing elite strategies, of attempting to suppress some issues and sublimate others into a limited part of the left–right spectrum. That approach can no longer accommodate what voters want to talk about and vote about.

Indeed from a Scottish, Welsh or Northern Irish perspective, where voters are concerned with issues relating to their immediate contexts, the concept of a UK or British party system has begun to look increasingly threadbare. While Westminster undoubtedly has an important impact on what happens in the three devolved territories, to voters in these regions the UK party system looks somewhat like an English-based party system no longer representing the broader UK state as a whole. Underlined by the SNP's extraordinary victory in the 2011 Scottish elections, according to an editorial in the normally reserved *Financial Times* (14 May 2011) the consequence of this dissonance is the most important constitutional issue facing the UK today.

What are the implications for students of party politics? Simply, it means that discussions relating to the UK party system now need to recognize the multi-level and multi-party complexity of today's politics instead of seeing it solely through the two- or three-party lens of Westminster. Dunleavy's (2005) notion of overlapping party systems is one way of beginning to consider this, while the work of Lynch (2007) and Mair (2009) also points to ways forward. Most importantly, in beginning to sketch a future research agenda for the study of party politics, there is an urgent need for students and analysts to further conceptualize both theoretically and empirically how the UK's multi-level party systems and party competition interact with each other.

Decline or Adaptation?

The question of whether political parties are in decline is revisited every few decades in the literature. In some ways, British parties have clearly been in decline. Chapters 2 and 9 have highlighted the decline in party membership and activism evident, while the discussion above underlines the declining ability of the mainstream parties to command voters' loyalties during elections. Seen as 'little short of precipitous' (Webb, 2009, p. 267), declining membership and activism is argued to have serious consequences for British democracy. This means that parties will have fewer and fewer people to act as volunteers, campaigning for the party at election time, acting as 'ambassadors in the community' (Scarrow, 1996), raising funds and sustaining them between elections. Consequently, parties are no longer performing an extensive integrative function in society. Whiteley (2009b) goes further and argues that a decline in partisanship, such as currently experienced in Britain, is likely to be closely correlated to declining levels of government effectiveness.

These are serious assertions. Yet, one of the difficulties in discussing parties in Britain is the tendency to see current developments through the lens of the recent past. While necessary to understand contemporary politics, a longer focus can provide considerable insight. Indeed, British political parties are always likely to have been in a parlous state. Popular literature from around a century ago bemoans the lack of interest in politics found amongst the working classes (Tressell, 1914 [1993]), while scholarly accounts of party organization written in the perceived 'golden age' of party politics in the 1950s highlight very similar concerns about declining memberships, collapsing organizations and the problems this was likely to cause for parties and democracy (Hanham, 1956). Consequently, Scarrow (1996) suggests that there was unlikely to have ever been such a 'golden age' of party politics and democratic engagement in Britain.

Instead of declining, it is therefore more useful to see British parties undergoing a constant process of adaptation to changing circumstances. A number of examples underline this. First, while parties undoubtedly trade on their ideological and policy reputations, competing for office is the core of what British parties now do. As Webb (2009, p. 270) notes, this is perhaps the least demanding perspective to assess parties from. Indeed, as Chapter 2 observes, despite declining membership there has nevertheless been a considerable extension of party candidates contesting elections at all levels. Where parties no longer have extensive local organization to sustain them, such candidates often now represent the main link between parties and the communities they claim to represent. Second, as highlighted in Chapter 10, party organizations have professionalized their campaign operations considerably from the pre-modern electioneering efforts of more personalized campaigning prior to the extensive availability of television, through the modern campaign which accommodated itself to the national television coverage and utilized sophisticated market research techniques, to the current post-modern campaign which is directly targeted at voters both nationally and locally and exploits the opportunities presented by new media to do so (Norris, 2000). Third, when elected the focus then moves to the politics of legis- lating and opposing. In other words, since parties are no longer rooted in their communities, their place in the institutions of government is now where parties draw their legitimacy, and often considerable resources, from (Katz and Mair, 1995).

On these questions, and despite writing almost two decades ago, the summary provided by Mair (1994, p. 19) remains highly pertinent. He argues that:

> The problem is not one of party decline per se, as is often imputed to be the case; rather it appears to be one in which the parties are at once stronger but also more remote; at once more in control, but also less powerful; and at once more privileged but also less legitimate.

This notion of legitimacy is at the heart of the problem. While parties have adapted to meet changing circumstances, the need for regime support has been central to understanding the persistence of political systems (Easton, 1965). A range of policy failures on both sides of the political spectrum, declining government effectiveness and the regular claims of parties to be unable to act for assorted economic reasons mean that voters no longer believe parties' claims to be able to make a decisive difference to their quality of life. Despite this, the demands and expecta- tions of parties and governments are higher than ever before. These are classic grounds for what might be termed a 'legitimacy deficit' (Beetham, 1991, p. 207). The result is declining partisanship and increasing distrust which is both quantitatively and qualitatively different from previous scepticism about the role of parties (Dalton and Weldon, 2005).

The Challenge to Parties

Political parties in the UK therefore face a variety of challenges in the aftermath of the 2010 general election. These are manifold and this section outlines six of the most important. The first relates to parties' links to society. It is worth focusing on one particular consequence of declining memberships. The narrower targeting of voters and marginal constituencies, largely now originating from a distant party HQ and call centre, is partly a consequence of the incentives offered by the Westminster electoral system. More importantly, parties are doing so out of necessity. Fewer members mean less intensive local efforts to contact voters during elections, and campaigns more generally can often appear tokenistic at best. Parties are utilizing the support of a more diffuse group of 'supporters' in some places to help them during elections. Given that voters can increasingly avoid election coverage in the UK's fragmented media market, this means that they are seldom getting the party message delivered to them by a dedicated partisan. This is hardly democratically desirable. Where small parties such as the BNP have been successful, it is because they have been able to exploit this gap between mainstream parties and society. Local efforts to combat such radical small parties have been shown to be effective, as in the 2010 case of campaigns against the BNP in places like Barking in London. As Chapter 10 has discussed, the evidence suggests that local campaign efforts can be effective in raising awareness among voters and mobilizing them to go to the polls.

A key challenge is therefore for parties to attempt to reinvigorate their local organizations, and for them to be seen to be active not just during elections, but between them. This has been said many times before. It is extremely difficult to do, and any such effort needs to be sustained. Recent debates in British politics have nevertheless emphasized the importance of community organizing. Such ideas have been picked up by parties; efforts in particular have been made by erstwhile Labour leadership contender David Miliband in this direction, although whether this proves to be lasting and effective remains to be seen.

A second challenge has also been argued to emanate from the decline of party memberships. Whiteley (2009a) suggests that declining memberships mean that parties are less able to counterbalance the claims of special interest groups, thereby making parties increasingly reliant on such sectional interests for policy ideas and other aspects of political support. Indeed, as often as not parties have often seemed to have been 'captured' by certain interests. Thus, lobbying by the food and drink industry is perceived to have led to a weakening of restrictions on food and licensing laws under both the coalition and the previous Labour government, while the banking industry has given large donations to the Conservative Party and is widely perceived to have escaped extensive regulation to ensure there is no repeat of the 2008 financial crisis (Watt and Treanor, 2011). It is important to recognize that there is no direct evidence of links between such donations and policy favours. In this sense British party politics remains relatively corruption-free (Fisher, 2008b). Moreover, due to parties' origins and ideological roots, some groups are likely to enjoy better access to some parties than others, with the trade unions and Labour being a case in point. However, if special interest groups are all that a party listens to and count as decisive when deciding upon policies, it is unlikely to make anything but partial policy, even if these groups may have considerable policy expertise. The contrary views of members and communities also need to be taken seriously. Parties would say that they do this already. Yet it is not always obvious to members or communities exactly why certain policy decisions have been made. Parties therefore need to explain their choices more clearly to their members and particularly the communities they are active in if they are to regain some degree of legitimacy.

Third, and related, both main parties have presided over large scale policy failures – most recently the economic crisis from 2008 onwards, and the university tuition fees controversy – while their policies have actually perpetuated social inequality, not made it better (Dorling, 2010). At a time when performance voting is perceived to be important (Clarke et al., 2009), this is unlikely to improve the standing of party politics among the electorate particularly when more is demanded of parties and government than ever before. Events will often conspire against parties in government, meaning that they appear, in former Chancellor Norman Lamont's memorable phrase, 'to be in office but not in power'. There is no single prescription that can resolve the issue of high profile policy failures. The challenge for parties in the UK is to not only design effective policy, thereby minimizing policy failure, it is also to convince the electorate that the policies being followed are necessary and in their best interests. Perhaps more importantly, it is also to demonstrate that contrary evidence has been duly heeded when making policy, and that these policies are not driven by narrow sectional and ideological motives. Importantly, when policies are manifestly shown to be failing, parties need to change course and do so recognizing their mistakes.

Fourth, parties suffer in the eyes of the public for being less than fully frank about their aims and plans. For instance, despite criticizing the 'old parties' in the 2010 election, senior Liberal Democrats appear to have claimed no manifesto commitments were sacrosanct given the situation they felt the country was in, the party fielding this as a justification for raising university tuition fees (see Cable, 2010). Similarly, the Conservatives claimed that there would be no top-down reorganizations of the NHS prior to being elected, yet were widely seen to have embarked on just such a reorganization with the 2011 Health and Social Care Bill. These sorts of examples further corrode public trust, low as it already was. Moreover, ministers seldom any longer feel the need to resign for failures or wrongdoing. Elections are regularly said to be the way in which the public can hold parties accountable for such behaviour. However, if the public cannot trust what their parties say and do both between and during elections, and the three main parties are implicated in such behaviour, it is little wonder that they attract public opprobrium. New Labour pollster Philip Gould (1998b) once argued that parties should never compromise on trust. While this did not last long, it is nevertheless a good motto for parties and their candidates to keep in mind.

A fifth challenge comes from the increasingly important field of identity politics. There are multiple levels to this. As highlighted above, the notion of a British party system is increasingly under pressure. However, the three main British parties all contest elections in Scotland and Wales as well as to Westminster. When they have appeared to emphasize both their unity and their Britishness rather than their Scottish or Welsh identity in devolved elections, they have encountered difficulties. Labour's 2007 Scottish campaign was hindered considerably by the British party's insistence that the then unpopular Tony Blair campaign for the Scottish party. Similarly, Nick Clegg's forays into the 2011 Scottish campaign were highly damaging for the Scottish Liberal Democrats. The balance to be struck with the three statewide parties is therefore between recognizing the imperatives of devolution and granting what is seen to be meaningful autonomy to their Scottish and Welsh organizations, while at the same time not undermining their 'Britishness'.

A closely related question is how parties deal with English identity. The issue of English identity has also spilled onto the streets with numerous rallies, often turning violent, by the English Defence League (EDL). Parties such as the BNP and UKIP have exploited identity questions through exclusionary anti-immigrant sentiment, and, despite the use of British symbols such as the Union Jack, rely predominantly on English voters for support. Both Conservatives and Labour have also seemed to tread on exclusionary territory designed to appeal to such sentiment, not least when discussing immigration policy. Such an approach to national identity is far from inevitable. For instance, the SNP promote an approach of civic nationalism, which means that the politics of identity in Scotland takes on a different tenor to that south of the border. In other words, parties can lead public opinion in this field should they wish to do so, and do not only need to follow it.

An additional aspect of identity politics is worth highlighting. This is the question of how representative parties really are of the UK as a whole? This has been touched on in discussions about candidate selection. Although occasionally noted as a problem by parties, it is worth repeating that the UK is increasingly diverse and few of the parties in parliament look representative of this diversity. This is not to claim that MPs cannot represent their constituents properly, since they manifestly can and do. It is however to claim that this lack of diversity limits the experiences of the political elite somewhat, which in turn can limit an awareness of the lived experiences and needs of a large proportion of the population. While some parties have had more success in increasing their diversity at the local level (Garbaye, 2005), this is nevertheless at least problematic at the national level since the UK is far from a homogeneous state.

The final challenge to the three main parties is managing the consequences of coalition government. This is difficult for each of them. For the Liberal Democrats, the challenges are to minimize their electoral losses resulting from participation in the coalition, minimize internal party disputes and to retain a distinct identity. With the Conservatives, it took a long time to become electable again after losing office in 1997. Their electability however was clearly restricted given the hung parliament result of the 2010 election. Far from heeding calls from the party's right to emphasize more Eurosceptic issues and further privatization and marketization, the Conservatives need to understand the limits that public opinion has put on their evident policy ambition. Since their programme of public spending austerity will hit many across the UK, they will also need all of their once renowned 'statecraft' to retain their popularity in the next general election.

The coalition government provided an opportunity, but also a difficulty for Labour. It was an opportunity because the coalition's policies mean that Labour has the chance to again appeal to many that the coalition's policies have hit badly. The centralist incentives provided by the electoral system mean that such a narrative will however need to be widely cast, thereby losing some of its force on the way. Ed Miliband's early leadership has seemed uncertain as to the party's direction. While this is understandable as a new leader finds their way, it will nevertheless need to be clarified well in advance of the next general election. Which party does Labour aim its opposition at? The Liberal Democrats may prove important again in the event of a hung parliament, while both Liberal Democrat and moderate Conservative voters could conceivably be enticed to vote Labour. Too much negative campaigning either way could potentially alienate both sets of swing voters.

These are major challenges for all three main parties. Numerous reforms have been suggested in an attempt to address some of these issues (see Ingle, 2008; Webb, 2009). Prominent among them include, for example, electoral reform and state funding for political parties. Neither are likely to have the impact their advocates suggest. In the aftermath of the parliamentary expenses scandal, state funding is likely to be highly unpopular with voters, and is far from the panacea some suggest; Germany has Europe's oldest system of state funding, yet still endures occasional party financing scandals. Electoral reform is clearly necessary since first-past-the-post continues to underpin an unrepresentative party system. However, the 2011 referendum on electoral reform was lost, thereby putting the issue off the agenda for some time. Moreover, other electoral systems have proved no barrier elsewhere to trust in parties declining.

Webb (2009) is therefore rightly pessimistic about any such reforms making a major difference to people's views about British parties. As he notes, in advanced democracies, parties are necessary for the aggregation of interests, and the presentation of programmes to the electorate. If there were no parties, something similar would spring up to take their place. Indeed, even where Independents have been elected to parliament or to local government, it is striking just how often they rely on parties for information and cues on how to vote (Berry, 2008; Cowley and Stuart, 2009). What then can be done? First, increased transparency into party activities remains necessary. While this was extended considerably by the Political Parties, Elections and Referendums Act (2000), it nevertheless remains the case that large aspects of political party life remain unreported. If parties really are the 'public utilities' some have argued them to be (van Biezen, 2004), increased transparency would not only help students of political parties understand the pressures parties are under, it will also help keep them accountable. Second, if voters are unhappy with their parties, they need to either become active in holding them to account, both locally and nationally, or be prepared to organize themselves to provide some alternative. This may be somewhat optimistic, but nevertheless if better governance is desirable then people will have to demonstrate to parties that they both want this to happen and that they are willing to contribute to doing so.

Comparative Perspectives

A number of the observations made above have come from analysts studying political parties comparatively (Dalton and Weldon, 2005; Holmberg, 2003; Mair, 1994). This suggests that many of the challenges encountered by the UK's parties are also faced by parties more generally (see Webb et al., 2002). Parties have been challenged by the rise in social movement organizations that are more able to focus on single issues and that can enable political participation without the need to promote a party's programme, leading some to ask whether politics without parties may be a growing trend (Della Porta and Diani, 2006; Jordan, 1998). The most prominent of these is perhaps the environmental movement. Similarly, many Western democracies have been beset by populist anti-politics parties claiming to be acting in support of ordinary people against the political elite. Often these parties are anti-immigrant and can be placed on the radical populist right. Examples include the French Front National, the secessionist Italian Lega Nord, the Belgian Vlaams Belang, the Austrian Freedom Party and the American Tea Party movement. A number of these have now served in government, or otherwise had considerable success. Through an analysis of 20 democracies, Mair and van Biezen (2001) also show that party membership is also in universal decline. To counter this, throughout Western Europe most major parties have been able to rely on state funding for resources and to a far greater extent than British parties have been able to.

To examine this systematically, Webb (2002, p. 439) sets out a range of indicators of party legitimacy. These include: electoral volatility; the effective number of parties; election turnout; partisan identification; party membership; and anti-party sentiment. In almost all of these categories across 16 democracies, he finds that the indicators indicate extensive legitimacy problems for parties. Thus, dealignment has been accompanied by anti-party sentiment in 14 of the countries, while 12 show evidence of electoral volatility, 12 countries have experienced falling turnout and 13 have seen a rise in the effective number of parties in electoral competition. Parties have tried to combat these challenges in a number of ways, for instance by providing further opportunities to participate in internal decision-making processes as an attempt to increase membership (Scarrow, 1999). However, it is not always clear that parties have been willing to give up meaningful policy-making power to members, and consequently these attempts had little lasting impact. While recognizing that changing socio-economic circumstances have contributed to the decline of party legitimacy, many analysts blame parties themselves for turning to the state for resources instead and thereby compounding the problem (Dalton and Wattenberg, 2000b, p. 284; Mair, 1994, p. 19).

Where might this lead? Two examples provide food for thought. First, the Italian party system collapsed in the early 1990s in the aftermath of widespread corruption among party elites. A new range of party alternatives emerged, exploiting anti-politics sentiment among voters with populist appeals disdaining, as the Lega Nord put it, 'the thieves of Rome'. Led by the media tycoon Silvio Berlusconi, a coalition involving some of these parties has governed Italy for much of the period since 1994. At the same time, Berlusconi and his coalition have been accused of various offences such as legislating in the interests of Berlusconi's business interests, thereby weakening many of the processes of Italian democracy as they have done so, while also failing to provide adequate public policy solutions to the many problems faced by their country (Bull and Newell, 2005). Second, in a 'political earthquake', the party that has governed Ireland for most of the period since the country's independence, Fianna Fail, suffered a huge defeat in the country's 2011 general election, its vote share declining by 24.2 percentage points and losing 58 of the 78 seats it had held. This was the result of Ireland's economic crash from 2008 onwards where the country eventually needed to be bailed out by the EU and IMF after trying and failing to support its bankrupt financial sector. Prior to the crash, Fianna Fail had presided over a long period of ultimately unsustainable economic boom that led Ireland to near economic collapse.

These examples, admittedly both extreme but apocryphal cases, tell us two things that voters and students of British parties should heed. First, from the Italian case comes the danger of simplistic populist appeals, leading to a government widely perceived to be acting in the interests of its leader rather than of society as a whole, controlling most of the broadcast media and prepared to make vocal attacks on institutions such as the rule of law. Anti-politics populist appeals may therefore gain considerable sympathy amongst the public; they seldom however produce a resolution to a country's difficulties or improve a country's governance. Second, although more countries than Ireland have suffered from the economic downturn, because of its proximity to the UK, its severe economic consequences and the virtual collapse of its major party, the Irish case perhaps most graphically demonstrates the consequences of not continually holding politicians and policy-makers up to the lens of sustained critical scrutiny beyond just the short election period and asking questions that go beyond the news headlines of the day. Politics then matters to party political outcomes. Noting the various challenges to party legitimacy described above, Dalton and Wattenberg (2000b, p. 284) highlight the implications by suggesting that responses need to work at a number of levels, with citizens, politicians and institutions all accepting and reacting to the challenge posed by partisan dealignment in advanced democracies. While this is important, and urgent, these responses are unlikely to make a huge difference. Indeed, dealignment is now a virtually permanent feature of advanced democracies. However, stopping such processes from falling further would be an achievement in and of itself. Parties have continually shown themselves to be adaptable organizations. How they do so as they attempt to restore at least some of their lost legitimacy will be fascinating for students of comparative politics to observe.

Conclusion

Interest in party politics has taken some new directions in the UK due to the unusual circumstances prevailing in the 2010 general election. The televised leaders' debates led to large audiences tuning in, and this was influential in driving campaign developments. The novel outcome – a Conservative–Liberal Democrat coalition government – was a high profile indication of the level of change that the UK party system has experienced in recent decades. The changes have been societal, electoral and institutional, while many of the policy problems parties have had to deal with have originated not just domestically but also in the international sphere. The challenges facing political parties in the UK are therefore complex and many have also been encountered by parties elsewhere. While much of the discussion in this book has been critical of parties, it is nevertheless worth noting in conclusion that many party politicians do go into public service in order to try to make a positive difference to political outcomes. This is the very essence of democratic politics and their contribution should be recognized. This is however not the same as saying there is no 'crisis of party' in the UK. The legitimacy gap is large and arguably growing. The parties and party system will undoubtedly adapt. Whether the onset of coalition government, the radical policies proposed by the coalition, initiatives such as party leaders' debates and continued process of devolution are enough to engage the public in political debate remains to be seen. What is for certain is that students of political parties in the UK will have numerous new, important and exciting issues to examine in the coming years.

References

Abedi, A. and Lundberg, T. C. (2009) 'Doomed to Failure? UKIP and the Organisational Challenges Facing Right-Wing Populist Anti-Political Establishment Parties', *Parliamentary Affairs*, vol. 62, no. 1, pp. 72–87.

Abts, K. and Rummens, S. (2007) 'Populism Versus Democracy', *Political Studies*, vol. 55, no. 2, pp. 405–24.

Alderman, K. and Carter, N. (2000) 'The Liberal Democrat Leadership Election of 1999', *Parliamentary Affairs*, vol. 53, no. 2, pp. 311–27.

Allen, N. and Bartle, J. (eds) (2011) *Britain at the Polls 2010* (London: Sage).

Allen, N., Bara, J. and Bartle, J. (2011) 'A Much Debated Campaign', in Allen, N. and Bartle, J. (eds), *Britain at the Polls 2010* (London: Sage), pp. 175–202.

Almond, G. A. and Powell, G. B. (1966) *Comparative Politics: A Developmental Approach* (Boston: Little, Brown).

American Political Science Association (APSA) Committee on Political Parties (1950) 'Part 1: The Need for Greater Party Responsibility', *American Political Science Review*, vol. 44, no. 3, Part 2 Supplement, pp. 15–36.

Ashcroft, M. A. (2005) *Smell the Coffee: A Wake-Up Call to the Conservative Party* (GB: Michael Ashcroft).

Ashcroft, M. A. (2010) *Minority Verdict: The Conservative Party, the Voters and the 2010 Election* (London: Biteback).

Ashdown, P. (2000) *The Ashdown Diaries: Volume One 1988–1997* (London: Penguin).

Ashdown, P. (2002) *The Ashdown Diaries: Volume Two 1997–1999* (London: Penguin).

Bale, T. (1999) 'Harold Wilson 1963–76', in Jefferys, K. (ed.), *Leading Labour: From Kier Hardie to Tony Blair* (London: I. B. Tauris), pp. 116–32.

Bale, T. (2008) '"A Bit Less Bunny-Hugging and a Bit More Bunny-Boiling?" Qualifying Conservative Party Change Under David Cameron', *British Politics*, vol. 3, no. 3, pp. 270–99.

Bale, T. (2010) *The Conservative Party: From Thatcher to Cameron* (Cambridge: Polity).

Bale, T. and Webb, P. (2011) 'The Conservative Party', in Allen, N. and Bartle, J. (eds), *Britain at the Polls 2010* (London: Sage), pp. 37–62.

Barnes, J. (1994) 'Ideology and Factions', in Seldon, A. and Ball, S. (eds), *Conservative Century: The Conservative Party Since 1900* (Oxford: Oxford University Press), pp. 315–45.

Bean, K. (2007) *The New Politics of Sinn Fein* (Liverpool: Liverpool University Press).

Beech, M. (2009) 'Cameron and Conservative Ideology', in Lee. S. and Beech, M. (eds), *The Conservatives Under David Cameron: Built to Last?* (Basingstoke: Palgrave Macmillan), pp. 18–30.

Beer, S. H. (2001) 'New Labour: Old Liberalism', in White, S. (ed.), *New Labour: The Progressive Future* (Basingstoke: Palgrave Macmillan), pp. 18–31.

Beetham, D. (1991) *The Legitimation of Power* (Basingstoke: Macmillan).

Bennie, L. (2004) *Understanding Political Participation: Green Party Membership in Scotland* (Aldershot: Ashgate).

Bennie, L. and Clark, A. (2003) 'Towards Moderate Pluralism: Scotland's Post-Devolution Party System, 1999–2002', in Rallings, C. et. al. (eds), *British Elections and Parties Review Volume 13* (London: Cass), pp. 134–55.

Bennie, L., Brand, J. and Mitchell, J. (1997) *How Scotland Votes: Scottish Parties and Elections* (Manchester: Manchester University Press).

Bennie, L., Curtice, J. and Rüdig, W. (1996) 'Party Members', in MacIver, D. (ed.), *The Liberal Democrats* (Hemel Hempstead: Prentice-Hall/Harvester Wheatsheaf), pp. 135–53.

Benoit, K. and Laver, M. (2006) *Party Policy in Modern Democracies* (London: Routledge).

Bentham, C. (2007) 'Liberal Democrat Policy-Making: An Insider's View, 2000–2004', *Political Quarterly*, vol. 78, no. 1, pp. 59–67.

Berry, R. (2008) *Independent: The Rise of the Non-Aligned Politician* (Exeter: Imprint Academic).

Bevir, M. (2000) 'New Labour: A Study in Ideology', *British Journal of Politics and International Relations*, vol. 2, no. 3, pp. 277–301.

Bevir, M. and Rhodes, R. A. W. (1998) 'Narratives of Thatcherism', *West European Politics*, vol. 21, no. 1, pp. 97–119.

Birch, S. (2009) 'Real Progress: Prospects for Green Party Support in Britain', *Parliamentary Affairs*, vol. 62, no. 1, pp. 53–71.

Blair, T. (1998) *The Third Way: New Politics for the New Century* (London: Fabian Society), Pamphlet 588.

Blair, T. (2007) 'Tony Blair's Media Speech: the Prime Minister's Reuters Speech on Public Life', *Political Quarterly*, vol. 78, no. 4, pp. 476–87.

Blond, P. (2010) *Red Tory: How the Left and Right Have Broken Britain and How We Can Fix It* (London: Faber & Faber).

Blondel, J. (1968) 'Party Systems and Types of Government in Western Democracies', *Canadian Journal of Political Science*, vol. 1, no. 2, pp.180–203.

Blumler, J. G. and Gurevitch, M. (2002) 'Public Service in Transition? Campaign Journalism at the BBC, 2001', in Bartle, J., Atkinson, S. and Mortimore, R. (eds), *Political Communications: The General Election Campaign of 2001* (London: Cass), pp. 215–35.

Blyth, M. and Katz, R. (2005) 'From Catch-All Politics to Cartelization: The Political Economy of the Cartel Party', *West European Politics*, vol. 28, no. 1, pp. 33–60.

Bochel, J. and Denver, D. (1983) 'Candidate Selection in the Labour Party: What the Selectors Seek', *British Journal of Political Science*, vol. 13, no. 91, pp. 45–69.

Bogdanor, V. (2004) 'The Constitution and the Party System in the Twentieth Century', *Parliamentary Affairs*, vol. 57, no. 4, pp. 717–33.

Borisyuk, G., Rallings, C., Thrasher, M. and van der Kolk, H. (2007) 'Voter Support for Minor Parties: Assessing the Social and Political Context of Voting at the 2004 European Elections in Greater London', *Party Politics*, vol. 13, no. 6, pp. 669–93.

Brack, D. (1996) 'Liberal Democrat Policy', in MacIver, D. (ed.), *The Liberal Democrats* (Hemel Hempstead: Prentice Hall/Harvester Wheatsheaf), pp. 85–110.

Brack, D. (2007a) 'Equality Matters', in Brack, D., Grayson, R. S. and Howarth, D. (eds), *Reinventing the State: Social Liberalism for the 21st Century* (London: Politicos), pp. 17–35.

Brack, D. (2007b) 'Liberal Democrat Leadership: The Cases of Ashdown and Kennedy', *Political Quarterly*, vol. 78, no. 1, pp. 78–88.

Brack, D., Grayson, R. S. and Howarth, D. (eds) (2007) *Reinventing the State: Social Liberalism for the 21st Century* (London: Politico's).

Bradbury, J., Mitchell, J., Bennie, L. and Denver, D. (2000) 'Candidate Selection, Devolution and Modernization: The Selection of Labour Party Candidates for the 1999 Scottish Parliament and Welsh Assembly Elections', in Cowley, P. et al. (eds), *British Elections and Parties Review Volume 10* (London: Cass), pp. 151–72.

Brand, J. (1978) *The National Movement in Scotland* (London: Routledge & Kegan Paul).

Briggs, R. (2007) 'Who's Afraid of the Respect Party? Dissent and Cohesion in Modern Britain', *Renewal*, vol. 15, no. 2/3, pp. 89–97.

British National Party (2007) *Statement of Accounts, Year Ended 31st December 2007* (Welshpool: BNP).

British National Party (2005), *Rebuilding British Democracy: General Election 2005 Manifesto*, www.bnp.org.uk, [25/5/07].

Bruce, S. (2009) *Paisley: Religion and Politics in Northern Ireland* (Oxford: Oxford University Press).

Buckler, S. and Dolowitz, D. P. (2009) 'Ideology, Party Identity and Renewal', *Journal of Political Ideologies*, vol. 14, no. 1, pp. 11–30.

Budge, I. (1999) 'Party Policy and Ideology: Reversing the 1950s?', in Evans, G. and Norris, P. (eds), *Critical Elections: British Parties and Voters in Long-Term Perspective* (London: Sage), pp. 1–21.

Bull, M. J. and Newell, J. (2005) *Italian Politics: Adjustment Under Duress* (Cambridge: Polity).

Bulpitt, J. (1986) 'The Discipline of New Democracy: Mrs Thatcher's Domestic Statecraft', *Political Studies*, vol. 34, no. 1, pp. 19–39.

Burch, M. (1980) 'Approaches to Leadership in Opposition: Edward Heath and Margaret Thatcher', in Layton-Henry, Z. (ed.), *Conservative Party Politics* (Basingstoke: Macmillan), pp. 159–85.

Butler, D. and Stokes, D. (1969) *Political Change in Britain* (London: Macmillan).

Butler, D. and Kavanagh, D. (1980) *The British General Election of 1979* (Basingstoke: Macmillan).

Butler, D. and Kavanagh, D. (1988) *The British General Election of 1987* (Basingstoke: Macmillan).

Butler, D. and Kavanagh, D. (1997) *The British General Election of 1997* (Basingstoke: Macmillan).

Butler, D. and Kavanagh, D. (2002) *The British General Election of 2001* (Basingstoke: Palgrave Macmillan).

Cable, V. (2004) 'Liberal Economics and Social Justice', in Marshall, P. and Laws, D. (eds) (2004) *The Orange Book: Reclaiming Liberalism* (London: Profile Books), pp. 132–73.

Cable, V. (2010) *House of Commons Debates*, Vol. 516, Col. 172, 12 October.

Callaghan, J. (2000) 'Rise and Fall of the Alternative Economic Strategy: From Internationalisation of Capital to "Globalisation"', *Contemporary British History*, vol. 14, no. 3, pp. 105–30.

Cameron, D. (2005a) 'A Voice for Hope, for Optimism and for Change', 6 December, www.conservatives.com, [22/4/10].

Cameron, D. (2005b) 'Until We're Represented by Men and Women in the Country, We Won't Be Half the Party We Could Be', 12 December, www.conservatives.com, [22/4/10].

Cameron, D. (2009a) 'A Europe Policy That People Can Believe In', 4 November, www.conservatives.com [10/11/09].

Cameron, D. (2009b) 'The Big Society', Hugo Young Lecture, 10 November, www.conservatives.com [11/11/09].

Cameron, D. (2011) 'PM's Speech on the Big Society', 14 February, www.number10.gov.uk, [4/3/11].

Carter, E. (2005) *The Extreme Right in Western Europe: Success or Failure?* (Manchester: Manchester University Press).

Carter, N. (2006) 'Party Politicisation of the Environment in Britain', *Party Politics*, vol. 12, no. 6, pp. 747–67.

Carter, N. (2008) 'The Green Party: Emerging from the Political Wilderness?', *British Politics*, vol. 3, no. 2, pp. 223–40.

Carty, R. K. (2004) 'Parties as Franchise Systems: The Stratarchical Organisational Imperative', *Party Politics*, vol. 10, no. 1, pp. 5–24.

Chadwick, A. (2011a) 'Britain's First Live Televised Party Leaders' Debate: From the News Cycle to the Political Information Cycle', *Parliamentary Affairs*, vol. 64, no. 1, pp. 24–44.

Chadwick, A. (2011b) 'The Political Information Cycle in a Hybrid News System: The British Prime Minister and the "Bullygate" Affair', *International Journal of Press/Politics*, vol. 16, no. 1, pp. 3–29.

Childs, S. (2003) 'The Sex Discrimination (Elections Candidates) Act 2002 and its Implications', *Representation*, vol. 39, no. 2, pp. 83–93.

Childs, S., Webb, P. and Marthaler, S. (2009) 'The Feminisation of the Conservative Parliamentary Party: Party Members' Attitudes', *Political Quarterly*, vol. 80, no. 2, pp. 204–13.

Clark, A. (2004) 'The Continued Relevance of Local Parties in Representative Democracies', *Politics*, vol. 24, no. 1, pp. 35–45.

Clark, A. (2006) 'Local Parties, Participation and Campaigning in Post-Devolution Scotland' (University of Aberdeen: Unpublished PhD Thesis).

Clark, A. (2008) 'Building Nationalist Success? A Political Ecology of Scottish National Party Organization in the 2003 and 2007 Scottish Parliament Elections', Paper presented to Elections, Public Opinion and Parties Conference, University of Manchester 12–14 September.

Clark, A. (forthcoming 2012) 'Party Organisation and Concurrent Multi-Level Local Campaigning: The 2007 Scottish Elections Under MMP and STV', *Party Politics*.

Clark, A., Bottom, K. and Copus, C. (2008) 'More Similar Than They'd Like to Admit? Ideology, Policy and Populism in the Trajectories of the British National Party and Respect', *British Politics*, vol. 3, no. 4, pp. 511–34.

Clarke, H. D., Sanders, D., Stewart, M. C. and Whiteley, P. F. (2004) *Political Choice in Britain* (Oxford: Oxford University Press).

Clarke, H. D., Sanders, D., Stewart, M. C. and Whiteley, P. F. (2009) *Performance Politics and the British Voter* (Cambridge: Cambridge University Press).

Clegg, N. (2004) 'Europe: A Liberal Future', in Marshall, P. and Laws, D. (eds) (2004) *The Orange Book: Reclaiming Liberalism* (London: Profile Books), pp. 69–103.

Clegg, N. (2009) 'Don't Waste Our Time …: Bring Forward Real Reform', *The Independent*, 16th November.

Coates, D. (2008) 'Darling, It is Entirely My Fault! Gordon Brown's Legacy to Alistair and Himself', *British Politics*, vol. 3, no. 1, pp. 3–21.

Cole, M. (2009) 'Growing Without Pains? Explaining Liberal Democrat MPs' Behaviour', *British Journal of Politics and International Relations*, vol. 11, no. 2, pp. 259–79.

Coleman, S. (2001) 'Online Campaigning', in Norris, P. (ed.), *Britain Votes 2001* (Oxford: Oxford University Press).

Committee on Standards in Public Life (1998) *The Funding of Political Parties in the United Kingdom*, Cm 4057-1 (London: TSO).

ConservativeHome (2010a) *ConservativeHome Members' Panel*, http://conservativehome.blogs.com/thetorydiary/conservativehome-members-panel/ [8/4/10].

ConservativeHome (2010b) *ConservativeHome's Seats and Candidates' Blog*, http://conservativehome.blogs.com/goldlist/2009/07/ [21/4/10].

ConservativeHome (2010c) *ConservativeHome The Tory Diary*, http://conservativehome.blogs.com/thetorydiary/2009/10/ [21/4/10].

ConservativeHome (2010d) *Lessons from the Tories' General Election Campaign: A 7,000 Word Report*, http://conservativehome.blogs.com/generalelectionreview/ [13/05/2010].

Conservative Party (2005) *A 21st Century Party: A Consultation Paper Setting Out Proposals to Reform the Conservative Party's Organisation* (London: Conservative Party).

Conservative Party (2006) *Built to Last: The Aims and Values of the Conservative Party* (London: Conservative Party).

Conservative Party (2010) *An Invitation to Join the Government of Britain: The Conservative Manifesto 2010* (London: Conservative Party).

Constitutional Affairs Committee (2006) *Party Funding: First Report of Session 2006–07*, HC-136-1 (London: TSO).

Cooke, A. (n.d.) *A Party of Change* (London: Conservative Party), www.conservatives.com, [9/8/11].

Copsey, N. (2007) 'Changing Course or Changing Clothes? Reflections on the Ideological Evolution of the British National Party, 1999–2006', *Patterns of Prejudice*, vol. 41, no. 1, pp. 61–82.

Copsey, N. (2008) *Contemporary British Fascism: The British National Party and the Quest for Legitimacy*, 2nd edn (Basingstoke: Palgrave Macmillan).

Copsey, N. and Macklin, G. (eds) (2011) *British National Party: Contemporary Perspectives* (London: Routledge).

Copus, C., Clark, A. and Bottom, K. (2008) 'Multi-Party Politics in England? Small Parties, Independents and Political Associations in English Local Politics', in Reiser, M. and Holtmann, E. (eds), *Farewell to the Party Model? Independent Local Lists in Eastern and Western European Countries* (Wiesbaden: VS Verlag), pp. 253–76.

Copus, C., Clark, A., Reynaert, H. and Steyvers, K. (2009) 'Minor Party and Independent Politics Beyond the Mainstream: Fluctuating Fortunes but a Permanent Presence', *Parliamentary Affairs*, vol. 62, no. 1, pp. 4–18.

Cowley, P. (2001) 'The Observer: Good at Observing, Less Good at Influencing?', *Political Studies*, vol. 49, no. 5, pp. 957–68.

Cowley, P. (2005) *The Rebels: How Blair Mislaid His Majority* (London: Politico's).

Cowley, P. (2009) 'The Parliamentary Party', *Political Quarterly*, vol. 80, no. 2, pp. 214–21.

Cowley, P. and Garry, J. (1998) 'The British Conservative Party and Europe: The Choosing of John Major', *British Journal of Political Science*, vol. 28, no. 3, pp. 473–99.

Cowley, P. and Green, J. (2005) 'New Leaders, Same Problems: The Conservatives', in Geddes, A. and Tonge, J. (eds), *Britain Decides: The UK General Election 2005* (Basingstoke: Palgrave Macmillan), pp. 46–69.

Cowley, P. and Stuart, M. (2008a) 'A Rebellious Decade: Backbench Rebellions Under Tony Blair, 1997–2007', in Beech, M. and Lee, S. (eds), *Ten Years of New Labour* (Basingstoke: Palgrave Macmillan), pp. 103–19.

Cowley, P. and Stuart, M. (2008b) 'A Long Way From Equidistance: Lib Dem Voting in Parliament, 1997–2007', Available online at www.revolts.co.uk/cat_briefing_papers.html, [1/12/09].

Cowley, P. and Stuart, M. (2009) 'There was a Doctor, a Journalist and Two Welshmen: the Voting Behaviour of Independent MPs in the United Kingdom House of Commons, 1997–2007', *Parliamentary Affairs*, vol. 62, no.1, pp. 19–31.

Cracknell, R., McGuinness, F. and Rhodes, C. (2010) *General Election 2010: Final Edition*, London: House of Commons Library Research Paper 10/036.

Crewe, I. (1993) 'The Thatcher Legacy', in King, A. (ed.), *Britain at the Polls 1992* (Chatham, NJ: Chatham House), pp. 1–28.

Crewe, I. and King, A. (1995) *SDP: The Birth, Life and Death of the Social Democratic Party* (Oxford: Oxford University Press).

Crosland, A. (2006 [1956]) *The Future of Socialism* (London: Constable).

Curtice, J. (2007) 'Elections and Public Opinion', in Seldon, A. (ed.), *Blair's Britain 1997–2007* (Cambridge: Cambridge University Press), pp. 35–53.

Curtice, J. and Ormston, R. (2011) 'So Who Is Winning the Debate? Constitutional Preferences in Scotland After Four Years of Nationalist Government', *Scottish Affairs*, vol. 74, pp. 24–44.

Curtice, J. and Park, A. (1999) 'Region: New Labour, New Geography?', in Evans, G. and Norris, P. (eds), *Critical Elections: British Parties and Voters in Long-Term Perspective* (London: Sage), pp. 124–47.

Curtice, J., Fisher, S. and Steed, M. (2005) 'Appendix 2: The Results Analysed', in Kavanagh, D. and Butler, D. (2005) *The British General Election of 2005* (Basingstoke: Palgrave Macmillan), pp. 235–59.

Cuthbert, J. and Cuthbert, M. (2009) 'SNP Economic Strategy: Neo-Liberalism with a Heart', in Hassan, G. (ed.), *The Modern SNP: From Protest to Power* (Edinburgh: Edinburgh University Press), pp. 105–19.

Cutts, D. (2006) '"Where We Work We Win": A Case Study of Local Liberal Democrat Campaigning', *Journal of Elections, Public Opinion and Parties*, vol. 16, no. 3, pp. 221–42.

Cutts, D. and Shryane, N. (2006) 'Did Local Activism Really Matter? Liberal Democrat Campaigning and the 2001 British General Election', *British Journal of Politics and International Relations*, vol. 8, no. 3, pp. 427–44.

Cutts, D., Childs, S. and Fieldhouse, E. (2008) 'This is What Happens When you Don't Listen: All Women Shortlists at the 2005 General Election', *Party Politics*, vol. 14, no. 5, pp. 575–95.

Daalder, H. (1991) 'A Crisis of Party?', *Scandinavian Political Studies*, vol. 15, no. 4, pp. 269–88.

Dahl, R. A. (1966) *Political Oppositions in Western Democracies* (London: Yale University Press).

Dahl, R. A. (1966) 'Patterns of Opposition', in Dahl, R. A. (ed.), *Political Oppositions in Western Democracies* (London: Yale University Press), pp. 332–47.

Dalton, R. J. and Wattenberg, M. P. (2000a) 'Unthinkable Democracy: Political Change in Advanced Industrial Democracies', in Dalton, R. J. and Wattenberg, M. P. (eds), *Parties Without Partisans: Political Change in Advanced Industrial Democracies* (Oxford: Oxford University Press), pp. 3–16.

Dalton, R. J. and Wattenberg, M. P. (2000b) 'Partisan Change and the Democratic Process', in Dalton, R. J. and Wattenberg, M. P. (eds), *Parties Without Partisans: Political Change in Advanced Industrial Democracies* (Oxford: Oxford University Press), pp. 261–84.

Dalton, R. J. and Weldon, S. A. (2005) 'Public Images of Political Parties: A Necessary Evil?', *West European Politics*, vol. 28, no. 5, pp. 931–51.

Davies, A. J. (1992) *To Build a New Jerusalem: The Labour Movement from the 1880s to the 1990s* (London: Michael Joseph).

Deacon, D. and Wring, D. (2002) 'Partisan Dealignment and the British Press', in Bartle, J., Atkinson, S. and Mortimore, R. (eds), *Political Communications: The General Election Campaign of 2001* (London: Cass), pp. 197–214.

Deacon, D., Golding, P. and Billig, M. (1998) 'Between Fear and Loathing: National Press Coverage of the 1997 British General Election', in Denver, D., Fisher, J., Cowley, P. and Pattie, C. (eds), *British Elections and Parties Review Vol. 8: The 1997 General Election* (London: Cass), pp. 135–49.

Deacon, R. (2007) 'The Welsh Liberal Democrats: From Government to Opposition and Then Back Again?', *Political Quarterly*, vol. 78, no. 1, pp. 156–64.

Della Porta, D. and Diani, M. (2006) *Social Movements: An Introduction,* 2nd edn (London: Blackwell).

Democratic Unionist Party (2007) *Getting It Right: Manifesto 2007* (Belfast: DUP).

Democratic Unionist Party (2010) *Let's Keep Northern Ireland Moving Forward: Manifesto 2010* (Belfast: DUP).

Democratic Unionist Party (2011) *Moving Forward: Manifesto 2011* (Belfast: DUP).

Denham, A. and Dorey, P. (2007) 'The "Caretaker" Cleans Up: The Liberal Democrat Leadership Election of 2006', *Parliamentary Affairs*, vol. 60, no. 1, pp. 26–45.

Denham, A. and O'Hara, K. (2007) 'The Three "Mantras": "Modernisation" and the Conservative Party', *British Politics*, vol. 2, no. 2, pp. 167–90.

Denham, A. and O'Hara, K. (2008) *Democratising Conservative Leadership Selection: From Grey Suits to Grassroots* (Manchester: Manchester University Press).

Denver, D. (1994) *Elections and Voting Behaviour in Britain*, 2nd edn (London: Harvester Wheatsheaf).

Denver, D. (2007) *Elections and Voters in Britain, Second Edition* (Basingstoke: Palgrave Macmillan).

Denver, D. and Bochel, H. (1994) 'Merger or Bust: Whatever Happened to Members of the SDP?', *British Journal of Political Science*, vol. 24, no. 3, pp. 403–17.

Denver, D. and Hands, G. (1993) 'Measuring the Intensity and Effectiveness of Constituency Campaigning in the 1992 General Election', in Denver, D. et al. (eds), *British Elections and Parties Yearbook 1993* (London: Harvester Wheatsheaf), pp. 229–42.

Denver, D. and Hands, G. (1997) *Modern Constituency Electioneering: Local Campaigning in the 1992 General Election* (London: Cass).

Denver, D. and Hands, G. (1998) 'Constituency Campaigning in the 1997 General Election: Party Effort and Electoral Effect', in I. Crewe et al. (eds) *Political Communications: Why Labour Won the General Election of 1997* (London: Cass), pp.75–92.

Denver, D. and Hands, G. (2004) 'Labour's Targeted Constituency Campaigning: Nationally Directed or Locally Produced?', *Electoral Studies*, vol. 23, no. 4, pp. 709–26.

Denver, D., Hands, G. and Henig, S. (1998) 'Triumph of Targeting? Constituency Campaigning in the 1997 Election', in Denver, D. et al. (eds), *British Elections and Parties Review Volume 8: The 1997 General Election* (London: Cass), pp. 171–90.

Denver, D., Hands, G., Fisher, J. and MacAllister, I. (2002a) 'The Impact of Constituency Campaigning in the 2001 General Election', in Bennie, L. et al. (eds), *British Elections and Parties Review Vol. 12: The 2001 General Election* (London: Cass), pp. 81–94.

Denver, D., Hands, G., Fisher, J., and MacAllister, I. (2002b) 'Constituency Campaigning in 2001: The Effectiveness of Targeting', in Bartle, J., Atkinson, S. and Mortimore, R. (eds), *Political Communications: The General Election Campaign of 2001* (London: Cass), pp. 159–80.

Denver, D., Hands, G. and MacAllister, I. (2004) 'The Electoral Impact of Constituency Campaigning in Britain, 1992–2001', *Political Studies*, vol. 52, no. 2, pp. 289–306.

Deschouwer, K. (2008) 'Comparing Newly Governing Parties', in Deschouwer, K. (ed.), *New Parties in Government: In Power for the First Time* (London: Routledge/ECPR), pp. 1–16.

Di Gennaro, C. and Dutton, W. (2006) 'The Internet and the Public: Online and Offline Political Participation in the United Kingdom', *Parliamentary Affairs*, vol. 59, no. 2, pp. 299–313.

Disraeli, B. (1927) *Sybil, or, The Two Nations* (London: Bodley Head).

Dorey, P. (2007) 'A New Direction or Another False Dawn? David Cameron and the Crisis of British Conservatism', *British Politics*, vol. 2, no. 2, pp. 137–66.

Dorey, P. (2009) '"Sharing the Proceeds of Growth": Conservative Economic Policy under David Cameron', *Political Quarterly*, vol. 80, no. 2, pp. 259–69.

Dorling, D. (2010) *Injustice: Why Social Inequality Still Exists* (Bristol: Policy Press).

Downs, A. (1957) *An Economic Theory of Democracy* (New York: Harper & Row).

Driver, S. and Martell, L. (2002) *Blair's Britain* (Cambridge: Polity Press).

Drucker, H. M. (1979) *Doctrine and Ethos in the Labour Party* (London: George Allen & Unwin).

Dunleavy, P. (1980) 'The Political Implications of Sectoral Cleavages and the Growth of State Employment: Parts 1 and 2', *Political Studies*, vol. 28, nos 3 & 4, pp. 364–83 and 527–49.

Dunleavy, P. (2005) 'Facing Up to Multi-Party Politics: How Partisan Dealignment and PR Voting Have Fundamentally Changed Britain's Party Systems', *Parliamentary Affairs*, vol. 58, no. 3, pp. 503–32.

Dutton, D. (2004) *A History of the Liberal Party in the Twentieth Century* (Basingstoke: Palgrave Macmillan).

Duverger, M. (1964) *Political Parties: Their Organization and Activity in the Modern State* (London: Methuen).

Easton, D. (1965) *A Systems Analysis of Political Life* (New York: Wiley).

Eatwell, R. (2000) 'The Extreme Right and British Exceptionalism: The Primacy of Politics', in Hainsworth, P. (ed.), *The Politics of the Extreme Right: From the Margins to the Mainstream* (London: Pinter), pp. 172–92.

Eatwell, R. and Goodwin, M. J. (eds) (2010) *The New Extremism in 21st Century Britain* (London: Routledge).

Elias, A. (2009) 'From Protest to Power: Mapping the Ideological Evolution of Plaid Cymru and the Bloque Nacionalista Galego', *Regional and Federal Studies*, vol. 19, nos 4–5, pp. 533–58.

Elliott, L. (2011a) '"Careless" Coalition Cuts Damaging Recovery, Says CBI Head', *The Guardian*, 25 January, p. 7.

Elliott, L. (2011b) 'George Soros Tells David Cameron: Change Direction or Face Recession', *The Guardian*, 26 January.

Elliott, F. and Hanning, J. (2009) *Cameron: The Rise of the New Conservative* (London: Harper Perennial).

Evans, E. (2008) 'Supply or Demand? Women Candidates and the Liberal Democrats', *British Journal of Politics and International Relations*, vol. 10, no. 4, pp. 590–606.

Evans, E. and Sanderson-Nash, E. (2011) 'From Sandals to Suits: Professionalization, Coalition and the Liberal Democrats', *British Journal of Politics and International Relations*, vol. 13, no. 4, pp.459–73.

Evans, G. and Norris, P. (eds) (1999) *Critical Elections: British Parties and Voters in Long-Term Perspective* (London: Sage).

Evans, J. A. J. and Tonge, J. (2005) 'Problems of Modernising an Ethno-Religious Party: The Case of the Ulster Unionist Party in Northern Ireland', *Party Politics*, vol. 11, no. 3, pp. 319–38.

Evans, S. (2008) 'Consigning its Past to History? David Cameron and the Conservative Party', *Parliamentary Affairs*, vol. 61, no. 2, pp. 291–314.

Evans, S. (2009) 'The Not So Odd Couple: Margaret Thatcher and One Nation Conservatism', *Contemporary British History*, vol. 23, no. 1, pp. 101–21.

Evans, S. (2010) 'Mother's Boy: David Cameron and Margaret Thatcher', *British Journal of Politics and International Relations*, vol. 12, no. 3, pp. 325–43.

Farrell, D. M. and Webb, P. (2000) 'Political Parties as Campaign Organizations', in Dalton, R. J. and Wattenberg, M. P. (eds), *Parties Without Partisans: Political Change in Advanced Industrial Democracies* (Oxford: Oxford University Press), pp. 102–28.

Fielding, S. (1997) 'Labour's Path to Power', in Geddes, A. and Tonge, J. (eds), *Labour's Landslide: The British General Election 1997* (Manchester: Manchester University Press), pp. 23–35.

Fielding, S. (2003) *The Labour Party: Continuity and Change in the Making of New Labour* (Basingstoke: Palgrave Macmillan).

Finlayson, A. (2003) *Making Sense of New Labour* (London: Lawrence & Wishart).

Fisher, J. (1996) *British Political Parties* (London: Prentice-Hall/Harvester Wheatsheaf).

Fisher, J. (2000) 'Small Kingdoms and Crumbling Organizations: Examining the Variation in Constituency Party Membership and Resources', in Cowley, P. et al. (eds), *British Elections and Parties Review Volume 10* (London: Cass), pp. 133–50.

Fisher, J. (2001) 'The Political Parties, Elections and Referendums Act 2000', *Representation*, vol. 38, no. 1, pp. 11–19.

Fisher, J. (2002) 'Next Step: State Funding for the Parties?', *Political Quarterly*, vol. 73, no. 4, pp. 392–9.

Fisher, J. (2008a) 'Whither the Parties?', in Hazell, R. (ed.), *Constitutional Futures Revisited: Britain's Constitution to 2020* (Basingstoke: Palgrave Macmillan), pp. 249–66.

Fisher, J. (2008b) 'Party Funding: Back to Square One (and a Half), or Every Cloud Has a Silver Lining?', *Political Quarterly*, vol. 79, no. 1, pp. 119–25.

Fisher, J. (2009) 'Hayden Phillips and Jack Straw: The Continuation of British Exceptionalism in Party Finance?', *Parliamentary Affairs*, vol. 62, no. 2, pp. 298–317.

Fisher, J. and Denver, D. (2008) 'From Foot-Slogging to Call Centres and Direct Mail: A Framework for Analysing the Development of District-Level Campaigning', *European Journal of Political Research*, vol. 47, no. 6, pp. 794–826.

Fisher, J., Denver, D. and Hands, G. (2006a) 'The Relative Electoral Impact of Central Party Co-ordination and Size of Party Membership at Constituency Level', *Electoral Studies*, vol. 25, pp. 664–76.

Fisher, J., Denver, D. and Hands, G. (2006b) 'Unsung Heroes: Constituency Election Agents in British General Elections', *British Journal of Politics and International Relations*, vol. 8, no. 4, pp. 569–86.

Foley, M. (2009) 'Gordon Brown and the Role of Compounded Crisis in the Pathology of Leadership Decline', *British Politics*, vol. 4, no. 4, pp. 498–513.

Foote, G. (1997) *The Labour Party's Political Thought: A History*, 3rd edn (Basingstoke: Macmillan).

Ford, R. (2010) 'Who Might Vote for the BNP? Survey Evidence on the Electoral Potential of the Extreme Right in Britain', in Eatwell, R. and Goodwin, M. J.

(eds), *The New Extremism in 21st Century Britain* (London: Routledge), pp. 145–68.

Gallagher, M. and Marsh, M. (eds) (1988) *Candidate Selection in Comparative Perspective: The Secret Garden of Politics* (London: Sage).

Gallagher, M. (2010) 'Election Indices', www.tcd.ie/PoliticalScience/staff/michael_gallagher/ElSystems/Docts/ElectionIndices.pdf [6 December 2010].

Galloway, G. (2005) *I'm Not the Only One* (London: Penguin).

Gamble, A. (1980) 'Economic Policy', in Layton-Henry, Z. (ed.), *Conservative Party Politics* (Basingstoke: Macmillan), pp. 26–49.

Gamble, A. (1994) *The Free Economy and the Strong State: The Politics of Thatcherism*, 2nd edn (Basingstoke: Macmillan).

Gamble, A. (1996) 'An Ideological Party', in Ludlam, S. and Smith, M. J. (eds), *Contemporary British Conservatism* (Basingstoke: Macmillan), pp. 19–36.

Garbaye, R. (2005) *Getting into Local Power: The Politics of Ethnic Minorities in British and French Cities* (London: Blackwell).

Garnett, M. (2003a) 'A Question of Definition? Ideology and the Conservative Party, 1997–2001', in Garnett, M. and Lynch, P. (eds), *The Conservatives in Crisis* (Manchester: Manchester University Press), pp. 107–24.

Garnett, M. (2003b) 'Win or Bust: the Leadership Gamble of William Hague', in Garnett, M. and Lynch, P. (eds), *The Conservatives in Crisis* (Manchester: Manchester University Press), pp. 49–65.

Garnett, M. (2005) 'Planning for Power, 1964–1970', in Ball, S. and Seldon, A. (eds), *Recovering Power: The Conservatives in Opposition since 1867* (Basingstoke: Palgrave Macmillan), pp. 192–218.

Garnett, M. and Lynch, P. (eds) (2003) *The Conservatives in Crisis* (Manchester: Manchester University Press).

Gavin, N. T., Sanders, D. and Farrall, N. (1996) 'The Impact of Television Economic News on Public Perceptions of the Economy and Government, 1993–94', in Farrell, D. M., Broughton, D., Denver, D. and Fisher, J. (eds), *British Elections and Parties Yearbook 1996* (London: Cass), pp. 68–84.

Gay, O. (2009) *Members Since 1979*, London: House of Commons Library Research Paper 09/31.

Geddes, A. (1997) 'Europe: Major's Nemesis', in Geddes, A. and Tonge, J. (eds), *Labour's Landslide* (Manchester: Manchester University Press), pp. 85–99.

Geddes, A. and Tonge, J. (eds) (2010) *Britain Votes 2010* Oxford: Oxford University Press).

Gibson, R. and Ward, S. (2000) 'An Outsider's Medium? The European Elections and UK Party Competition on the Internet', in Cowley, P., Denver, D., Russell, A. and Harrison, L. (eds), *British Elections and Parties Review Vol. 10* (London: Cass), pp. 173–91.

Gibson, R. K., Lusoli, W. and Ward, S. (2005) 'Online Participation in the UK: Testing a "Contextualised" Model of Internet Effects', *British Journal of Politics and International Relations*, vol. 7, no. 4, pp. 561–83.

Gibson, R. K., Williamson, A. and Ward, S. (2010) *The Internet and the 2010 Election: Putting the Small 'p' Back in Politics?* (London: Hansard Society).

Giddens, A. (1998) *The Third Way: the Renewal of Social Democracy* (Cambridge: Polity Press).

Giddens, A. (2000) *The Third Way and its Critics* (Cambridge: Polity Press).

Goodwin, M. J. (2011) *New British Fascism: The Rise of the BNP* (London: Routledge).

Gould, P. (1998a) *The Unfinished Revolution: How the Modernisers Saved the Labour Party* (London: Abacus).

Gould, P. (1998b) 'Why Labour Won', in Crewe, I., Gosschalk, B. and Bartle, J. (eds), *Political Communications: Why Labour Won the General Election of 1997* (London: Cass), pp. 3–11.

Grayson, R. S. (2007a) 'Social Democracy or Social Liberalism? Ideological Sources of Liberal Democrat Policy', *Political Quarterly*, vol. 78, no. 1, pp. 32–9.

Grayson, R. S. (2007b) 'Reforming the NHS: A Local and Democratic Voice', in Brack, D., Grayson, R. S. and Howarth, D. (eds), *Reinventing the State: Social Liberalism for the 21st Century* (London: Politico's), pp. 269–86.

Grayson, R. S. (2010) *The Liberal Democrat Journey to a Lib–Con Coalition: And Where Next?* (London: Compass).

Gunther, R. and Diamond, L. (2003) 'Species of Political Parties: A New Typology', *Party Politics*, vol. 9, no. 2, pp. 167–99.

Hainsworth, P. (2000) 'Introduction: The Extreme Right', in Hainsworth, P. (ed.), *The Politics of the Extreme Right: From the Margins to the Mainstream* (London: Pinter), pp. 1–17.

Hanham, H. J. (1956) 'The Local Organisation of the British Labour Party', *Western Political Quarterly*, vol. 9, no. 2, pp. 376–88.

Hansard Society (2010) *What's Trust Got To Do With It? Public Trust in and Expectations of Politicians and Parliament* (London: Hansard Society).

Harmel, R. and Roberston, J. D. (1985) 'Formation and Success of New Parties: A Cross National Analysis', *International Political Science Review*, vol. 6, no. 4, pp. 501–23.

Harris, J. (2011) 'Call This a Party?', *The Guardian G2*, 13 January, pp. 4–8.

Harrison, L. (2007) 'How "Local" Are the Liberal Democrats? Recent Evidence from Electoral Performance and Campaigning', *Political Quarterly*, vol. 78, no. 1, pp. 139–46.

Harrop, M. and Miller, W. L. (1987) *Elections and Voters: A Comparative Introduction* (Basingstoke: Macmillan).

Hay, C. (1999) *The Political Economy of New Labour: Labouring Under False Pretences?* (Manchester: Manchester University Press).

Hay, C. (2006) 'Whatever Happened to Thatcherism?', *Political Studies Review*, vol. 5, no. 2, pp. 183–201.

Hay, C. (2007) *Why We Hate Politics* (Cambridge: Polity).

Hayton, R. and Heppell, T. (2010) 'The Quiet Man of British Politics: The Rise, Fall and Significance of Iain Duncan Smith', *Parliamentary Affairs*, vol. 63, no. 3, pp. 425–45.

Heath, A., Jowell, R. and Curtice, J. (1985) *How Britain Votes* (London: Pergamon).

Heath, A., Jowell, R. and Curtice, J. (1994) *Labour's Last Chance? The 1992 Election and Beyond* (Aldershot: Dartmouth Publishing).

Heath, A., McLean, I., Taylor, B. and Curtice, J. (1999) 'Between First and Second Order: A Comparison of Voting Behaviour in European and Local Elections in Britain', *European Journal of Political Research*, vol. 35, no. 3, pp. 389–414.

Heffernan, R. (2001) *New Labour and Thatcherism: Political Change in Britain* (Basingstoke: Palgrave Macmillan).

Heffernan, R. (2007) 'Tony Blair as Labour Party Leader', in Seldon, A. (ed.), *Blair's Britain 1997–2007* (Cambridge: Cambridge University Press), pp. 143–63.

Heffernan, R. (2009) 'Political Parties', in Flinders, M., Gamble, A., Hay, C. and Kenny, M. (eds), *The Oxford Handbook of British Politics* (Oxford: Oxford University Press), pp. 441–60.

Heppell, T. (2007a) 'Weak and Ineffective? Reassessing the Party Political Leadership of John Major', *Political Quarterly*, vol. 78, no. 3, pp. 382–91.

Heppell, T. (2007b) 'A Crisis of Legitimacy: The Conservative Party Leadership of John Major', *Contemporary British History*, vol. 21, no. 4, pp. 471–90.

Heppell, T. (2010) 'Labour Leadership Elections from Wilson to Brown: Ideological Factions and Succession Planning Strategies', *Representation*, vol. 46, no. 1, pp. 69–79.

Heppell, T. and Hill, M. (2009) 'Transcending Thatcherism? Ideology and the Conservative Party Leadership Mandate of David Cameron', *Political Quarterly*, vol. 80, no. 3, pp. 388–99.

Herbert, S., Burnside, R., Earle, M., Liddell, G. and McIver, I. (2011) *Election 2011* (Edinburgh: Scottish Parliament Information Centre).

Herzog, H. (1987) 'Minor Parties: The Relevancy Perspective', *Comparative Politics*, vol. 19, no. 3, pp. 317–29.

Hindmoor, A. (2004) *New Labour at the Centre: Constructing Political Space* (Oxford: Oxford University Press).

Hobhouse, L. T. (1964 [1911]) *Liberalism* (Oxford: Oxford University Press).

Holmberg, S. (2003) 'Are Political Parties Necessary?', *Electoral Studies*, vol. 22, no. 2, pp. 287–99.

Holmes, A. (2007) 'Devolution, Coalition and the Liberal Democrats: Necessary Evil or Progressive Politics', *Parliamentary Affairs*, vol. 60, no. 4, pp. 527–47.

Holmes, P. (2007) 'The Limits of the Market', in Brack, D., Grayson, R. S. and Howarth, D. (eds), *Reinventing the State: Social Liberalism for the 21st Century* (London: Politico's), pp. 211–29.

Hopkin, J. and Bradbury, J. (2006) 'British Statewide Parties and Multilevel Politics', *Publius: The Journal of Federalism*, vol. 36, no. 1, pp. 135–52.

Howarth, D. (2007) 'What is Social Liberalism?', in Brack, D., Grayson, R. S. and Howarth, D. (eds), *Reinventing the State: Social Liberalism for the 21st Century* (London: Politico's), pp. 1–15.

Howell, D. (2006) *Attlee* (London: Haus Publishing).

Howson, J. (2007) 'The State and Education', in Brack, D., Grayson, R. S. and Howarth, D. (eds), *Reinventing the State: Social Liberalism for the 21st Century* (London: Politico's), pp. 255–68.

Hug, S. (2000) 'Studying the Electoral Success of New Political Parties: A Methodological Note', *Party Politics*, vol. 6, no. 2, pp. 187–97.

Huhne, C. (2007) 'The Case for Localism: The Liberal Narrative', in Brack, D., Grayson, R. S. and Howarth, D. (eds), *Reinventing the State: Social Liberalism for the 21st Century* (London: Politico's), pp. 241–54.

Ignazi, P. (1992) 'The Silent Counter-Revolution: Hypotheses on the Emergence of Extreme Right-Wing Parties in Europe', *European Journal of Political Research*, vol. 22, no. 1, pp. 3–34.

Ingle, S. (1996) 'Party Organisation', in MacIver, D. N. (ed.), *The Liberal Democrats* (Hemel Hempstead: Prentice-Hall/Harvester Wheatsheaf), pp. 113–33.

Ingle, S. (2008) *The British Party System: An Introduction, Fourth Edition* (Abingdon: Routledge).

Inglehart, R. (1990a) 'The Nature of Value Change', in Mair, P. (ed.), *The West European Party System* (Oxford: Oxford University Press), pp. 247–52.

Inglehart, R. (1990b) 'From Class-Based to Value-Based Politics', in Mair, P. (ed.), *The West European Party System* (Oxford: Oxford University Press), pp. 266–82.

Ipsos MORI (2010) *Ipsos MORI Issues Index* (London: Ipsos MORI). http://www.ipsos-mori.com/researchpublications/researcharchive/poll.aspx?oItemId=2595 [26 January 2011].

Jackson, N. (2006) 'Political Parties, Their E-Newsletters and Subscribers: "One Night Stand" or "Match Made in Heaven"?', in Davies, P. J. and Newman, B. I. (eds), *Winning Elections with Political Marketing* (Binghampton, NJ: Haworth Press), pp. 149–75.

Jefferys, K. (ed.) (1999) *Leading Labour: From Kier Hardie to Tony Blair* (London: I. B. Tauris).

Jenkins, S. (2007) *Thatcher and Sons: A Revolution in Three Acts* (London: Penguin).

John, P., Margetts, H., Rowland, D. and Weir, S. (2006) *The BNP: The Roots of its Appeal* (Colchester: Democratic Audit).

John, P. and Margetts, H. (2009) 'The Latent Support for the Extreme Right in British Politics', *West European Politics*, vol. 32, no. 3, pp. 496–513.

Johns, R., Mitchell, J., Denver, D. and Pattie, C. (2009) 'Valence Politics in Scotland: Towards an Explanation of the 2007 Election', *Political Studies*, vol. 57, no. 1, pp. 207–33.

Johnston, R. J. and Pattie, C. J. (1995) 'The Impact of Spending on Party Constituency Campaigns at Recent British General Elections', *Party Politics*, vol. 1, no. 2, pp. 261–73.

Johnston, R. and Pattie, C. (2007) 'Conservative Constituency Parties' Funding and Spending in England and Wales, 2004–2005', *Political Quarterly*, vol. 78, no. 3, pp. 392–411.

Johnston, R. and Pattie, C. (2011) 'The Local Campaigns and the Outcome', in Allen, N. and Bartle, J. (eds), *Britain at the Polls 2010* (London: Sage), pp. 203–41.

Johnston, R. J., Pattie, C. J. and Allsopp, J. G. (1988) *A Nation Dividing? The Electoral Map of Great Britain 1979–1987* (London: Longman).

Jones, T. (1996) 'Liberal Democrat Thought', in MacIver, D. (ed.), *The Liberal Democrats* (Hemel Hempstead: Prentice-Hall/Harvester Wheatsheaf), pp. 63–83.

Jones, P. and Hudson, J. (1996) 'The Quality of Political Leadership: A Case Study of John Major', *British Journal of Political Science*, vol. 26, no. 2, pp. 229–44.

Jordan, G. (1998) 'Politics Without Parties: A Growing Trend?', *Parliamentary Affairs*, vol. 51, no. 3, pp. 314–28.

Kaletsky, A. (2011) 'Osborne Bets the Farm on an Untested Theory', *The Times*, 26 January, p. 21.

Katz, R. S. and Mair, P. (1995) 'Changing Models of Party Organization and Party Democracy: The Emergence of the Cartel Party', *Party Politics*, vol. 1, no. 1, pp. 5–28.

Kaufmann, E. and Patterson, H. (2006) 'Intra-Party Support for the Good Friday Agreement in the Ulster Unionist Party', *Political Studies*, vol. 54, no. 3, pp. 509–32.

Kavanagh, D. A. (1970) *Constituency Electioneering in Britain* (London: Longmans).

Kavanagh, D. (1995) *Election Campaigning: The New Marketing of Politics* (Oxford: Blackwell).

Kavanagh, D. and Butler, D. (2005) *The British General Election of 2005* (Basingstoke: Palgrave Macmillan).

Kavanagh, D. and Cowley, P. (2010) *The British General Election of 2010* (Basingstoke: Palgrave Macmillan).

Kelly, R. N. (1989) *Conservative Party Conferences: The Hidden System* (Manchester: Manchester University Press).

Kelly, R. (2001) 'Farewell Conference, Hello Forum: The Making of Labour and Tory Policy', *Political Quarterly*, vol. 72, no. 3, pp. 329–34.

Kelly, R. (2002) 'The Party Didn't Work: Conservative Reorganisation and Electoral Failure', *Political Quarterly*, vol. 73, no. 1, pp. 38–43.

Kelly, R. (2004) 'The Extra-Parliamentary Tory Party: McKenzie Revisited', *Political Quarterly*, vol. 75, no. 4, pp. 398–404.

Kennedy, C. (2004) 'Foreword', in Marshall, P. and Laws, D. (eds) (2004) *The Orange Book: Reclaiming Liberalism* (London: Profile Books).

Kettell, S. and Kerr, P. (2008) 'One Year On: The Decline and Fall of Gordon Brown', *British Politics*, vol. 3, no. 4, pp. 490–510.

King, A. (1969) 'Political Parties in Western Democracies: Some Sceptical Reflections', *Polity*, vol. 2, no. 2, pp. 111–41.

King, A. (2002) 'The Outsider as Political Leader: The Case of Margaret Thatcher', *British Journal of Political Science*, vol. 32, no. 3, pp. 435–54.

Kirchheimer, O. (1966) 'The Transformation of the Western European Party Systems', in LaPalombara, J. and Weiner, M. (eds), *Political Parties and Political Development* (Princeton: Princeton University Press), pp. 177–200.

Kitschelt, H. (1994) *The Transformation of European Social Democracy* (Cambridge: Cambridge University Press).

Kitschelt, H. (1997) *The Radical Right in Western Europe: A Comparative Analysis* (Ann Arbor: Michigan University Press).

Koole, R. A. (1994) 'The Vulnerability of the Modern Cadre Party in the Netherlands', in Katz, R. S. and Mair, P. (eds), *How Parties Organize: Change and Adaptation in Party Organizations in Western Democracies* (London: Sage), pp. 278–303.

Kuhn, R. (2007) *Politics and the Media in Britain* (Basingstoke: Palgrave Macmillan).

Labour Party (2010) *A Future Fair For All: The Labour Party Manifesto 2010* (London: Labour Party).

Labour Party (2011) *Refounding Labour: A Party for the New Generation* (London: Labour Party).

Laffin. M. (2007a) 'Coalition Formation and Centre–Periphery Relations in a National Political Party: The Liberal Democrats in a Devolved Britain', *Party Politics*, vol. 13, no. 6, pp. 651–68.

Laffin, M. (2007b) 'The Scottish Liberal Democrats', *Political Quarterly*, vol. 78, no. 1, pp. 147–55.

LaPalombara, J. and Weiner, M. (1966) 'The Origin and Development of Political Parties', in LaPalombara, J. and Weiner, M. (eds), *Political Parties and Political Development* (Princeton: Princeton University Press), pp. 3–42.

Laver, M. and Schofield, N. (1990) *Multiparty Government: The Politics of Coalition in Europe* (Oxford: Oxford University Press).

Laws, D. (2004a) 'Reclaiming Liberalism: A Liberal Agenda for the Liberal Democrats', in Marshall, P. and Laws, D. (eds) (2004) *The Orange Book: Reclaiming Liberalism* (London: Profile Books), pp. 18–42.

Laws, D. (2004b) 'UK Health Services: A Liberal Agenda for Reform and Renewal', in Marshall, P. and Laws, D. (eds) (2004) *The Orange Book: Reclaiming Liberalism* (London: Profile Books), pp. 191–210.

Laws, D. (2010) *22 Days in May: The Birth of the Lib Dem–Conservative Coalition* (London: Biteback).

Leach, S. (2006) *The Changing Role of Local Politics in Britain* (Bristol: Policy Press).

Lee, S. (2008) 'The British Model of Political Economy', in Beech, M. and Lee, S. (eds), *Ten Years of New Labour* (Basingstoke: Palgrave Macmillan), pp. 17–34.

Lee, S. (2009) 'The Rock of Stability? The Political Economy of the Brown Government', *Policy Studies*, 30, (1), pp17–32.

Lees-Marshment, J. and Quayle, S. (2001) 'Empowering the Members or Marketing the Party? The Conservative Reforms of 1998', *Political Quarterly*, vol. 72, no. 2, pp. 204–12.

Leith, M. S. and Steven, M. (2010) 'Party Over Policy? Scottish Nationalism and the Politics of Independence', *Political Quarterly*, vol. 81, no. 2, pp. 263–9.

Levy, R. (1994) 'Nationalist Parties in Scotland and Wales', in Robins, L., Blackmore, H. and Pyper, R. (eds), *Britain's Changing Party System* (London: Leicester University Press), pp. 147–65.

Liberal Democrats (2005) *Liberal Democrats: The Real Alternative* (London: Liberal Democrats).

Liberal Democrats (2006) *Trust in People: Make Britain Free, Fair and Green* (London: Liberal Democrats).

Liberal Democrats (2009) *The Constitutions of the Liberal Democrats* (London: Liberal Democrats).

Liberal Democrats (2010) *Liberal Democrat Manifesto 2010* (London: Liberal Democrats).

Lijphart, A. (1999) *Patterns of Democracy: Government Forms and Performance in Thirty-Six Countries* (New Haven: Yale University Press).

Lipset, S. M. and Rokkan, S. (1967) 'Cleavage Structures, Party Systems and Voter Alignments: An Introduction', in Lipset, S. M. and Rokkan, S. (eds), *Party Systems and Voter Alignments* (London: Collier-Macmillan), pp. 1–64.

Lloyd, J. (2004) *What The Media Are Doing to Our Politics* (London: Constable).

Lowi, T. (1963) 'Towards Functionalism in Political Science: the Case of Innovation in Party Systems', *American Political Science Review*, vol. 57, no. 3, pp. 570–83.

Ludlam, S. (1996) 'The Spectre Haunting Conservatism: Europe and Backbench Rebellion', in Ludlam, S. and Smith, M. J. (eds), *Contemporary British Conservatism* (Basingstoke: Macmillan), pp. 98–120.

Ludlam, S. (2001) 'The Making of New Labour', in Ludlam, S. and Smith, M. J. (eds), *New Labour in Government* (Basingstoke: Macmillan), pp. 1–31.

Lusoli, W. and Ward, S. (2004) 'Digital Rank-and-File: Party Activists' Perceptions and Use of the Internet', *British Journal of Politics and International Relations*, vol. 6, no. 4, pp. 453–70.

Lynch, Peter. (1996) 'Professionalization, New Technology and Change in a Small Party: The Case of the Scottish National Party', in Farrell, D. M., Broughton, D., Denver, D. and Fisher, J. (eds), *British Elections and Parties Yearbook 1996* (London: Cass), pp. 217–33.

Lynch, Peter (2009) 'From Social Democracy Back to No Ideology? The Scottish National Party and Ideological Change in a Multi-Level Setting', *Regional and Federal Studies*, vol. 19, nos 4–5, pp. 619–38.

Lynch, Philip (2007) 'Party System Change in Britain: Multi-Party Politics in a Multi-Level Polity', *British Politics*, vol. 2, no. 3, pp. 323–46.

Mackay, F. and Kenny, M. (2007) 'Women's Representation in the 2007 Scottish Parliament: Temporary Setback or Return to the Norm?', *Scottish Affairs*, vol. 60, pp. 80–93.

Mair, P. (1991) 'The Electoral Universe of Small Parties in Postwar Western Europe', in Müller-Rommel, F. and Pridham, G. (eds), *Small Parties in Western Europe: Comparative and National Perspectives* (London: Sage), pp. 41–70.

Mair, P. (1994) 'Party Organizations: From Civil Society to the State', in Katz, R. S. and Mair, P. (eds), *How Parties Organize: Change and Adaptation in Party Organizations in Western Democracies* (London: Sage), pp. 1–22.

Mair, P. (2009) 'The Party System', in Flinders, M., Gamble, A., Hay, C. and Kenny, M. (eds), *The Oxford Handbook of British Politics* (Oxford: Oxford University Press), pp. 283–301.

Mair, P. and van Biezen, I. (2001) 'Party Membership in Twenty European Democracies, 1980–2000', *Party Politics*, vol. 7, no. 1, pp. 5–21.

Mandelson, P. and Liddle, R. (1996) *The Blair Revolution: Can New Labour Deliver?* (London: Faber & Faber).

Marshall, J. (2009) *Membership of UK Political Parties*, London: House of Commons Library Standard Note SN/SG/5125.

Marshall, P. and Laws, D. (eds) (2004) *The Orange Book: Reclaiming Liberalism* (London: Profile Books).

Massetti, E. (2008) *The Scottish and Welsh Party Systems Ten Years After Devolution: Format, Ideological Polarisation and Structure of Competition*, Brighton: University of Sussex SEI Working Paper No 107.

Maxwell, S. (2009) 'Social Justice and the SNP', in Hassan, G. (ed.), *The Modern SNP: From Protest to Power* (Edinburgh: Edinburgh University Press), pp. 120–34.

May, J. D. (1973) 'Opinion Structure of Political Parties: The Special Law of Curvilinear Disparity', *Political Studies*, vol. 21, no. 2, pp. 135–51.

McAllister, L. (2001) *Plaid Cymru: The Emergence of a Political Party* (Bridgend: Seren Books).

McEwen, N. (2002) 'The Scottish National Party After Devolution: Progress and Prospects', in Hassan, G. and Warhurst, C. (eds), *Tomorrow's Scotland* (London: Lawrence & Wishart), pp. 49–65.

McIlveen, R. (2009) 'Ladies of the Right: An Interim Analysis of the A-List', *Journal of Elections, Public Opinion and Parties*, vol. 19, no. 2, pp. 147–57.

McKenzie, R.T. (1963) *British Political Parties: The Distribution of Power Within the Conservative and Labour Parties, Second (Revised) Edition* (London: Heinemann).

McKenzie, R. (1982) 'Power in the Labour Party: The Issue of Intra-Party Democracy', in Kavanagh, D. (ed.), *The Politics of the Labour Party* (London: George, Allen & Unwin), pp. 191–201.

McNair, B. (1995) *An Introduction to Political Communication* (London: Routledge).

McSmith, A. (1999) 'John Smith 1992–94', in Jefferys, K. (ed.), *Leading Labour: From Kier Hardie to Tony Blair* (London: I. B. Tauris), pp. 193–207.

Meadowcroft, J. (2000) 'Is There a Liberal Alternative? Charles Kennedy and the Liberal Democrats' Strategy', *Political Quarterly*, vol. 71, no. 4, pp. 436–42.

Mellows-Facer, A., Cracknell, R. and Lightbown, S. (2009) *European Parliament Elections 2009*, London: House of Commons Library Research Paper 09/53.

Michels, R. (1959 [1915]) *Political Parties: A Sociological Study of the Emergence of Leadership, the Psychology of Power, and the Oligarchic Tendencies of Organization* (New York: Dover Publications).

Ministry of Justice (2008) *Party Finance and Expenditure in the United Kingdom: The Government's Proposals*, CM-7329 (London: TSO).

Minkin, L. (1978) *The Labour Party Conference: A Study in the Politics of Intra-Party Democracy* (London: Allen Lane).

Mitchell, P., Evans, G. and O'Leary, B. (2009) 'Extremist Outbidding in Ethnic Party Systems is Not Inevitable: Tribune Parties in Northern Ireland', *Political Studies*, vol. 57, no. 2, pp. 397–421.

Morgan, K. O. (1992) *Labour People: Leaders and Lieutenants, Hardie to Kinnock* (Oxford: Oxford University Press).

Morgan, K. O. (1999) 'James Callaghan 1976–80', in Jefferys, K. (ed.), *Leading Labour: From Kier Hardie to Tony Blair* (London: I. B. Tauris), pp. 133–50.

Morgan, K. O. (2004) 'United Kingdom: A Comparative Case Study of Labour Prime Ministers Attlee, Wilson, Callaghan and Blair', *Journal of Legislative Studies*, vol. 10, no. 2/3, pp. 38–52.

Mudde, C. (2007) *Populist Radical Right Parties in Europe* (Cambridge: Cambridge University Press).

Mughan, A. (1996) 'Television Can Matter: Bias in the 1992 General Election', in Farrell, D. M., Broughton, D., Denver, D. and Fisher, J. (eds), *British Elections and Parties Yearbook 1996* (London: Cass), pp. 128–42.

Müller-Rommel, F. (1991) 'Small Parties in Comparative Perspective: The State of the Art', in Müller-Rommel, F. and Pridham, G. (eds), *Small Parties in Western Europe: Comparative and National Perspectives* (London: Sage), pp. 1–22.

Murray, G. and Tonge, J. (2005) *Sinn Fein and the SDLP: From Alienation to Participation* (London: Hurst).

Naughtie, J. (2002) *The Rivals: The Intimate Story of a Political Marriage* (London: Fourth Estate).

Neumann, S. (1956) 'Toward a Comparative Study of Political Parties', in Neumann, S. (ed.), *Modern Political Parties: Approaches to Comparative Politics* (London: University of Chicago Press), pp. 395–421.

Newton, K. and Brynin, M. (2001) 'The National Press and Party Voting in the UK', *Political Studies*, vol. 49, no. 2, pp. 265–85.

Norman, J. (2010) *The Big Society: the Anatomy of the New Politics* (Buckingham: University of Buckingham Press).

Norris, P. (1990) 'Thatcher's Enterprise Society and Electoral Change', *West European Politics*, vol. 13, no. 1, pp. 63–78.

Norris, P. (2000) *A Virtuous Circle: Political Communications in Postindustrial Societies* (Cambridge: Cambridge University Press).

Norris, P. (2001) *Digital Divide: Civic Engagement, Information Poverty and the Internet Worldwide* (Cambridge: Cambridge University Press).

Norris, P. (2003) 'Preaching to the Converted? Pluralism, Participation and Party Websites', *Party Politics*, vol. 9, no. 1, pp. 21–45.

Norris, P., Curtice, J., Sanders, D., Scammell, M. and Semetko, H. A. (1999) *On Message: Communicating the Campaign* (London: Sage).

Norris, P. and Lovenduski, J. (1995) *Political Recruitment: Gender, Race and Class in the British Parliament* (Cambridge: Cambridge University Press).

Norton, P. (1993) 'The Conservative Party from Thatcher to Major', in King, A. (ed.), *Britain at the Polls 1992* (Chatham, NJ: Chatham House), pp. 29–69.

Norton, P. (2011) 'The Politics of Coalition', in Allen, N. and Bartle, J. (eds), *Britain at the Polls 2010* (London: Sage), pp. 242–65.

Osborne, G. (2009a) 'Progressive Reform in an Age of Austerity', Speech to Demos, 11 August, www.conservatives.com [12/1/10].

Osborne, G. (2009b) 'We Will Lead the Economy Out of Crisis', Speech to Conservative Party Conference, 6 October, www.conservatives.com [12/1/10].

Osborne, G. (2010a) 'A New Economic Model', 2 February, www.conservatives.com [3/2/10].

Osborne, G. (2010b) 'A New Economic Model', The MAIS Lecture, 24 February, www.conservatives.com [1/3/10].

Osborne, G. (2010c) 'Unleashing the Forces of Enterprise', Speech to Conservative Party Spring Conference, 27 February, www.conservatives.com [1/3/10].

Pack, M. (2007) 'Using Community Politics to Build a Liberal Society', in Brack, D., Grayson, R. S. and Howarth, D. (eds), *Reinventing the State: Social Liberalism for the 21st Century* (London: Politico's), pp. 131–43.

Panebianco, A. (1988) *Political Parties: Organization and Power* (Cambridge: Cambridge University Press).

Panitch, L. V. (1971) 'Ideology and Integration: the Case of the British Labour Party', *Political Studies*, vol. XIX, no. 2, pp. 184–200.

Parkinson, C. (2003) 'The Reform of the Conservative Party', in Garnett, M. and Lynch, P. (eds), *The Conservatives in Crisis* (Manchester: Manchester University Press), pp. 217–20.

Paterson, L., Brown, A., Curtice, J., Hinds, K., McCrone, D., Park, A., Sproston K. and Surridge, P. (2001) *New Scotland, New Politics?* (Edinburgh: Polygon).

Pattie, C., Whiteley, P., Johnston, R. and Seyd, P. (1994) 'Measuring Local Campaign Effects: Labour Party Constituency Campaigning at the 1987 General Election', *Political Studies*, vol. 42, no. 3, pp. 469–79.

Pattie, C. J. and Johnston, R. J. (2003a) 'Hanging on the Telephone? Doorstep and Telephone Canvassing at the British General Election of 1997', *British Journal of Political Science*, vol. 33, no. 2, pp. 303–22.

Pattie, C. J. and Johnston, R. J. (2003b) 'Local Battles in a National Landslide: Constituency Campaigning at the 2001 British General Election', *Political Geography*, vol. 22, no. 4, pp. 381–414.

Pattie, C. J. and Johnston, R. J. (2004) 'Party Knowledge and Candidate Knowledge: Constituency Campaigning and Voting and the 1997 British General Election', *Electoral Studies*, vol. 23, no. 4, pp. 795–819.

Pattie, C. and Johnston, R. (2009) 'The Conservatives' Grassroots "Revival"', *Political Quarterly*, vol. 80, no. 2, pp. 193–203.

Pearce, R. (1999) 'Clement Attlee 1935–55', in Jefferys, K. (ed.), *Leading Labour: From Kier Hardie to Tony Blair* (London: I. B. Tauris), pp. 80–96.

Pedersen, M. N. (1982) 'Towards a New Typology of Party Lifespans and Minor Parties', *Scandinavian Political Studies*, vol. 5, no. 1, pp. 1–16.

Pedersen, M. N. (1990) 'Electoral Volatility in Western Europe, 1948–1977', in Mair, P. (ed.), *The West European Party System* (Oxford: Oxford University Press), pp. 195–207.

Phillips, H. (2007) *Strengthening Democracy: Fair and Sustainable Funding of Political Parties – The Review of the Funding of Political Parties* (London: TSO).

Political Parties, Elections and Referendums Act (PPERA) (2000) (London: TSO).

Price, A. (2010) *Why Vote Plaid Cymru?* (London: Biteback Publishing).

Price, L. (2010) *Where Power Lies: Prime Ministers v. the Media* (London: Simon & Schuster).

Pulzer, P. G. (1967) *Political Representation and Elections in Britain* (London: George Allen & Unwin).

Quinn, T. (2004) 'Electing the Leader: The British Labour Party's Electoral College', *British Journal of Politics and International Relations*, vol. 6, no. 3, pp. 333–52.

Quinn, T. (2005) 'Leasehold or Freehold? Leader-Eviction Rules in the British Conservative and Labour Parties', *Political Studies*, vol. 53, no. 4, pp. 793–815.

Quinn, T. (2010) 'New Labour and the Trade Unions in Britain', *Journal of Elections, Public Opinion and Parties*, vol. 20, no. 3, pp.357–80.

Rallings, C. and Thrasher, M. (1997) *Local Elections in Britain* (London: Routledge).

Rallings, C. and Thrasher, M. (2000) *British Electoral Facts 1832–1999* (Aldershot: Ashgate).

Rallings, C. and Thrasher, M. (2003) 'Explaining Split-ticket Voting and the 1979 and 1997 General and Local Elections in Britain', *Political Studies*, vol. 51, no. 3, pp. 558–72.

Rallings, C. and Thrasher, M. (2009) 'The 2008 Local Elections: A False Dawn for the Conservatives?', *Representation*, vol. 45, no. 1, pp. 53–65.

Randall, E. (2007) 'Yellow Versus Orange – Never a Fair Fight: An Assessment of Two Contributions to Liberal Politics Separated by Three-Quarters of a Century', *Political Quarterly*, vol. 78, no. 1, pp. 40–9.

Randall, N. (2003) 'Understanding Labour's Ideological Trajectory', in Callaghan, J., Fielding, S. and Ludlam, S. (eds), *Interpreting the Labour Party: Approaches to Labour Politics and History* (Manchester: Manchester University Press), pp. 8–22.

Randall, N. (2009) 'No Friends in the North? The Conservative Party in Northern England', *Political Quarterly*, vol. 80, no. 2, pp. 184–92.

Rasmussen, J. (1991) 'They Also Serve: Small Parties in the British Political System', in Müller-Rommel, F. and Pridham, G. (eds), *Small Parties in Western Europe: Comparative and National Perspectives* (London: Sage), pp. 152–73.

Rawnsley, A. (2001) *Servants of the People: The Inside Story of New Labour* (London: Penguin).

Rawnsley, A. (2010) *The End of the Party: The Rise and Fall of New Labour* (London: Penguin).

Reif, K. and Schmitt, H. (1980) 'Nine Second-Order National Elections: A Conceptual Framework for the Analysis of European Election Results', *European Journal of Political Research*, vol. 8, no. 1, pp. 3–44.

Renton, D. (2005) 'A Day to Make History? The 2004 Elections and the British National Party', *Patterns of Prejudice*, vol. 39, no. 1, pp. 25–45.

Rentoul, J. (1999) 'Tony Blair 1994–', in Jefferys, K. (ed.), *Leading Labour: From Kier Hardie to Tony Blair* (London: I. B. Tauris), pp. 208–28.

Respect (2006) *Respect: The Unity Coalition: Financial Statements for the Year Ended 31 December 2006* (London: Respect).

Rhodes, J. (2009) 'The Political Breakthrough of the BNP: The Case of Burnley', *British Politics*, vol. 4, no. 1, pp. 22–46.

Rhodes, R. A. W. (1996) 'The New Governance: Governing Without Government', *Political Studies*, vol. 44, no. 4, pp. 652–67.

Roddin, E. (2004) 'Has the Labour Party or the Liberal Democrats Proved More Successful in the Partnership for Scotland Coalition? An Initial Assessment', *Scottish Affairs*, vol. 48, pp. 24–49.

Rohrschneider, R. (2002) 'Mobilising Versus Chasing: How Do Parties Target Voters in Election Campaigns?', *Electoral Studies*, vol. 21, no. 3, pp. 367–82.

Rose, R. (1984) *Do Parties Make a Difference? Expanded Second Edition* (London: Macmillan).

Russell, A. (2010) 'Inclusion, Exclusion or Obscurity? The 2010 General Election and the Implications of the Con–Lib Coalition for Third-Party Politics in Britain', *British Politics*, vol. 5, no. 4, pp. 506–24.

Russell A. and Fieldhouse, E. (2005) *Neither Left Nor Right? The Liberal Democrats and the Electorate* (Manchester: Manchester University Press).

Russell, A., Fieldhouse, E. and Cutts, D. (2007a) '*De Facto* Veto? The Parliamentary Liberal Democrats, *Political Quarterly*, vol. 78, no. 1, pp. 89–98.

Russell, A., Cutts, D. and Fieldhouse, E. (2007b) 'National–Regional–Local: the Electoral and Political Health of the Liberal Democrats in Britain', *British Politics*, vol. 2, no. 2, pp. 191–214.

Russell, M. (2005) *Building New Labour: The Politics of Party Organisation* (Basingstoke: Palgrave Macmillan).

Sanders, D. (2006) 'Reflections on the 2005 General Election: Some Speculations on How the Conservatives Can Win Next Time', *British Politics*, vol. 1, no. 2, pp. 170–94.

Sanders, D. and Norris, P. (1998) 'Does Negative News Matter? The Effect of Television News on Party Images in the 1997 British General Election', in Denver, D., Fisher, J., Cowley, P. and Pattie, C. (eds), *British Elections and Parties Review Vol. 8: The 1997 General Election* (London: Cass), pp. 150–70.

Sarlvik, B. and Crewe, I. (1983) *Decade of Dealignment: the Conservative Victory of 1979 and Electoral Trends in the 1970s* (Cambridge: Cambridge University Press).

Sartori, G. (2005 [1976]) *Parties and Party Systems: A Framework for Analysis* (Colchester: ECPR Press).

Sartori, G. (2005) 'Party Types, Organisation and Functions', *West European Politics*, vol. 28, no. 1, pp. 5–32.

Scammell, M. (1995) *Designer Politics: How Elections Are Won* (Basingstoke: Macmillan).

Scammell, M. (2000) 'New Media, New Politics', in Dunleavy, P., Gamble, A., Holliday, I. and Peele, G. (eds), *Developments in British Politics 6* (Basingstoke: Macmillan), pp. 169–84.

Scarrow, S. E. (1996) *Parties and Their Members: Organizing for Victory in Britain and Germany* (Oxford: Oxford University Press).

Scarrow, S. E. (1999), 'Parties and the Expansion of Direct Democracy: Who Benefits?', *Party Politics*, vol. 5, no. 3, pp. 348–9.

Schattschneider, E. E. (1942) *Party Government* (New York: Rinehart).

Schedler, A. (1996) 'Anti-Political-Establishment Parties', *Party Politics*, 2, (3), pp. 291–312.

Schumpeter, J. A. (1965 [1942]) *Capitalism, Socialism and Democracy, Fourth Edition* (London: Unwin).

Seawright, D. (2010) *The British Conservative Party and One Nation Politics* (London: Continuum).

Seldon, A. and Ball, S. (eds) (1994) *Conservative Century: The Conservative Party Since 1900* (Oxford: Oxford University Press).

Seldon, A. (2007) 'The Net Blair Effect, 1994–2007', in Seldon, A. (ed.), *Blair's Britain 1997–2007* (Cambridge: Cambridge University Press), pp. 645–50.

Select Committee on Public Administration (1998) *Minutes of Evidence, Questions 400–419* (London: House of Commons).

Seyd, P. (1999) 'New Parties/New Politics? A Case Study of the British Labour Party', *Party Politics*, vol. 5, no. 3, pp. 383–405.

Seyd, P. and Whiteley, P. (1992) *Labour's Grassroots: The Politics of Party Membership* (Oxford: Oxford University Press).

Seyd, P. and Whiteley, P. (2002a) *New Labour's Grassroots: The Transformation of the Labour Party Membership* (Basingstoke: Palgrave Macmillan).

Seyd, P. and Whiteley, P. F. (2002b) *Survey of Labour Party Members, 1997 and 1999* [computer file]. Colchester, Essex: UK Data Archive [distributor], SN: 4466.

Seyd, P. and Whiteley, P. (2004) 'British Party Members: An Overview', *Party Politics*, vol. 10, no. 4, pp. 355–66.

Shaw, E. (1994) *The Labour Party Since 1979: Crisis and Transformation* (London: Routledge).

Shaw, E. (1996) *The Labour Party Since 1945: Old Labour, New Labour* (Oxford: Blackwell).

Shaw, E. (1999) 'Michael Foot 1980–83', in Jefferys, K. (ed.), *Leading Labour: From Kier Hardie to Tony Blair* (London: I. B. Tauris), pp. 151–70.

Shaw, E. (2001) 'New Labour: New Pathways to Parliament', *Parliamentary Affairs*, vol. 54, no. 1, pp. 35–53.

Sinn Féin (2007) *Delivering for Ireland's Future: Saoirse, Ceart agus Siochain* (Dublin: Sinn Féin).

Sinn Féin (2011) *Leadership Across Ireland: Assembly Election Manifesto 2011* (Belfast: Sinn Féin).

Smith, G. (1989) 'Core Persistence: Change and the People's Party', *West European Politics*, vol. 12, no.4, pp. 157–68.

Smith, J. K. (2009) 'Campaigning and the Catch-All Party: The Process of Party Transformation in Britain', *Party Politics*, vol. 15, no. 5, pp. 555–72.

Smith, M. J. (1996) 'Reforming the State' in Ludlam, S. and Smith, M. J. (eds), *Contemporary British Conservatism* (Basingstoke: Macmillan), pp. 143–65.

Smith, M. J. and Ludlam, S. (1996) 'Introduction', in Ludlam, S. and Smith, M. J. (eds), *Contemporary British Conservatism* (Basingstoke: Macmillan), pp. 1–18.

Snowdon, P. (2010) *Back from the Brink: The Inside Story of the Tory Resurrection* (London: Harper Press).

SNP (2003) *The Case for a Better Scotland: Manifesto 2003* (Edinburgh: Scottish National Party).

SNP (2010) *Elect A Local Champion: Manifesto 2010* (Edinburgh: Scottish National Party).

Stuart, M. (2006) 'Managing the Poor Bloody Infantry: The Parliamentary Labour Party under John Smith, 1992–94', *Parliamentary Affairs*, vol. 59, no. 3, pp. 401–19.

Taggart, P. (2000) *Populism* (Buckingham: Open University Press).

Talshir, G. (2005) 'Knowing Right From Left: The Politics of Identity Between the Radical Left and Far Right', *Journal of Political Ideologies*, vol. 10, no. 3, pp. 311–35.

Tavits, M. (2006) 'Party System Change: Testing a Model of New Party Entry', *Party Politics*, vol. 12, no. 1, pp. 99–119.

Tawney, R. H. (1964) *Equality* (London: Unwin Books).

Taylor, A. (1994) 'The Party and the Trade Unions', in Seldon, A. and Ball, S. (eds), *Conservative Century: The Conservative Party Since 1900* (Oxford: Oxford University Press), pp. 499–543.

Taylor, M. (2001) 'Too Early to Say? New Labour's First Term', *Political Quarterly*, vol. 72, no. 1, pp. 5–18.

Taylor, M. (2007) 'Global Giants', in Brack, D., Grayson, R. S. and Howarth, D. (eds), *Reinventing the State: Social Liberalism for the 21st Century* (London: Politico's), pp. 55–74.

Tetteh, E. (2008) *Election Statistics: UK 1918–2007*, London: House of Commons Library Research Paper 08/12.

Tetteh, E. (2010) *Local Elections 2010*, London: House of Commons Library Research Paper 10/44.

Thatcher, M. (1993) *The Downing Street Years, 1979–1990* (London: Harper-Collins).

Theakston, K. and Gill, M. (2006) 'Rating 20th Century British Prime Minsters', *British Journal of Politics and International Relations*, vol. 8, no. 2, pp. 193–213.

Tonge, J. (2004) *The New Northern Irish Politics* (Basingstoke: Palgrave Macmillan).

Torfing, J. (2007) 'Introduction: Democratic Network Governance', in Marcussen, M. and Torfing, J. (eds), *Democratic Network Governance in Europe* (Basingstoke: Palgrave Macmillan), pp. 1–22.

Toynbee, P. and Walker, D. (2001) *Did Things Get Better? An Audit of Labour's Successes and Failures* (London: Penguin).

Toynbee, P. and Walker, D. (2010) *The Verdict: Did Labour Change Britain?* (London: Granta).

Tressell, R. (1914 [1993]) *The Ragged Trousered Philanthropists* (London: Flamingo Modern Classics).

van Biezen, I. (2004) 'Parties as Public Utilities', *Party Politics*, vol. 10, no. 6, pp. 701–22.

van Biezen, I. and Saward, M. (2008) 'Democratic Theorists and Party Scholars: Why They Don't Talk to Each Other and Why They Should', *Perspectives on Politics*, vol. 6, no. 1, pp. 21–35.

Vincent, A. (1994) 'British Conservatism and the Problem of Ideology', *Political Studies*, vol. 42, no. 2, pp. 204–27.

Walker, G. (2004) *A History of the Ulster Unionist Party: Protest, Pragmatism and Pessimism* (Manchester: Manchester University Press).

Ward, S. (2005) 'The Internet, E-democracy and the Election: Virtually Irrelevant?', in Geddes, A. and Tonge, J. (eds), *Britain Decides: The UK General Election 2005* (Basingstoke: Palgrave Macmillan), pp. 188–206.

Ward, S. and Gibson, R. (2003) 'On-Line and On Message? Candidate Websites in the 2001 General Election', *British Journal of Politics and International Relations*, vol. 5, no. 2, pp. 188–205.

Ware, A. (1996) *Political Parties and Party Systems* (Oxford: Oxford University Press).

Watt, N. and Treanor, J. (2011) 'Revealed: 50% of Tory Funds Come from City', *The Guardian*, 8 February.

Watts, D. (1997) *Political Communication Today* (Manchester: Manchester University Press).

Webb, P. D. (1992) 'The United Kingdom', in Katz, R. S. and Mair, P. (eds), *Party Organisations: A Data Handbook on Party Organisations in Western Democracies, 1960–90* (London: Sage), pp. 837–70.

Webb, P. D. (1994) 'Party Organizational Change in Britain: The Iron Law of Centralisation?', in Katz, R. S. and Mair, P. (eds), *How Parties Organise: Change and Adaptation in Party Organisations in Western Democracies* (London: Sage), pp. 109–33.

Webb, P. D. (1995) 'Are British Political Parties in Decline?', *Party Politics*, vol. 1, no. 3, pp. 299–322.

Webb, P. (2000) *The Modern British Party System* (London: Sage).

Webb, P. (2002) 'Conclusion: Political Parties and Democratic Control in Advanced Industrial Societies', in Webb, P., Farrell, D. and Holliday, I. (eds) *Political Parties in Advanced Industrial Democracies* (Oxford: Oxford University Press), pp. 438–60.

Webb, P. (2005) 'The Continuing Advance of the Minor Parties', *Parliamentary Affairs*, vol. 58, no. 4, pp. 757–75.

Webb, P. (2009) 'The Failings of Political Parties: Reality or Perception', *Representation*, vol. 45, no. 3, pp. 265–75.

Webb, P. and Farrell, D. M. (1999) 'Party Members and Ideological Change', in Evans, G. and Norris, P. (eds), *Critical Elections: British Parties and Voters in Long-Term Perspective* (London: Sage), pp. 44–63.

Webb, P., Farrell, D. and Holliday, I. (eds) (2002) *Political Parties in Advanced Industrial Democracies* (Oxford: Oxford University Press).

Webb, P. and Fisher, J. (1999) 'The Changing British Party System: Two-Party Equilibrium or the Emergence of Moderate Pluralism?', in Broughton, D. and Donovan, M. (eds), *Changing Party Systems in Western Europe* (London: Pinter), pp. 8–29.

Webb, P. and Fisher, J. (2003) 'Professionalisation and the Millbank Tendency: The Political Sociology of New Labour's Employees', *Politics*, vol. 23, no. 1, pp. 10–20.

Webb, P. and Childs, S. (2011) 'Wets and Dries Resurgent? Intra-Party Alignments Among Contemporary Conservative Members', *Parliamentary Affairs*, vol. 64, no. 3, pp. 383–402.

Westlake, M. (1999) 'Neil Kinnock 1983–92', in Jefferys, K. (ed.), *Leading Labour: From Kier Hardie to Tony Blair* (London: I. B. Tauris), pp. 171–92.

Whiteley, P. (1983) *The Labour Party in Crisis* (London: Methuen).

Whiteley, P. (2009a) 'Government Effectiveness and Political Participation in Britain', *Representation*, vol. 45, no. 3, pp. 247–57.

Whiteley, P. (2009b) 'Where Have All the Members Gone? The Dynamics of Party Membership in Britain', *Parliamentary Affairs*, vol. 62, no. 2, pp. 242–57.

Whiteley, P. F. and Seyd, P. (1994) 'Local Party Campaigning and Electoral Mobilization in Britain', *Journal of Politics*, vol. 56, no. 1, pp. 242–52.

Whiteley P. and Seyd, P. (2003) 'How to Win a Landslide by Really Trying: The Effects of Local Campaigning on Voting at the 1997 British General Election', *Electoral Studies*, vol. 22, no. 2, pp. 301–24.

Whiteley, P., Seyd, P. and Billinghurst, A. (2006) *Third Force Politics: Liberal Democrats at the Grassroots* (Oxford: Oxford University Press).

Whiteley, P., Seyd, P. and Richardson, J. (1994) *True Blues: The Politics of Conservative Party Membership* (Oxford: Oxford University Press).

Wickham-Jones, M. (1997) 'How the Conservatives Lost the Economic Argument', in Geddes, A. and Tonge, J. (eds), *Labour's Landslide* (Manchester: Manchester University Press), pp. 100–19.

Wilks-Heeg, S. (2009) 'The Canary in the Coalmine? Explaining the Emergence of the British National Party in English Local Politics', *Parliamentary Affairs*, vol. 62, no. 3, pp. 377–98.

Wilks-Heeg, S. and Crone, S. (2010) *Funding Political Parties in Great Britain: A Pathway to Reform* (Liverpool: Democratic Audit).

Willetts, D. (1992) *Modern Conservatism* (London: Penguin).

Wilson, D. and Game, C. (2006) *Local Government in the United Kingdom,* 4th edn (Basingstoke: Palgrave Macmillan).

Wilson, G. (2006) 'Cameron "Heir to Disraeli as a One Nation Tory"', *Daily Telegraph*, 28 December, www.telegraph.co.uk [6/4/10].

Wolinetz, S. (1979) 'The Transformation of Western European Party Systems Revisited', *West European Politics*, vol. 2, no. 1, pp. 4–27.

Wright, W. E. (1971) 'Comparative Party Models: Rational Efficient and Party Democracy', in Wright, W. E. (ed.), *A Comparative Study of Party Organization* (Columbus, Ohio: Merrill Publishing), pp. 17–54.

Wring, D. and Deacon, D. (2010) 'Patterns of Press Partisanship in the 2010 General Election', *British Politics*, vol. 5, no. 4, pp. 436–54.

Wring, D. and Ward, S. (2010) 'The Media and the 2010 Campaign: The Television Election', *Parliamentary Affairs*, vol. 63, no. 4, pp. 802–17.

Wyn Jones, R. and Scully, R. (2006) 'Devolution and Electoral Politics in Scotland and Wales', *Publius: The Journal of Federalism*, vol. 36, no. 1, 115–34.

Yelland, D. (2010) 'The Rise of Clegg Could Lock Murdoch and the Media Elite Out of UK Politics', *The Guardian*, 19 April, p. 28.

Young, R. (2008) *London Elections 2008*, London: House of Commons Library Research Paper 08/47.

Index